Concepts of Programming Languages

CONCEPTS OF PROGRAMMING LANGUAGES

by Mark Elson

SCIENCE RESEARCH ASSOCIATES, INC.
Chicago, Palo Alto, Toronto
Henley-on-Thames, Sydney, Paris

A Subsidiary of IBM

LIBRARY OF CONGRESS CATALOG CARD NUMBER: 72–94972

ACKNOWLEDGMENTS

Appendix 3, ALGOL 60 Syntax—Reprinted from *Communications of the ACM*, Volume 6, Number 1, January 1963, pages 1–17; also appeared in *Numerische Mathematik* and *The Computer Journal*.

Appendix 4, The LISP Interpreter—Reprinted from *LISP 1.5 Programmer's Manual* by McCarthy, J.; Abrahams, P. W.; Edwards, D. J.; Hart, T. P.; and Levin, J. I. by permission of The M.I.T. Press, Cambridge, Massachusetts.

PREFACE

This book is intended to accommodate the needs of a spectrum of individuals ranging from the neophyte FORTRAN programmer to the language designer versed in languages and programming. But use of the book should vary somewhat through this spectrum.

The book's organization is discussed thoroughly in the Introduction; the unifying theme is the localized study of each particular language concept, rather than of each of a number of particular languages. This message is elaborated in chapters 5 through 15 and 18. Chapters 1 through 4, 16, and 17, and the appendices provide introductions to particular languages and some elementary formalism appropriate as background to the more systematic study. Thus, use of the book should be governed, in part, by the student's prior exposure to this background.

At the lower end of the reader spectrum, the material covered should include the language introductions, the comparative programming example following them, and the material in appendices 1, 2 and 3. In the case of the language introductions, supplementary reading may be desirable if a significant degree of actual coding is involved. Because of the deemphasis of syntax, these chapters are not adequate by themselves as programming guides. References to sources of more detailed tutorial coverage are given with the language introductions. Similarly, references are given to more in-depth coverages of the appendix materials.

It is advisable to cover next the chapters on LISP (along with appendix 4) and SNOBOL as an introduction to specialized application languages. Again, more detailed material may be used to augment these presentations, particularly for SNOBOL, if much coding is involved. About thirty lecture hours are required for this scope of coverage. If time remains, the chapters on information binding, data structures, control structures, and language extensibility should be studied. About fifteen lecture hours are needed for these additions.

This meandering approach is recommended only for the reader with limited language exposure. The reader with a good language background may already be familiar with the material on specific languages and in the appendices. In this case a more straightforward reading of chapters 5 through 18 is best. This coverage should require about forty-five lecture hours. If time is insufficient for all, it is still best to conclude with chapter 18.

Exercises are provided wherever appropriate, rather than only at ends of chapters, but are numbered consecutively within each chapter. Many are intended to test comprehension of what has preceded, but others are designed to be more thought-provoking and subjective, more amenable to creative answers.

We recommend, as a project accompanying this language study, the design and, if possible, implementation by the reader of a small, special-purpose, application language for work within some discipline of interest to him. Emphasis should be on design of the language as a communication aid, rather than on creation of application routines usable with a common language such as FORTRAN. Encouragement should be given for languages far from the realm of number crunching, in order to stress the utility of computers and languages in widely disparate areas of endeavor.

A word of caution applies to the six particular languages discussed in this book. All have been implemented on a variety of machines, and there are multiple dialects of each. We have felt free to discuss features commonly associated with certain dialects of the languages but not available in all implementations. In the case of FORTRAN, for example, we discuss several features that are not available in ASA Standard FORTRAN but are commonly supported by implementations. They are significant language features that should be understood. But for none of the languages do we guarantee the availability of the features, character sets, or program formats that we have used in illustration. Actual programs must be sensitive to the dialect and implementation available.

Sincere thanks are due Lew Bastian, Marilyn Bohl, Frank DeRemer, Joyce Friedman, James Horning, James Leathrum, Dieter Paris, Tad Pinkerton, Terry Pratt, Frank Prosser, Bert Raphael, William Viavant, and Neil Webre, for their constructive criticisms. IBM Boulder provided automated text development aids invaluable to composition of the manuscript. And Rosalie typed, retyped, edited, admonished, and inspired.

TABLE OF CONTENTS

APPENDICES

INTRODUCTION

In the last fifteen years, there have emerged from within the world of automation several hundred different entities characterizable as high-level programming languages. Such christening of a language implies that its expressive powers make it either a valuable communication vehicle, from the standpoint of a computer user, or an unrecognizable collection of nonsense, from the standpoint of a computing machine. A large number of high-level languages possess only the latter quality; a moderate number pass on both counts; a few possess only the first property.

The problem is the extreme mismatch in the neurological constitution of people and computing machines. We just don't think the way they do. I can spend ten minutes solving a system of equations, deciding on a chess move, or appreciating a piece of music. A computing machine may spend milliseconds on the first of these, ten minutes on the second, and an eternity wondering what is meant by the third.

The problem of designing programming languages for effective communication between people and machines is and will continue to be a difficult one, as long as this mismatch remains. But a critical balance is shifting. In the early days of programming languages, the high costs of data storage and machine instruction execution meant that the sacrifice of convenience usually fell on the shoulders of programmers; languages were designed to be easily adaptable to the machines on which they were used. Now such costs are rapidly decreasing in relation to those of programmer time. It is becoming more important that languages be easily usable by programmers, even at the cost of a more difficult adaptation to machines. This trend will continue, as hardware technology advances and language use extends to the world of nontechnicians.

Even in an ideal world of infinite storage and infinitesimal times for program translation and execution, the mismatch between user languages and machine languages would be overwhelming. The process of producing language translators is still primarily a human one, though steps toward automation of translation are being made. Progress in overcoming the problem of communication between people and machines requires moving the level of machine languages toward that of user languages, so that translations can be made more easily. This migration need not initially be effected by physically changing the level of machine languages; it can be achieved by introducing an intermediate language to serve as the conceptual machine language targeted by compilers. Diagrammatically we have the following:

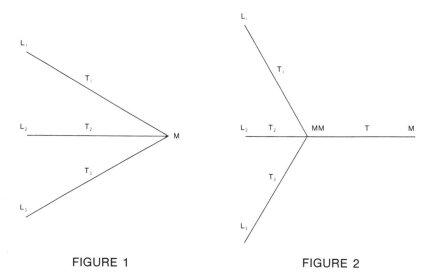

FIGURE 1   FIGURE 2

Figures 1 and 2 illustrate the mismatch between user languages L_1, L_2, and L_3, and a target machine language M. In figure 1, three correspondingly complex translators T_1, T_2, and T_3 are required to translate the user languages to machine language. In figure 2, an intermediate language MM is introduced as the target language for the translators; MM is nearer the level of the user languages, and translators T_1, T_2, and T_3 are simplified. Although we have introduced a new translator T for translating MM to M, we have reduced the total translation problem. The saving grows in proportion to the number of languages L_i supported.

Another advantage indicated by figure 2 is the possibility of modifying the actual hardware machine with which M is used (and modifying T) until eventually T disappears and M converges to MM. This process may proceed without disturbing the T_i's, to which such migration is totally transparent. Thus hardware migration may proceed independently of initial user-language translator creation.

At this point, we may envision the possibility, for any machine language M, of building a language MM with the characteristics indicated. Let us be more audacious and observe that MM need not even be related to a given machine language M. That is, let us introduce the possibility of developing an intermediate language MM, independent of any real machine, to which user languages are compiled in a hardware machine-independent manner. Since we are assuming that development of new user languages is a more frequent occurrence than development of new hardware machine languages, our goal is to place MM as near the level of user languages (as far left in figure 3) as possible.

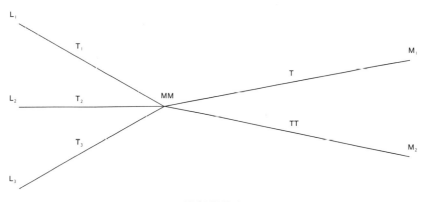

FIGURE 3

If one takes the pessimistic view that the semantics of most high-level languages have little in common, then he will conclude that MM, as a common target language for translators, will be very low level, and that building of translators T_i will be little easier than translating directly into machine language. But the thesis of this book is that user-language semantics have much in common at a high level, and that an MM can be developed reflecting that commonality at a high level.

It is not ostensibly the purpose of this book to develop or describe such an intermediate language. Our primary purpose is to study the important structural characteristics of various prominent high-level languages. But this study will, quite necessarily, produce as a byproduct a set of guidelines for such design. These guidelines should be comprehensive in breadth of coverage, though not in depth. The book, viewed in this light, may therefore be of use to any system designer who is interested in developing such a language for use in a particular environment.

This presumption follows from the organization of the book's contents, which at the outer level factors by language concepts, not by individual languages. Thus, for example, discussion of control mechanisms in high-level languages is localized and refers to many different languages; discussion of PL/I as a particular language is, on the other hand, spread across several chapters. This approach helps to clarify, rather than camouflage, the important semantic similarities and differences among the various languages. To minimize interlanguage terminology barriers, a common terminology is evolved and applied to all languages described. Since this terminology is intended to serve as a vehicle of exposition, it must satisfy two constraints: (1) it must be general enough to describe the phenomena of a number of languages; and (2) it must be high-level enough to allow simple and painless descriptions of parochial aspects of particular languages in its terms. These constraints lead us to hope that it might closely reflect the concepts of an intermediate language such as we have characterized.

The book does not present a comprehensive treatment of any individual language. Trivia of syntax and semantics are omitted in favor of emphasis on more interesting structural characteristics. The dividend for the reader should be a broadened insight into the functional characteristics of various programming languages, and a heightened sensitivity for recognizing the semantic requirements of a problem-solving task and for selecting a programming language appropriate for that task. A language critic or designer may develop a keener insight into what lies below the surface of various language constructs. In short, we hope that the reader may emerge as more a linguist than a multilingual journeyman.

Ideally it might be possible to embark on this study without prior familiarization with any particular languages, their semantic constructs, syntax, or descriptive terminology. Unfortunately, in practice, structured treatment of any discipline must usually follow an acquaintance involving at least a superficial working knowledge. For this reason, the first portion of this book provides brief, informal introductions to a cross-section of prominent languages that are later drawn on for illustration. These introductions are not comprehensive or detailed, and they include frequent errors of simplification, but they give a flavor for the various languages, their problem-solving features, and their descriptive terminology.

The remainder of the book assumes a casual familiarity with the languages introduced. We occasionally rely on the reader's intuitive understanding of informal use of terms such as *block structure, subroutine, array, structure, loop, interrupt,* and *format.* We also take the liberty of considering such terms nontechnical. Just as an English dictionary is comprehensible only to those who read and understand English, the remainder of this book is comprehensible only to those who have some knowledge of programming.

The second and third parts of this book provide the analysis of language features; they differ from each other, not in style of treatment, but in degree of generality of concepts discussed. The third part includes introductions to two special-purpose languages.

The appendices provide ancillary information ranging from elementary automata theory to language-syntax description to compilation techniques. The concepts discussed are not directly related to the remainder of the language study, but they are ones with which any computer-language scientist will eventually come in contact and require familiarization.

A bibliography of programming-language literature is provided, and references to this literature are included wherever relevant throughout the book. Each reference is given by the first three letters of an author's name, followed by the last two digits of the year of publication. The reference is enclosed in brackets.

For earlier discussions of the high-level language approach described in this Introduction, see [Str58], [Con58], and [Ste61].

SECTION I

Introductions to Programming Languages

CHAPTER 1

FORTRAN

FORTRAN is a user language developed for the solution of scientific problems involved primarily with numerical computation. It is of interest to us as one of the earliest and the most widely used high-level languages for scientific problem solving. Many of its design characteristics have been carried over into a host of modern languages; Its Influence on language development cannot be overstated.

In this chapter, we shall discuss the FORTRAN IV language, since it is richer in features than its predecessors, FORTRAN I and FORTRAN II.

1.1 ARITHMETIC

FORTRAN arithmetic expressions may in most contexts be of arbitrary complexity, and may use a variety of built-in functions and the following operators:

+	addition
−	subtraction
*	multiplication
/	division
**	exponentiation

Each of these operators works on pairs of data items, each of which may be either of two types: REAL or INTEGER. INTEGER data (whether variables or constants) must be integral, but the domain of REAL data is all real numbers.

The type of a variable is determined in either of two ways. If the programmer gives no type specification for it, the first character of its name determines its type. Names beginning with any of the letters from I through N are taken to be INTEGER, all others REAL. It is, however, possible to specify explicitly the type of a variable. The declarations

        REAL MINUTES
        INTEGER DAY, YEAR

indicate that the variable MINUTES may take on all real values, while DAY and YEAR accept only integer values.

The type of a constant is determined by whether it is written with a decimal point.

        73   integer constant of value 73
        73.   real constant of value 73
        73.2E-4   real constant of value .00732

The type of a constant is important because of the general restriction that operators other than $**$ may not take on operands of different types. Thus, in absence of type declarations, the following expressions are legal:

        I + 40
        A + 2.

but the ones below are illegal:

        A + 2
        I + .4E + 2

Since expressions can be of arbitrary complexity, we can write $A + B * 3.4$ as a valid expression. Without further evaluation rules, however, this might be interpreted as either "the multiplication of the sum of A and B by 3.4" or "the addition of A to the product of B and 3.4." An evaluation order can be forced by use of parentheses, as in $(A + B) * 3.4$ or $A + (B * 3.4)$. Operations within parentheses are performed first, but default rules are otherwise used to resolve ambiguity. These rules are discussed further in chapter 6 and appendix 1.

The result of an expression evaluation is typically retained by storing it in a variable specified to the left of the symbol = in an assignment statement. Thus

        $E = RM * C ** 2$

evaluates the expression on the right of the = and assigns the result value to the variable E.

1.2 ARRAYS

A variable name may identify an array of data items of the same type rather than only a single data item. Thus the declaration

DIMENSION A (2,3)

identifies A as a two-dimensional array (a matrix) of real numbers, with elements graphically arranged as follows:

$$A_{1,1} \quad A_{1,2} \quad A_{1,3}$$
$$A_{2,1} \quad A_{2,2} \quad A_{2,3}$$

An element of an array is referred to by specifying the array name and a set of subscripts (indices), one for each dimension of the array. Thus, given the above declaration, A(2,I) retrieves $A_{2,1}$, $A_{2,2}$, or $A_{2,3}$, depending on the value of I.

1.3 LOOPS, BRANCHES, AND CONDITIONALS

Suppose we have a one-dimensional array A of 100 elements, and we wish to compute the sum of the values of those elements. One way is to execute the statement

SUM = A(1)+A(2)+ . . . +A(100)

but this is evidently tedious for large arrays. Alternatively we can use the following sequence of statements.

```
     SUM = 0
     I = 1
10   SUM = SUM+A(I)
     I = I+1
     IF(I−100) 10, 10, 20
20   next statement
```

We initialize SUM to 0 and set I to the subscript value of the first array element. The third statement is labeled in the FORTRAN manner by the integer 10. This statement assigns to SUM the current value of SUM plus the value of A(I), which in this first execution is A(1). I is increased by 1 and then a test is made by the IF statement. If the value of I−100 is negative, we go to statement 10 (the first label given in the IF statement); if it is 0, we also go to 10 (the second label); if it is positive, we go to 20. This last case occurs only when I is greater than 100 and our sum is complete.

We have seen here the conditional branching capability of the arithemtic IF. There is, of course, an unconditional branch statement. For example, GOTO 30 always causes a transfer to statement 30.

A second type of IF statement is also available. The logical IF conditionally executes a statement, depending on the truth or falseness of a proposition. We could replace our arithmetic IF statement above by the logical IF statement

    IF(I .LE. 100)GOTO 10

This statement would cause a transfer to 10 if I were less than or equal to 100.

Repetitive looping (iteration) over a sequence of statements is common enough to be specifiable with a more stylized statement. The following code is equivalent to our above sequence:

```
        SUM = 0
        DO 10 I = 1,100,1
10          SUM = SUM + A(I)
20   next statement
```

Here SUM is again initialized to 0. The DO statement specifies that a sequence of code (in this case, a single statement) up to the statement with a given label (10) is to be executed repeatedly. The first time I is to have the first value following "I = " (1); successive iterations are to be performed by incrementing I each time by the third value (1); the iterations are to terminate when the value of I exceeds the second value (100). I is known as the control variable for the loop.

1.4 INPUT/OUTPUT

In this section, we cover the simplest varieties of input/output involving standard external devices. The programmer is able to define and use more specialized data files, but we need not go into those features.

The statements used for input and output of data are READ and PRINT, respectively. Each identifies the data items to be transmitted and a FORMAT statement describing the layout of the data on the external device. Consider the following program:

```
        READ(9,1) A,B,I,X
        Y = A*B+X**I
        PRINT(10,2) Y
        STOP
```

```
1   FORMAT(2E16.8,I10,E10.7)
2   FORMAT(E16.8)
    END
```

The READ statement causes input of values for the four indicated variables according to the FORMAT statement labeled 1, from the device represented by 9. This format specifies that the first two items, A and B, will be in the form of real numbers in successive sixteen-column fields. If either field contains no decimal point, a point eight columns to the left of its end will be assumed. The next variable, I, will be in the form of an integer, located within the next ten columns. X will be in real form in the next ten columns.

The calculation $A*B+X**I$ is performed. Then the result, Y, is printed, according to the FORMAT statement labeled 2, on device 10 (in a sixteen-column field in real form). It will be printed as an eight-digit number of magnitude less than 1, with an exponent providing the needed power.

STOP terminates program execution, and END indicates the physical end of the program text. Thus this example gives a complete, even if not especially interesting, program.

The DATA statement provides for compile-time assignment of values to variables, thus avoiding the execution-time overhead experienced when values are obtained from an external device. It can be used when the values are known at progrom compile-time.

```
DATA A,B,I/3.2E-4,25.6,15/
```

The statement above causes the ordered assignments to A, B, and I to take place at compile-time. Thus the variables will have the indicated values at the beginning of program execution.

A strong dynamic power of FORTRAN is the ability to read FORMAT statements, so that formats need not be decided upon prior to execution. Consider the following example:

```
DIMENSION FORM(20)
READ(9,1) FORM
  .
  .
  .
  .
WRITE(10,FORM) A,B,C
  .
  .
1   FORMAT(20A4)
```

The READ statement brings in twenty words, each comprising four characters, into the array FORM. That collection of characters is subsequently interpreted as a format specification for the WRITE statement.

The NAMELIST statement provides for reading in data items according to their self-identification on the input file. Thus, the NAMELIST statement below identifies ITEMS as a list of names, namely, the list A, B, C. Values for these variables can be read by the READ statement that refers to ITEMS.

    NAMELIST/ITEMS/A,B,C
    .
    .
    READ(9,ITEMS)

Suppose that when the READ is executed, the input file contains:

    $INPUT
    C = 23.5,A = 4.6E − 2
    $END

The values for A and C will be read in, but B will be unchanged. Thus, NAMELIST provides an increased ability for program execution to be driven by data rather than by instructions. We discuss this subject further in chapter 12.

1.5 EXTENDED BRANCHING FEATURES

We have mentioned that GOTO and IF statements provide for transfer of control to indicated statements. Additional features available with GOTO permit determination of the target of a branch to be deferred until execution. Consider the following examples.

    I = 3
    .
    .
    GOTO(10,20,30,40),I

The GOTO statement above is called a *computed* GOTO. Its effect is to evaluate I (in this case 3), and transfer to the statement number given as the Ith (here third) list entry. (In this case, transfer would be to statement 30.)

    ASSIGN 30 TO I
    .
    .
    GOTO I (10,20,30,40)

The *assigned* GOTO above also causes a branch to statement 30. The list in this statement identifies statements to which control might be transferred, and is used by the FORTRAN compiler in setting up the executable program.

1.6 FUNCTIONS, SUBROUTINES, AND PARAMETERS

Functions and subroutines are programs that may be invoked to execute from any point in another program. Either may receive parameters from a calling program, but they differ in whether or not a result is returned.

```
        .
        .
CALL X(A,I)       SUBROUTINE X(B,J)
        .               .
        .               .
                    RETURN
                        .
                    END
```

The CALL statement in the program on the left causes execution of the subroutine X, and passes the variables A and I as arguments to the corresponding parameters B and J. Then X executes and, at some point, issues a RETURN statement. This terminates X and returns control to the statement following the CALL in the calling program.

```
        .
        .
A = C + X(A,I) + Z  FUNCTION X(B,J)
        .               .
                    X = B*3.+H**J
                        .
                    RETURN
                        .
                    END
```

Here the calling effect is similar, but, in this case, X is a function that returns a result. Note that X is invoked when encountered in the assignment statement. Its returned value is the last value assigned to X prior to its return. That value is used in the expression, whose evaluation is then continued.

Either a function or a subroutine may have entry points in addition to the normal entry point at its start. Furthermore, different entry points to a routine may accept values for different parameters. In the following example, the subroutine x is entered at the ENTRY statement, rather than at the top of the subroutine.

```
                .
                .
CALL  Y         SUBROUTINE  X(P)
  .                 .
  .                 .
                ENTRY  Y
                    .
                    .
                END
```

Another return feature allows a return to be made from a subroutine to a statement label passed as an argument by the calling program. Thus, the caller below passes statements 10 and 20 as possible return points from x. These are provided for by asterisks in x's parameter list. The IF statement conditionally causes return from x to statement 10 (the first statement-label parameter), or return is made later to statement 20.

```
CALL  X(A,B,10S,20S)   SUBROUTINE  X(Y,Z,*,*)
                          .
                          .
                       IF(G .EQ. H)RETURN 1
                          .
                          .
                       RETURN  2
                          .
                          .
                       END
```

Array dimensions must normally be given as constant values, since storage is obtained for them prior to execution. But if an array is passed as an argument to a function or subroutine, that routine need not know in advance the bounds of the array. The calling program can pass as arguments the dimensions of any array arguments, and the called routine can use its corresponding parameters to indicate dimensions of its array parameters.

```
DIMENSION A(10)       SUBROUTINE  X(B,N)
       .              DIMENSION  B(N)
       .
CALL X(A,10)
```

The reader should now study the FORTRAN program at the end of section I (see page 57).

1.7 ADDITIONAL DATA TYPES

In addition to REAL and INTEGER data, FORTRAN recognizes several other data types that we shall look at briefly.

LOGICAL data takes on the Boolean values .TRUE. and .FALSE. as values. The operators .NOT., .AND., and .OR. are available for use with such data.

COMPLEX data are definable as pairs of real quantities. The arithmetic operators work on such data according to the normal mathematical rules for complex numbers.

Data may be declared DOUBLE PRECISION, in which case the amount of storage allotted for the data is double that otherwise allotted. This feature is of use when the normal precision available for numeric quantities is not adequate.

1.8 DATA SHARING AMONG PROGRAMS

We have seen how argument-parameter relations allow sharing of data among programs. It is possible to provide for such sharing among any number of routines without the explicit parameter-passing mechanism. Suppose each of three programs contains the following declaration. This indicates that the arrays A, B, and C are to be accessible commonly to each of them.

    COMMON A(100), B(20), C(50,10)

1.9 OVERLAYING OF DATA

Suppose that a program requires use of two large arrays, A(50,50) and B(3000), during its execution. Suppose further that use of A is completed before use of B begins. If storage space is at a premium, the same storage area can be used for both arrays. This can be accomplished by the EQUIVALENCE statement

    EQUIVALENCE (A(1,1), B(1))

This statement specifies that the starting location for the array A (the location of A(1,1)) is to be the same as the starting location for B. The storage is thus shared during execution, with B overlaying A.

This use of EQUIVALENCE is highly oriented to pragmatics of machine storage space, and is not of particular interest linguistically. But let us consider another way of using the feature that is not motivated by the desire to save storage space.

Assume that an application uses an array of 100 data items. Certain portions of the program work on the array as though it were a 10×10 matrix, performing operations along rows or columns. Other parts of the program treat the array as a vector of 100 elements. Given the following declarations, the names A and B can be used interchangeably to refer to the same data. A is used when a vector interpretation is desired; B is used when a matrix interpretation is needed.

```
DIMENSION A(100), B(10,10)
EQUIVALENCE (A(1), B(1,1))
```

Note that use of the feature in this way presupposes a knowledge of the storage order of array elements, so that the desired associations are obtained. Different FORTRAN dialects use different orderings, but we shall assume that FORTRAN arrays are stored in row-major order, meaning, in the case of B above, the order

$$B_{1,1}, B_{1,2},\dots B_{1,10}, B_{2,1}, B_{2,2},\dots B_{2,10},\dots B_{10,1}, B_{10,2},\dots B_{10,10}$$

In general, row-major order denotes that the rightmost subscript varies most rapidly, then the second rightmost, and so on. With such mapping knowledge, the programmer can effectively remap data aggregates to his convenience, simply by using different names for each mapping and EQUIVALENCE specifications.

1.10 SUMMARY

This completes our look at FORTRAN. Descriptions have been relatively general, as they will be in subsequent language discussions. It is hoped that the reader previously unfamiliar with FORTRAN has obtained some flavor of the language and a feel for its capabilities. Such comprehension is sufficient for continuing this study. Those interested in a more detailed specification of the FORTRAN IV language should see [Stu69], [Lec66], and [Gol65].

CHAPTER 2

ALGOL 60

ALGOL 60 may, at a gross functional level, be viewed as similar to FORTRAN. It is intended for solution of numeric and scientific problems. The importance of the ALGOL language, however, lies not so much in its functional capabilities as in the underlying structure that hosts those capabilities. As we shall see, ALGOL programs operate under a discipline contrasting sharply with the simplicity of FORTRAN. This discipline establishes a protocol that provides useful guidelines for program creation.

2.1 ARITHMETIC

ALGOL's arithmetic capabilities, in terms of both data types and operators, are similar to those of FORTRAN. The same basic operators and a similar set of built-in functions are provided, and data may be of REAL or INTEGER type. All variables in an ALGOL program must have a type declaration.

```
REAL ALPHA, B, MAG;
INTEGER GAMMA;
```

These statements declare ALPHA, B, and MAG to be real variables and GAMMA to be an integer variable.

As in FORTRAN, expressions may be arbitrarily complex, with a combination of precedence rules and parentheses dictating an evaluation order. We have, in fact, overstated the expression complexity allowed in FORTRAN; that language has a number of contexts, such as subscripts, in which only a restricted variety of expressions can be specified. ALGOL is much more liberal; it allows an arbitrary expression wherever a numeric value is required.

2.2 ARRAYS

ALGOL's features for defining arrays are broader than those of FORTRAN in two ways:

1. Whereas FORTRAN always assumes a lower bound of 1 on each dimension, ALGOL allows specification of both upper and lower bounds. Given the declaration

   REAL ARRAY A[3:5,-4:-3];

we may visualize A as follows:

$$A_{3,-4} \quad A_{3,-3}$$
$$A_{4,-4} \quad A_{4,-3}$$
$$A_{5,-4} \quad A_{5,-3}$$

2. Whereas array dimensions in FORTRAN must be given as constants (except for array parameters), ALGOL allows use of arbitrary expressions for dimension specifications:

   INTEGER ARRAY B[N + 1:3∗N + 4];

At time of definition of B, which is not in general prior to program execution, N is evaluated and the bounds of B are set accordingly.

2.3 LOOPS, BRANCHES, AND CONDITIONALS

ALGOL has somewhat more powerful features for conditional execution than FORTRAN does. In the example below, if the sum of A and B is less than 100, control is transferred to the statement labeled REPEAT (note that labels are given as names rather than integers). Otherwise A is incremented by 10 (the symbol : = is the ALGOL assignment operator), and execution continues with the next statement.

   IF A+B<100 THEN GO TO REPEAT ELSE A: = A+10;

It is also possible in ALGOL that the statement following THEN, the one

Red's Towing Service

6201 MICHIGAN AVENUE
DETROIT, MICHIGAN 48210
897-7746 • 897-7747

N° 2503

NAME

STREET_____ PHONE

CITY_____ DATE 5-27-77

MAKE AND YEAR	LICENSE NO.	MILEAGE
Dodge 2009	N6X-762	

	AMOUNT
TOWING	17 50
DOLLY BLOCKS	
STORAGE	
LABOR	_Paid_
SERIAL #	_cash_
ABA	
FROM 94 WB E of Trumbull	
TO Mich & Livernois	
RECEIVED BY TOTAL	

following ELSE, or both be a collection of statements (a compound statement).

We note at this point, after observing evaluation of truth-valued expressions, that Boolean variables are declarable in ALGOL and can take on true or false values. The operators used with such data are ~(not), ∧ (and), ∨ (or), ⊃ (implies), and ≡ (equivalent to).

Iteration in ALGOL is functionally similar to that in FORTRAN, but is rather different in form.

```
SUM: = 0;
FOR I: = J STEP K UNTIL N+2 DO
    SUM: = SUM+A[I];
```

This sequence of statements adds selected elements of array A, depending on the values of J, K, and N. I is initialized to the value of J and incremented by the value of K. The iteration stops when I exceeds N+2 (or if K is negative, when N+2 exceeds I). Again the summation statement could be a compound statement.

Another form of ALGOL loop allows iteration while a given condition is true. Thus, the iteration below continues as long as A = B, with I having the value 1.

```
FOR I: = 1 WHILE A = B DO
    statement;
```

More dynamic branching specification is available in ALGOL, as in FORTRAN, via assigned or computed GOTO's.

```
SWITCH L: = LAB1,LAB2,LAB3;
    .
    .
    .
GO TO L[I+J];
```

In this example, L is declared as a switch with a list of three statement labels. The GO TO evaluates I+J (presumably to one of the values 1, 2, or 3) and branches accordingly to the first, second, or third label given in L's declaration list.

2.4 CONDITIONAL EXPRESSIONS

We have looked at the conditional statement; now we observe more general ways in which conditional specification may be used.

```
A: = B+IF I>J THEN C ELSE D+5;
```

A is to be assigned the sum of B and either of two values, one of which is selected by evaluation of the conditional expression I>J. If I is greater than J, A is assigned the value of B+C; otherwise A is assigned the value of B+D+5.

GO TO IF I = J THEN L1 ELSE L2;

If I is equal to J, then transfer is made to L1; otherwise transfer is made to L2.

GO TO IF D+5>J THEN L3 ELSE L4;

If D+5 is greater than J, then transfer is made to L3; otherwise transfer is made to L4.

2.5 PROGRAM STRUCTURE

We turn now to the important structural characteristics of the ALGOL language.

2.5.1 THE BLOCK CONCEPT

A complete ALGOL program, which we shall also designate a block, consists of the keyword BEGIN, a sequence of declarations, a sequence of statements, and finally the keyword END. Thus the following statements are an example of an ALGOL program. (In ALGOL, ↑ is the exponentiation operator; WRITE is the output statement.)

```
BEGIN
     REAL A, B;
     INTEGER I;
     B: = A↑I;
     WRITE(B);
END
```

The above program is also an example of a block, which is itself a valid type of ALGOL statement. And we just said that a program, or block, consists of, among other things, a sequence of statements. This phenomenon leads us to the notion of a nest of blocks, since any block may contain, as one of its statements, another block. Such nests are the basis of the ALGOL program structure.

The text below denotes a series of ALGOL statements, highlighting block initiations (labeled) and terminations. The drawing illustrates the logical block nestings implied.

We can graphically depict the ALGOL block structure as follows:

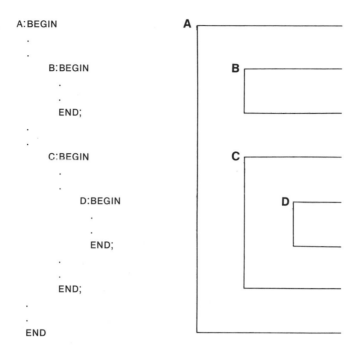

```
A:BEGIN
    .
    .
        B:BEGIN
            .
            .
        END;
    .
    .
        C:BEGIN
            .
            .
                D:BEGIN
                    .
                    .
                END;
            .
            .
        END;
    .
    .
END
```

2.5.2 SCOPE OF NAMES

We have seen that a block may include declarations of names to be used in the block. Let us now investigate the relation of these declarations to names referred to within a block.

As one might expect, if a reference to a name declared in a block occurs within that block, the reference is to the data item described by the declaration. In the following example, the reference to x denotes the x given in the declaration, regardless of the context in which block A occurs in a program.

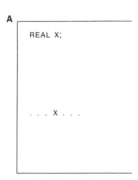

```
A
    REAL X;



    . . . X . . .
```

Now consider a somewhat more complex situation:

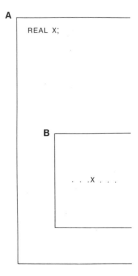

Block B contains reference to X but no declaration for it. However, B's containing block, A, contains a declaration for X, so the reference to X in B is resolved to this declaration.

Now consider the following program:

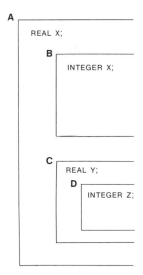

The names X, Y, and Z are known within blocks and resolved to declarations as indicated below.

Block	Resolution
A	X declared in A
B	X declared in B
C	X declared in A
	Y declared in C
D	X declared in A
	Y declared in C
	Z declared in D

The general rule for resolving a name to a declaration is as follows:

> If the name is declared in the block containing the reference, then that is the appropriate declaration, and the data item is said to be *local* to the block. Otherwise the containing block is searched for a declaration, then its containing block, and so on, until a declaration of the name is found. The reference is resolved to the first declaration found. In these cases, the data item is said to be *non-local* to the block in which the reference occurs.

We can now speak of the scope of a declaration of a name as being the block in which the declaration appears, plus all contained blocks not providing a new declaration of the same name. This stratification of the naming process provides a flexible means for selective sharing or privacy of names within blocks.

2.5.3 ALLOCATION OF STORAGE FOR DATA

The block structuring of ALGOL hosts another language flexibility that we shall consider first in terms of storage management. Recall from chapter 1 that storage for all FORTRAN data is allocated prior to program execution. This makes techniques (such as EQUIVALENCE) that allow reuse of storage during execution useful and even necessary. It also excludes the possibility of dynamically calculating the size of an array and then allocating the array accordingly; in general, dimensions have to be constant.

In ALGOL, storage for a variable is allocated only upon entry to the block in which the variable is declared; that storage is freed upon exit from the block. Since dynamic allocation is possible, storage for data is required only while that data is needed in a program.

Now let us look at the language implications of this storage picture. Its most significant value is that one can calculate the dimensions of an array before entering the block in which that array is declared. Upon entry to the block, the array comes into being with the desired bounds.

```
BEGIN
     INTEGER N;
     READ (N);
     BEGIN
          REAL A[1:N,1:N+1];
          .
          .
     END;
     .
     .

END
```

In the example above the outer block calculates N, in this case by reading it, and then the block using array A is entered. At the time of entry, N and N+1 are evaluated to provide the bounds for A.

A second important language aspect of storage management can also be seen in the above example. Since storage for A is freed when the inner block has finished execution and terminated, any values assigned to elements of A are lost. If the block is reentered later in execution, a new A comes into being; the old A, and the values of its elements, are not restored.

This loss of data values does, in some cases, cause problems. Suppose that a certain block, nested deeply within an ALGOL program, must record information about its executions during a program run. (It may of course be executed any number of times.) No other block needs this information, so use of private data variables declared in the block seems in order. Yet each time the block's execution is terminated, the values of these data elements will be lost. One solution is to require an outer block to make the declarations (and to ensure that no other containing blocks modify the data elements or redeclare the names).

A better solution adopted in ALGOL is use of OWN variables. If a variable is declared to be OWN, the scope of its name is as usual, but its value is not lost upon termination of an execution of the declaring block. Thus the variable can be used to store information across executions of the block, and its name can still be known only to that block.

2.6 PROCEDURES AND PARAMETERS

Proper procedures and *function procedures* are ALGOL analogs of FORTRAN *subroutines* and *functions*, respectively. A procedure is closely related to a block, from the standpoint of program structure as we have been describing it; in fact, the body of a procedure is a block. But procedures differ from blocks in their mode of initiation and termination, and in their ability to accept parameters from a calling block.

```
REAL PROCEDURE P(X,Y);
      VALUE X;
      REAL X;
      REAL ARRAY Y;
      BEGIN
         .
         .
         .
      END;
```

In the example above, P, a function procedure, has two formal parameters, X and Y. (Recall that FORTRAN *arguments* are passed by a caller to corresponding *parameters* in the called routine; in ALGOL, *actual parameters* are passed to *formal parameters*.) X is a formal parameter by VALUE, Y a formal parameter by NAME. This difference is discussed in detail in chapter 5, but we can outline it as follows: If a formal parameter is to be received by value, every reference to that parameter in the called procedure yields the value of the actual parameter at the time of the call. If a formal parameter is received by name, every such reference yields the value of the actual parameter at the time of the reference.

X is declared to represent a REAL quantity, Y a REAL ARRAY. Note that no bounds are given for Y. Instead, the bounds are passed as a logical part of the array actual parameter, so that subscripted references to Y can be interpreted correctly.

The body of the procedure follows as a normal ALGOL block. The returned value of the procedure is the last value assigned to the name P.

An ALGOL procedure is invoked only as a result of an explicit reference to it, either within an expression (for a function procedure) or in an invoking statement consisting solely of the procedure name and actual parameter list (for a proper procedure). A procedure definition is skipped if encountered during normal sequential statement execution.

The point of return from a function procedure or proper procedure is analogous to that in FORTRAN. Labels can be passed to proper procedures and used as return points by means of GO TO's containing label formal parameters.

A procedure name is considered to be declared in the block containing the procedure definition; its scope is as for any other name. It can, of course, be invoked only from a point in the program at which its name is known.

The reader should now study the ALGOL program at the end of section I (see page 58).

2.7 RECURSION

An ALGOL procedure can call itself during its execution just as it can call other procedures. This type of call is known as a *recursive call*.

```
INTEGER PROCEDURE FACTORIAL (N);
    INTEGER N;
    FACTORIAL: = IF N<3 THEN N ELSE N ∗ FACTORIAL (N–1);
```

FACTORIAL evaluates the factorial of its positive-integer formal parameter N. If N<3 then FACTORIAL (N) = N. Otherwise FACTORIAL (N) = N ∗ FACTORIAL (N − 1). Thus, for example,

$$
\begin{aligned}
\text{FACTORIAL } (4) &= 4 \ast \text{FACTORIAL } (3) \\
&= 4 \ast (3 \ast \text{FACTORIAL } (2)) \\
&= 4 \ast (3 \ast 2) \\
&= 24
\end{aligned}
$$

We are not intending here to explain recursion as a programming technique, or to advocate its use in computing factorials. We wish only to point out the availability of the mechanism. When a procedure calls itself recursively, it is as though it were calling an identical copy of itself located at the same point in the block structure. Thus new copies of local data are created for each level of a recursive call. We look in detail at recursion in chapter 13.

2.8 SUMMARY

ALGOL is functionally similar to FORTRAN (recursion is one of the few added features). But as the reader should sense, its structural aspects introduce programming disciplines and protocols that make it a much more sophisticated vehicle for problem solution. The reader who desires more detail of ALGOL 60 should see [Bau64], [Lec67], and [Ekm65]. A complete formal syntactic description of the language is given in appendix 3.

CHAPTER 3

PL/I

PL/I was developed during the middle 1960s in an attempt to bring to-gether the features of a number of earlier, less general-purpose lan-guages. At this time FORTRAN and ALGOL were widely used for numeric applications, and assembly languages were preferred for systems pro-gramming. Commercial applications, involving primarily data-file manip-ulations, were processed chiefly in COBOL ([Lys68] and [Ros67]), while more specialized applications such as string manipulation and list proc-essing might be done in special-purpose languages such as LISP and SNOBOL, which we discuss in chapters 16 and 17.

This proliferation of languages was thought by many to be intoler-able for two reasons: (1) an installation might have a difficult time sup-porting and maintaining a large number of languages and educating people in several of them; and (2) increasingly sophisticated application programs were beginning to require features spreading across several languages.

The PL/I philosophy was that it should be possible to create a single programming language containing, in a unified way, features ade-quate for programming any kind of application. That total set of features would not necessarily make PL/I as easy to use in a specialized applica-tion as a language designed only for that purpose; but features would be present to make programming for that application feasible. And for any application broad enough to require features of several previous lan-guages, PL/I would be the optimum language to use.

As one might expect, the language resulting from such an intent is very large by any standard: number of data types, number of operators, number of statements, and the like. It is, after all, a language designed to be totally general purpose by incorporating features from many disciplines. There is an alternative approach toward building a language adequate for many types of applications: extensibility, which we discuss in chapter 18. That approach is built around incorporating only the barest essentials into the base language, but providing within that language the ability to define new constructs in terms of basic ones in order to enrich the language in particular directions. The result of that approach is a small core language adequate in itself for only limited use, but having a powerful set of basic features allowing extensions. As we have explained, PL/I was not designed according to this approach; it is a single large language, not easily extensible, but adequate in itself for many types of applications.

3.1 DESIGN PROBLEMS

The goals established for PL/I led to several large design problems, the most serious of which revolved around the size of the language. A person using the language within a particular application area should not have to understand language features irrelevant to his needs; on the other hand, a person using the language more broadly should be able to use all of its features in a smooth and integrated manner. In other words, the language must be *modular*, or *orthogonal:* different sets of features must be usable independently; and yet it must be *integrated:* features used together must mesh easily.

A second problem related to language size was that of keywords within the language. Previous languages reserved such terms (DO, BEGIN, DIMENSION, WHILE, and so forth), not allowing them to be used as programmer-selected names. This restriction avoided problems of syntactic ambiguity that might otherwise result (for example, was a particular occurrence of WHILE a use of the keyword WHILE or of a variable?). But in PL/I, the large number of keywords, and the desire to permit users to know only parts of the language required for their needs, made this approach unattractive. So keywords were in general not reserved, with the result that a number of unusual syntactic forms were introduced to ensure that no ambiguities would arise.

A third problem stemmed from a desire that the language be usable for systems programming. Such languages (usually, assembly languages) are, as a rule, highly specific to the particular machines for which they are designed. Systems programming is, after all, the tailoring of a particular machine for certain uses. Other applications, such as arithmetic problem-solving, are quite independent of machine considerations. Therefore, languages like FORTRAN and ALGOL are defined in a manner relatively independent of particular hardware machines and can be implemented satisfactorily on many of them. Could PL/I be designed in such a way that it was usable for systems programming yet easy to implement on numerous machines for problem solving?

This dilemma resulted in language features compromising the two needs. For example, an UNSPEC built-in function was provided to return the internal representation of a datum. The formats of both the operator and the result of UNSPEC are defined independent of a particular machine, but the content of the result (a string of bits) is not defined in the language. It is defined only by a particular implementation of the language on a particular machine, and is thus said to be implementation-dependent.

A further problem arose because of the realization that the language would have to be augmented over a number of years following its initial use. The first attempt at a language so all-encompassing would not include every desirable feature. The problem was to ensure that PL/I programs running satisfactorily would not run differently when additions were made. It often seemed that a certain feature should be defined in one way if a certain extended feature were present, but in a different way if that feature were not. This desire had to be suppressed, resulting sometimes in defining constructs to be illegal, sometimes in precluding certain types of extensions, and sometimes in awkward incorporation of extensions.

All of these problems arose because of the size and general-purpose characteristic of the language. PL/I is not always esthetically pleasing, but it is useful to study because of the wide variety of features that it offers.

3.2 DATA TYPES AND OPERATIONS

It is only a slight exaggeration to say that the data types available in a language completely determine the rest of the language. Therefore, we center much of our discussion of PL/I language features around the data types to which those features relate. For this discussion we assume that PL/I has a block structure similar to that of ALGOL. In section 3.6 we look further at this structure. Attributes of PL/I data items are given in DECLARE statements, which in general are processed at block entry time, although DECLARE's may appear at any point in a block. Normally all the attributes of a variable are declared together (e.g., DECLARE A FIXED DECIMAL EXTERNAL, B FLOAT COMPLEX EXTERNAL), but one also can factor attributes common to a number of variables. (DECLARE (A FIXED DECIMAL, B FLOAT COMPLEX) EXTERNAL is equivalent to the above declaration.)

Remember throughout this discussion of attributes and data types that default assumptions are made for virtually every class of attributes in the language; variables need not ever be declared, in which case a complete set of defaults are applied. In addition, there are many cases where the use of a variable in a certain context implies certain characteristics for it. If the variable has not been declared, these are assumed instead of the usual defaults. For example, the usual default characteristics for undeclared variables not starting with one of the letters from I through N are FLOAT DECIMAL REAL. However, if the identifier P is first encountered as an undeclared variable in the statement CALL P, then P is contextually declared to be of type ENTRY.

It is useful to separate PL/I data into two classes: (1) problem data, the strings and numbers to be processed; and (2) program data (labels, pointers, and so forth), the language tools used in this processing.

One type of PL/I problem data is arithmetic data. Arithmetic data items have four primary characteristics: *base,* DECIMAL or BINARY; *scale,* FIXED or FLOAT; *mode,* REAL or COMPLEX; and *precision,* (p,q) for FIXED or (p) for FLOAT. For constants, these attributes are not declarable but are taken from the form of the constant. One might argue that, of these four, only mode and precision belong in the realm of language; base and scale are too heavily oriented toward machine and implementation. But these attributes do not actually dictate internal representations. Nothing in PL/I semantics depends on the internal representation of a FLOAT DECIMAL variable; these attributes are, however, reflected in the external forms of presentation of data.

A few words of explanation should be given about the precision attribute. For FIXED data, (p,q) indicates the total number of decimal digits or binary bits and the number of these to the right of the point; for FLOAT data, (p) indicates the mantissa length (there is no provision for specifying characteristic length). Suppose one adds 2.34 (precision (3,2)) and 9.1 (precision (2,1)). Should the precision of the result, 11.44, be (4,2) or (3,1)? That is, should the result include the rightmost 4? Unfortunately, the answer varies with the programmer, depending on whether or not he considers 9.1 equivalent to 9.10. In PL/I, they are considered to be the same; the smaller precision operand is assumed to have trailing zeroes so that the precisions of the operands match, and this longer precision is also taken as the precision of the result. All precision rules are based on the assumption that quantities are exact.

The PL/I arithmetic operators are quite standard: prefix $+$ and $-$; and inflx $+$, $-$, $*$ (multiplication), $/$, and $**$ (exponentiation). PL/I also includes a large number of built-in functions.

We turn now to a second type of PL/I problem data, strings, separable into two subcategories, BIT and CHARACTER. Character strings are used to hold alphanumeric information, while bit strings serve both to hold binary information in string form and to hold truth-functional information.

Strings can be declared to be of either fixed or varying length. For either, a length must be given (in the latter case, representing the maximum length that the string may attain). The length can in general be given by any expression.

Several operators are available for use with string data. The bit-string operators are the three logical connectives: & (and), | (or), and ¬

(not). Bit-string, or logical, operations are performed bit-by-bit, yielding a result of the same length as the operand(s). An operator for use with both bit and character strings is ‖ (concatenation). In addition, for both types of strings, a number of built-in functions are available. For example, SUBSTR(string,m,n) returns a string, of length n, starting at the mth character or bit of the given string. This function may also appear on the left side of an assignment statement (or in other positions of assignment), in which case the expression on the right is stored into the designated portion of the string. (Functions that can be used in this way are called *pseudo-variables*.) INDEX(string1,string2) returns an integer giving the position in string1 where string2 begins. These string operators and built-in functions provide, in theory, for all requirements of building and dissecting strings. A language devoted exclusively to string manipulation would have more operations available, simply for the convenience of the user, but PL/I is not intended to be such a language.

There is one other group of operators, the relational operators, which test equalities and inequalities. They compare algebraically for arithmetic and bit-string operands (bit strings are interpreted as binary integers) and lexically for character strings.

There is also one type of problem data that has not been mentioned, PICTURE data, which we shall not treat in detail. Basically, the programmer is given the ability, through editing characters, to specify precisely the format of strings or numbers. When a desired format does not conform to any specifications available in the language, he can set up his own specifications.

Most of the types of program data are discussed in conjunction with specific language features, but one should be mentioned now because of its general applicability. This is LABEL data. PL/I has label constants appearing as statement prefixes and in GO TO statements. Label variables are also allowed. They may be assigned label constants or variables as values, through assignment statements, and then may be specified in GO TO statements. Label variables are a generalization of the assigned and computed GOTO's of FORTRAN, and of ALGOL switches.

```
        .
        .

    DECLARE LAB LABEL;
        .

        .
    LAB = L1;
        .

        .
    GO TO LAB;
        .

        .
L1:   . . . . . .
```

In the above example, transfer will be made to the statement labeled L1, since L1 is the current value of the label variable LAB.

3.3 DATA CONVERSION

We have discussed the types of problem data and the associated operations that are possible. This area is relatively integrated in PL/I, in that any of the operators may be applied to data of any of the types. This is possible because of the complete set of automatic conversions among data types.

The implication here is that there must be specified not only a precedence table for all of the operators, since they may appear in any combination in an expression, but also precedence rules for conversions—if a variable of type FIXED is added to one of type FLOAT, which should be converted to the type of the other? Often the operand type is determined completely by the operator (e.g., operands used with the bit-string operators must be bit strings); sometimes it is partially determined (the arithmetic operators need arithmetic operands, but base, scale, and mode are not implied); and sometimes it is limited hardly at all (the relational operators derive their semantics from the types of their operands). But wherever an operator does not completely determine its operands, rules for determining conversions are required.

We need not discuss all of the specific conversions, nor even all of the precedence rules for conversions or operators. A few special cases are, however, of interest.

It was a slight exaggeration to say that all conversions are possible, regardless of the data and operators. The exceptional case is that of conversion from character string to either bit string or arithmetic. Roughly, the restriction is that the character string must "look like" some member of the type to which it is being converted—if it is being converted to a bit string, it must contain only zeroes and ones; if to arithmetic, it must contain only characters that can represent, according to PL/I rules, a valid arithmetic constant.

This point on character strings raises a related point dealing with implementation requirements of compilers. If a compiler encounters the expression S+A, where S is a character-string variable and A is, for example, a real arithmetic variable, it must know whether to compile a real or complex addition. Yet it cannot generally determine whether S will at execution time contain a string representing a real or complex number; if the latter, then precedence dictates that the addition be performed in complex mode. This problem has no ideal solution short of complete interpretation in the compiled code, so PL/I specifies a compromise assumption, worth quoting carefully:

> The string will be converted, for the addition, to
> whatever a FIXED DECIMAL REAL variable of maxi-

mum precision would have been converted to if it
had appeared instead.

The conversion from BIT to FIXED BINARY is particularly important, because
it allows truth-functional values to be used in an arithmetic context.

A = 2+(B>C);

The expression B>C yields a BIT value of 1 or 0. This result is converted
to the FIXED BINARY value 1 or 0, and the addition yields a result of either 3
or 2, accordingly.

Another use for this conversion is to simulate conditional expressions that are not available in PL/I. An ALGOL program might contain a
statement of the form

A: = IF e1 THEN e2 ELSE e3;

An analogous PL/I statement has the form

A = e1 * e2 + ¬ e1 * e3;

Unfortunately, this analog is not adequate in many cases, since it requires
evaluation of both e2 and e3.

ALGOL	PL/I
IF B = 0 THEN C ELSE D/B	(B = 0)*C + (B¬ = 0)*D/B

Here the PL/I statement involves a division by 0 if B = 0, whereas the
ALGOL statement evaluates D/B only if B≠0.

3.4 AGGREGATES

Two techniques for grouping data elements are offered in PL/I: (1) *arrays*
(similar to those in ALGOL and FORTRAN) and (2) *structures*. There are
two primary language differences between them. First, arrays must be
homogeneous (contain only elements of the same type), while structures
may be heterogeneous (may contain elements of different types). Second,
array elements are referred to by giving numerical locators relative to a
base, while structure elements are themselves named and referred to by
identifiers.

Let us look at a simple PL/I structure declaration:

DECLARE 1 MAN,
     2 NAME,
          3 FIRST CHARACTER(10),
          3 MIDDLE CHARACTER(10),

3 LAST CHARACTER(10),
2 MANNUMBER FIXED BINARY,
2 SALARY FIXED BINARY;

MAN is a structure with three components (the level-2 entries): NAME, MANNUMBER, and SALARY. The latter two of these are data elements but NAME is itself a substructure with three components (its level-3 entries). We can graphically depict this structure as a tree:

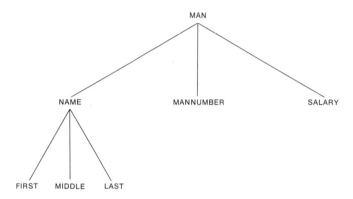

One purpose of grouping data elements into either structures or arrays is unity. It is often desirable to move an aggregate, either through assignment or during input/output, as a single data item. For this reason, PL/I allows the specification of a structure or array name in most contexts, to designate that the action indicated is to apply to all elements of the aggregate.

It is usually advantageous, when data are of the same data type, to form arrays rather than structures if the number of elements is fairly large. The programmer must generate fewer names, and iteration through the aggregate is easier to effect, since subscripts can be used.

PL/I structures represent only one very limited type of list structure. They are trees whose linkages are frozen at compile-time; they have no growth capabilities. A component may have characteristics computed at execution time (e.g., an array with variable bounds), but if the programmer needs a more general list structure, he must build his own using the list-processing features discussed later in this chapter.

Arrays are characterized by a much greater flexibility than structures, though still not all that might be desired in a general array-manipulation language. The number of dimensions of an array must be known at compile-time, and the length of each dimension is frozen when storage is allocated for the array. Thus, for example, one cannot dynamically add rows or columns to a matrix, nor can he add a dimension to a matrix to acquire a three-dimensional array.

The programmer can refer to a *cross section of an array* by putting asterisks in the appropriate subscript positions to indicate iterations over the entire subscript ranges for those dimensions. Thus, A(5, ∗) is a reference to a one-dimensional array, the fifth row of A. A(∗, ∗) is of course equivalent to A.

Arrays may appear in most contexts normally occupied by *scalars* (single data elements); the implication is just an iteration of the indicated action over all of the elements. Thus, for example, the statement A = B + 2, where A and B are arrays with the same bounds, is equivalent to a group of nested loops over the subscript ranges, with the scalar assignment statement A(. . .) = B(. . .) + 2 inside. A frequent, incorrect assumption is that these array operations are carried out in parallel, rather than by sequential iteration. But, for example, the statement A = A / A(1) will not normalize the vector A, described by DECLARE A(10); it will set the first element of A to 1, and then divide all others by that new first element, with no notable impact.

3.5 STORAGE ALLOCATION

In the latitude given the user for specifying when storage for his data is to be allocated and freed, PL/I went somewhat beyond other languages in turning system dictations into user decisions. PL/I data may be specified to have any of four different storage-class attributes. The first of these is STATIC, which specifies (as for all FORTRAN variables) that storage is to be allocated at program load time and not freed until program termination. The second is AUTOMATIC, the ALGOL norm, which specifies that storage is to be allocated upon entry to the block in which a variable is declared, and freed upon exit from the block.

Allocation and freeing of storage for data in the CONTROLLED storage class is entirely under the jurisdiction of the programmer, and is independent of block boundaries. The statements ALLOCATE and FREE provide for explicit allocation and freeing.

```
      .
    .
    DECLARE A CONTROLLED;
    .

    .

    .
    BEGIN;
        .

        .

        .
        ALLOCATE A;
        .

        .

        .
    END;
```

.

.

      FREE A;

.

.

Here storage for the CONTROLLED variable A is allocated when the ALLOCATE statement in the inner block is executed. It is freed when the FREE statement is executed (rather than upon termination of the inner block).

CONTROLLED storage has a subsidiary characteristic of some importance. Suppose that one executes the statement ALLOCATE A, followed prior to a corresponding FREE A by another ALLOCATE A. This sequence produces a new generation of A with the first stacked, to be popped up later when a FREE A is encountered. Thus push-down stacks are available in PL/I. We look in more detail at stacks in chapter 7.

The fourth storage class, BASED storage, is discussed in detail in section 3.7. A variable of this class need never have storage assigned; in this case, it serves through its other attributes as a descriptor of data.

Finally, we mention the INITIAL attribute, whose semantics are tied closely to storage-class considerations. This attribute specifies an initial value to be given to a variable whenever storage is allocated for it (the attribute may appear not only in a declaration, but also in an ALLOCATE statement for a CONTROLLED variable). In most cases this attribute serves only as a shorthand, replacing a subsequent assignment statement. In one important instance, however, its value is somewhat more tangible; this is the case in which a STATIC variable is given an INITIAL attribute. Suppose, for example, one wishes to count the depth to which a procedure invokes itself recursively. This is easily done by including in the procedure the declaration DECLARE I STATIC INITIAL(0), and then having as the first executable statement $I = I + 1$ and as the last, $I = I - 1$. At any time, I contains the present depth of the recursion. This feature, a procedure appearing to remember information, cannot otherwise be obtained without introducing an enclosing procedure whose only function is to initialize I.

3.6 SCOPE OF NAMES

Most languages have inextricably linked the concepts of scope and storage by assuming that wherever a variable's name is known it must have storage assigned for it, and usually vice versa. In PL/I, this notion disappears as, for example, in the case of CONTROLLED variables. Such a variable's name must be known in order to specify it in an ALLOCATE statement, which is the only way to get storage for it. And in the case of BASED variables, as we mentioned before, storage may never be assigned, though certainly the normal scope rules are in effect.

PL/I recognizes two scope attributes, EXTERNAL and INTERNAL, which apply both to data and to procedures. Their applicability to procedures is marginal and bears little resemblance to the interpretation of data scopes. We shall discuss the two roles of scope attributes separately, in order to discourage the observance of analogies that do not hold.

As we begin our discussion of procedure scope, it is necessary to give a gross picture of what a PL/I program actually looks like. We have stated thus far only that PL/I has a block structure similar to that of ALGOL. Actually, a PL/I program consists of a linear collection of EXTERNAL procedures, one of which is specified as being the first to be invoked (the EXTERNAL procedure is the unit of compilation in PL/I). These procedures, like all PL/I procedures, may have parameters and may be invoked as either *functions* or *subroutines*.

Each EXTERNAL procedure may contain, to any depth, well-nested BEGIN. . .END blocks and INTERNAL procedure blocks (any procedure contained in another procedure is INTERNAL). Note that we speak of procedures as blocks. This is because BEGIN. . .END and PROCEDURE. . .END sequences are autonomous to the same degree; both may contain declarations, and they relate identically to scope and storage-class semantics of data. Since the attribute EXTERNAL or INTERNAL is forced for a procedure by that procedure's physical location in a program, neither need ever be specified.

We now consider data scope, a somewhat more interesting topic. When a variable is declared in a block to be INTERNAL, it is known in that block and in all contained blocks except those in which its name is redeclared. This corresponds with normal ALGOL scope rules. An EXTERNAL variable is known in all of the above contexts and, in addition, is identified with any other variable in the program having the same name and the EXTERNAL attribute. This represents a generalization of the FORTRAN COMMON declaration, in that it can equate variables, in the same procedure or in different external procedures, that would be distinct if each had not been given the EXTERNAL attribute.

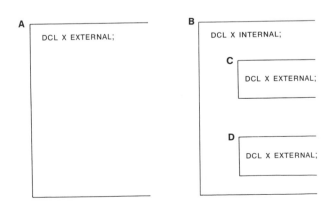

Here A and B are external procedures; B has internal blocks C and D. Because of the EXTERNAL declarations for x in blocks A, C, and D, these blocks use the same x, which is distinct from the x declared to be INTERNAL in B. If all declarations had been INTERNAL, all blocks would use different x's.

The reader should now study the PL/I program at the end of section I (see page 60).

3.7 LIST PROCESSING

We discuss list processing in detail in chapters 5 and 16. For now, we view it as a type of programming application in which logical linkages among data items must be specifiable and modifiable during program execution. These linkages provide the structuring for collections of data not describable as simple aggregates such as arrays or structures.

PL/I's list-processing features are extremely simple and extremely general. The tradeoff for these advantages is that the features are given at quite a low level as building blocks rather than as sophisticated structures. Basically, one new data type, (POINTER), one new storage class (BASED), and two built-in functions (ADDR and NULL) are involved. We describe each of these briefly, and then discuss a simple program that illustrates their interaction.

A POINTER variable identifies, in language terms, some generation of a scalar, array, or structure; in implementation, it contains an address, but this fact is transparent to the language semantics.

A BASED variable acts primarily as a data descriptor, through its data attributes. In addition, it may itself be allocated and freed. The important point here is that a distinction is made between the data characteristics of a variable and its storage location. Normally a reference to a variable provides two pieces of information: its location and its characteristics. For a based variable B, however, a reference is given as P->B, where P is a pointer. P gives the location of the data item of interest, and B provides the data interpretation for that item.

ADDR returns a pointer that identifies its argument; NULL returns a pointer that is guaranteed not to identify any data.

As a first example, we consider a procedure that builds a forward-linked list. The list can be depicted graphically as follows:

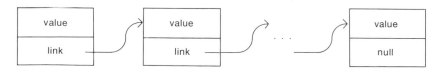

Each box in the above diagram corresponds to an area of storage described by a structure declaration. A pointer in each area (other than the last one) shows the location of the next area; thus, a forward-linked list is formed. The procedure below constructs such a list, adding to the list each new argument that it receives. (The numbers at the left are included only for the discussion that follows.)

```
1.   FORWARD_LINK:   PROCEDURE(PTR);
2.                   DECLARE 1 ELEMENT BASED (PTR),
                        2 VALUE FIXED DECIMAL(6,3),
                        2 LINK POINTER;
3.                   DECLARE SAVE POINTER
                        STATIC INITIAL (NULL);
4.                   LINK = NULL;
5.                   IF SAVE = NULL THEN
                        SAVE = ADDR(ELEMENT);
                     ELSE DO;
                        SAVE->LINK = ADDR(ELEMENT);
                        SAVE = ADDR(ELEMENT);
                     END;
6.                   RETURN;
7.                   END FORWARD_LINK;
```

1. Context determines that PTR is a programmer-selected identifier, rather than the allowable abbreviation for the keyword POINTER.

2. ELEMENT is a BASED structure describing the data referred to by the pointer arguments. Subsequent references to ELEMENT or either of its components will be to PTR->ELEMENT, LINK, or VALUE unless a different pointer is specified in the reference. Notice that PTR is never declared. Its context in the declaration of ELEMENT is sufficient to establish that it is of type POINTER.

   Each argument passed to this procedure will refer to a two-component structure, the first component of which contains the data item to be added, and the second of which will be filled in as it is added to the list.

3. SAVE, since it is STATIC, will be initialized to NULL only once, rather than at each invocation.

4. PTR->LINK is set to NULL, since this is the last element received.

5. SAVE retains the address of the current element, so that on the next invocation, the LINK of this element can be set to point to the next element. The simple DO. . .END group delimits the scope of the ELSE clause, which otherwise would be assumed to be a single statement.

6. The RETURN statement causes execution of FORWARD_LINK to be terminated.

7. The END statement indicates the end of the procedure.

At the time of first incorporation of list processing into the PL/I language, the only additional list-processing facility was that of allocating a BASED variable. This can be done by a statement of the form

> ALLOCATE variable SET (pointer);

Storage is actually allocated for the variable, and the indicated pointer is set to identify that *generation* (i.e., that allocation of the variable).

A problem with PL/I list processing as we have so far described it is that in implementation, pointers are just absolute core addresses. Thus, for example, if one forms, then writes out, and then later reads in the forward-linked list above, the pointers of the list are no longer reliable. While the language speaks specifically of pointers as "identifying generations of variables," rather than pointing to parts of storage, the implementation reflects precisely the opposite semantics.

The solution to the problem, which required a language assist to be realized in implementation, was the introduction of the concept of a relative pointer, called an OFFSET. An OFFSET variable is interpreted relative to the start of the storage area into which it points. That storage area, as a whole, is referred to by means of an AREA variable. Thus one might declare an AREA A and an OFFSET OFF, and then for some data item X execute

> ALLOCATE X IN (A) SET (OFF);

This statement allocates storage for X in area A and points to it with OFF (in implementation, OFF contains the displacement of X from the start of area A). If A is written out and read back in, OFF still identifies X correctly.

3.8 INTERRUPT HANDLING

PL/I goes somewhat beyond most languages in giving the programmer the ability to specify and control execution-time interrupt conditions. These conditions range from standard hardware traps, such as OVERFLOW, to conditions not recognized in hardware but no less relevant as program errors, such as SUBSCRIPTRANGE (signaled when the value computed for a subscript is outside its prescribed range), to conditions not necessarily associated with errors but useful in program checkout, such as CHECK(variable) (signaled whenever the specified variable is assigned a value or, if it is a label, whenever the associated statement is executed).

There are two distinct parts to the interrupt-handling feature, and it is important that these not be confused. The first is the specification of the enabled or disabled status of a condition. If a condition is enabled when it occurs, the occurrence can be fielded and acted upon by the programmer through means discussed below. If it is disabled, however, the occurrence is not recognized, and no trapping occurs. In most cases the result of occurrence of a disabled condition is undefined.

The above information for a condition is given statically in a program by statement prefixes. The prefix (UNDERFLOW): specifies that the UNDERFLOW condition is to be enabled, while (NOUNDERFLOW): indicates that it is to be disabled. (There are, of course, default settings for all the conditions.) If such a prefix is attached to a PROCEDURE or BEGIN statement, its scope of applicability is that entire block, exclusive of any contained blocks or statements for which the enabling (or disabling) is changed. A prefix attached to any other statement is in effect only for the duration of that statement.

The second part of the interrupt-handling feature is programmer specification of the action to be performed if a condition occurs when it is enabled. Such a specification is dynamic in scope and is given as an executable statement of the form

ON condition-name action-specification

The action specification may be a single statement or a BEGIN. . .END block.

Once executed, an ON statement is in effect for the rest of the execution of the block in which it occurs, and all dynamically descendant blocks entered (contained BEGIN. . .END blocks or any invoked procedures). The action specification for a condition may, however, be overridden temporarily in a descendant block, or respecified later in execution of the same block.

The use of this interrupt-handling feature extends beyond error checking and debugging. Perhaps the best example in a different area is the ENDPAGE condition, which can be used with print files to specify actions to be taken when a page of output has been completed. One can write a statement of the form

ON ENDPAGE action-specification

where the action specification might be, for example, to put out a line (the footing), start a new page, put out a number (the new page number), put out another line (the heading), and then return control.

3.9 MULTITASKING

In chapter 15, we discuss *multiprocessing*, an execution-time situation in which multiple procedures may execute simultaneously. In PL/I, this is called *multitasking*. PL/I language features for multitasking are introduced below.

The PL/I concept of a task is most easily understood by relating and contrasting a task to a procedure. A procedure in PL/I is statically describable as a unit of code; its attributes are independent of its execution (the world is full of procedures that have never been executed). A task, on the other hand, is explicable only dynamically; we define it to be an execution of a procedure. There may be many tasks representing different executions of a single procedure.

There is one other important defining characteristic of a task, dealing with the creation of new tasks within a task. When a PL/I program is first invoked through one of its external procedures, a task is created (the major task). But each subsequent procedure call does not create a new task relating to execution of that procedure. Rather an invoked procedure is in general considered to be a part of the same task. A new task (subtask) is created only by invocation of a procedure with the constraint that it be executed concurrently with the invoking task; this stipulation provides the association between tasks and multiprocessing. A PL/I program usually consists of only one task, the major task, although it may contain many procedures.

A TASK variable identifies a task naming an execution of a procedure. Thus this association is made at call time by an option on the CALL statement, for example,

CALL A(X,Y) TASK (B);

This statement specifies that A is to be executed concurrently with the calling task, and that B is to be the name of the newly created task.

We look next at how concurrently executing tasks can communicate with one another to synchronize or to determine progress. They can, of course, communicate via external data or parameters, but interrogation of either requires processor time. A feature is needed to allow one task to wait dormant until another reaches a desired point of synchronization—the former should not need to waste processor time in interrogation; it should simply be notified when the desired point is reached.

The solution to this problem in PL/I is a new data type, the EVENT variable. The content of an EVENT variable is primarily a completion status, given by a bit string '0'B (incomplete) or '1'B (complete). This status can be set or interrogated by built-in functions.

An EVENT variable normally is initialized and set to '0'B, then passed to an invoked task and later interrogated. At some point, the invoked task sets it to '1'B and this information is passed back to the invoking task. There are two ways in which an EVENT variable can be passed. The first is as a parameter or external variable, to be set to '1'B at some agreed point by the invoked procedure. The second is by an option similar to the TASK option on the CALL statement. Consider, for example,

CALL A(X,Y) EVENT (C);

This statement specifies that C will contain the completion status of this execution of A; it will be initialized implicitly to '0'B, and set implicitly to '1'B when A is completed.

Now we look at the means of interrogation of EVENT variables. Certainly, the calling task can use statements of the form

IF EVENT(event name) = '1'B THEN. . .;

As mentioned before, this technique requires processor time. It may not be applicable if the intent is simply to wait for transpiration of the indicated event. Thus a new statement is provided. Its form is

WAIT(event name);

This statement relinquishes processor time for the interrogating task until the prescribed event's completion status has been set, either implicitly or explicitly in the invoked task, to '1'B. Thus, this statement provides the required synchronization capability.

3.10 PROCEDURE INVOCATIONS

Thus far in our discussion, we have said little about specific characteristics of procedures. We now tie together some of the points already mentioned and emphasize others, particularly, those dealing with transfer of information between procedures.

We have said that procedures may be either internal or external. An external procedure can be invoked from anywhere in a program (unless its name has been redeclared). An internal procedure is said to be declared in the block where it appears, and it can be invoked only from within that block (exceptional cases may arise when a procedure is passed as an argument and later invoked by its parameter name).

As was also noted, a procedure can be invoked either as a subroutine or as a function; in the former case, its execution normally terminates with RETURN; in the latter, with RETURN(expression). A procedure may, however, terminate with a GO TO specifying a label constant, variable, or parameter; STOP, terminating the program; or EXIT, terminating the task in which the statement is executed.

Recursive procedures are permitted in PL/I as in ALGOL, and multiple entry points may be specified (possibly, with different parameters) for a single procedure. Data is shared through external variables or argument passing.

We have not discussed the relations established between arguments and parameters at the time of a procedure invocation. PL/I does not differentiate explicitly between parameters received by name and those received by value. In fact, all parameters are received by address, which is in most cases equivalent to receiving by name. (We examine this further in chapter 5.) In PL/I, receiving by value is effected by creating a copy of the argument, and passing that copy to the called procedure.

The simplest example of copying occurs when an argument is either a constant or an expression involving operators or parentheses. (A variable can be passed by value simply by enclosing it in parentheses.) A more interesting case occurs when the data attributes of an argument do not match those of the corresponding parameter. This possibility can be provided for by specification of the declarable attribute ENTRY for an entry point of a procedure.

```
P:   PROCEDURE;
     DECLARE A ENTRY (FIXED BINARY, COMPLEX)
          RETURNS (POINTER);
     DECLARE X FLOAT, Y REAL;
     .

     .

     .
     . . .A(X,Y). . .
     .

     .

     .
     END P;
A:   PROCEDURE (P,Q);
     DECLARE P FIXED BINARY, Q COMPLEX;
     .

     .

     .
     END A;
```

The above entry declaration in P asserts that A is an entry point of a procedure (the name of the procedure is a special case of such an entry point), and that it expects two arguments, of types FIXED BINARY and COMPLEX, respectively (defaults are assumed when the specification for an argument is incomplete). When A is invoked, the arguments passed to it are converted to these types, and the resultant dummy arguments are passed. If no such declaration were given, the data types of all arguments would be assumed to match those of corresponding parameters.

This declaration also indicates that if A is invoked as a function, it returns a value of type POINTER. Had this not been specified, default data attributes determined in accord with the entry name A would be assumed for the returned value.

One other feature is provided for specifying argument-parameter relationships, that of generic procedures:

DECLARE A GENERIC (B ENTRY(FIXED), C ENTRY(FLOAT));

A is declared to be the generic name for entries B and C. If a reference is made to A with a FIXED argument, then B is invoked; if the argument is FLOAT, C is invoked instead.

Many PL/I built-in functions are generic. They accept a variety of argument characteristics, and the appropriate routine or entry point is chosen from the type of the argument.

3.11 DATA MAPPING

We saw, in FORTRAN, features for sharing of storage among data aggregates. PL/I has generalized these features by allowing the specification of mappings that describe the relations between elements of different aggregates.

Suppose a FORTRAN program contains the following statements:

```
DIMENSION A(10,10), B(100)
EQUIVALENCE (A(1,1), B(1))
```

What is the purpose of the above? Either storage sharing between two unrelated arrays is desired, or an array is being renamed for programming convenience. PL/I's DEFINED attribute also serves both these purposes, with particular emphasis on renaming. Another attribute, CELL, can be used when only storage sharing is desired.

We shall consider two kinds of defining in PL/I, *correspondence defining* and *overlay defining*. Correspondence defining is in effect when two aggregates not only share the same storage, but also are related by a mapping between their elements.

DECLARE A(10,10) FLOAT, B(10,10) FLOAT DEFINED A;

Here B is declared to share A's storage; this is possible whenever A and B have the same data attributes. Since no mapping function has been given between elements, their aggregate structures must be identical (both are 10 × 10 arrays). The natural one-to-one mapping function will be used.

Now we look at two statements in which mapping functions are given.

```
DECLARE A(5,5), B(5) DEFINED A(1SUB,1SUB);
DECLARE A(25), B(5,5) DEFINED A(5*1SUB + 2SUB−5);
```

In each case, storage is allocated only for A, and it is required that a reference to an element of B yield through the mapping function an element of A. iSUB refers to the ith subscript in a reference to an element of B. In the first example, then, a reference to B(n) will actually be to A(n,n), so B represents the diagonal of A. In the second case, the function gives the first five elements of A as the first row of B, the second five as the second row, and so on.

Overlay defining allows one to partition a string into different elements, and, in so doing, it necessarily involves the notion of contiguity of all elements of an aggregate.

DECLARE A(50) BIT(1) UNALIGNED, B BIT(50) DEFINED A;

Here A is an array of fifty elements, each a bit; B represents the same storage, but views it as a single string of fifty bits. To provide for this, the UNALIGNED attribute has been given to A. If A were instead ALIGNED, the defining would not be possible, because in implementation the elements of A might not be packed contiguously, but rather put on nonadjacent boundaries to ensure efficient addressing. Overlay defining is possible only on UNALIGNED aggregates.

In all uses of the DEFINED attribute, the data attributes of the related aggregates must match. This is because of the renaming aspect of defining and the desire to avoid machine-dependent mapping relationships. But PL/I also has a feature for storage sharing between different data types, where it is understood that a reference to such storage under one of its names produces undefined results if data was placed into the storage via another name.

```
DECLARE 1 A CELL,
            2 B(50) FLOAT,
            2 C(70) FIXED,
            2 D(30) LABEL;
```

This declaration, which syntactically resembles that of a structure, indicates that A is a CELL. It can contain any of the data alternatives at the next level in the declaration and is large enough to accommodate any of them. But the effect of attempting to use any part of B, C, or D following assignment to some part of another of them is undefined. Thus the only alternative that should be referred to at any time is that to which assignment was made most recently.

3.12 INPUT/OUTPUT

Early PL/I specifications recognized a data file as a character string with no inherent structure; appropriate partitioning was achieved by format specifications accompanying the transmission statements. This approach was very elegant from a language standpoint, but the implementation inefficiency was often intolerable. Even when the user wanted to transmit large records of data in internal form, the implementation would pick off each data element in turn, examine it to see whether its type matched the associated format item, and finally transmit it. The need for a transmission mode that recognized records, buffers, and unedited transmission in a more direct fashion became evident. From this need grew the present dichotomy between STREAM and RECORD transmission.

In STREAM transmission, a data set is considered to be a continuous stream of characters, transmitted by GET and PUT statements and edited so that each data item conforms to its associated format item in external character-string form.

STREAM transmission can be subdivided into three types: LIST-directed, DATA-directed, and EDIT-directed. In LIST-directed transmission, the data on the external medium are transmitted in order to/from the variables specified in the GET or PUT statement, with type conversions occurring as necessary. In DATA-directed I/O, the external medium contains not only each value to be transmitted but also the name of the variable to which each value must be assigned. There need be no order correspondence between data in the stream and names specified in the GET or PUT statement. In fact, one can use the statement GET DATA with no variable list, in which case all variables known at that point and present in the stream (up to the next semicolon delimiter) will be read in. EDIT-directed transmission is analogous to normal FORTRAN I/O, in which both data and control format items direct the transmission.

In RECORD transmission, a data set is interpreted as a collection of discrete records, accessed either sequentially or directly. Records of information are transmitted without editing, and the programmer can control this transmission and record building through addressable buffers. PL/I READ and WRITE statements cause RECORD transmission of data.

3.13 COMPILE-TIME FEATURES

PL/I has incorporated a number of features to allow program modification prior to time of compilation. These features involve a shorthand means of specification that is translated, at compile-time, into an expanded PL/I form. The shorthand is a language that looks much like a subset of PL/I.

The features that we see here represent a very simple kind of language extensibility: the definition of new constructs in terms of existing ones. But the limitations of these features are severe, so it is best to consider them only as compile-time shorthand or, in assembly-language terms, as macro-definition features. As noted earlier, we discuss language extensibility at length in chapter 18.

The compile-time features are best defined in terms of the execution, at compile-time, of a PL/I macro-processor. This macro-processor operates by scanning the source text of a PL/I program, normally passing it unchanged, to the PL/I compiler. If, however, a compile-time statement is encountered, that statement is executed. Compile-time statements may be intermixed freely with source text. They are identifiable by the leading symbol %, but are otherwise syntactically identical to other statements of PL/I.

The best way to illustrate the type of feature offered is through a simple example. A programmer may want to execute the following loop at execution time:

```
DO I = 1 TO 10;
    A(I) = B(I) + C(I);
END;
```

The following code would accomplish the same thing, but without the execution-time requirements of incrementing and testing:

```
%DECLARE I FIXED;
%I = 1;
%L:;
A(I) = B(I) + C(I);
%I = I + 1;
%IF I < = 10 %THEN %GO TO L;
%DEACTIVATE I;
```

The % prefixed to a statement indicates that the action specified by the statement is to be carried out at the time it is encountered by the macro-processor. I is first declared to be a compile-time variable of type FIXED (CHARACTER and ENTRY are also allowed). Then it is given the value 1. This assignment also specifies that, unless the programmer indicates otherwise (note the later appearance of the %DEACTIVATE statement), subsequent occurrences of the identifier I in the source text are to be replaced in the text being formed by the string '1'. The statement %L:; is a compile-time null statement used as the transfer target for the %GO TO statement that appears later.

The text string A(I) = B(I) + C(I); is a source-program statement. Since the variable I has been the value 1, the first scan of this string causes the string A(1) = B(1) + C(1); to be inserted into the text being formed. I is then incremented by 1, after which the compile-time IF statement instructs the macro-processor to test the value of I. If I is not greater than 10, the scan is to resume at the compile-time statement labeled L; otherwise, the scan is to continue with the text immediately following the %GO TO statement.

The %DEACTIVATE statement is interpreted as follows: Subsequent occurrences of the variable I in the source text are not to be replaced by the string '11' in the text being formed (note that ı has the value 11 at the time the %DEACTIVATE statement is encountered); instead each ı is to be left unmodified.

As a result of the above compile-time activity, the following PL/I statements are generated in the text passed to the compiler:

$$A(1) = B(1) + C(1);$$
$$A(2) = B(2) + C(2);$$
$$.$$
$$.$$
$$.$$
$$A(10) = B(10) + C(10);$$

These statements will be compiled into executable code.

Another useful compile-time feature is the INCLUDE statement. Its argument identifies a string of text on some external medium. This string is then scanned by the macro-processor in the same way that it scans source text (executing compile-time statements and making insertions into the constructed text).

We have seen that it is possible to declare compile-time variables and have their text occurrences replaced by their values. One can also declare compile-time procedures, to be executed when encountered during source-text scan; the result of the execution replaces the text occurrence of the procedure reference, provided that the procedure is "activated."

It is possible to specify that a large amount of processing be done at compile-time. But the only permissible text modifications are replacement of variable or procedure references, and introduction of INCLUDE text. Thus the features for extending the language are very primitive. The PL/I goal is, as we have emphasized, that the language itself be adequate for a wide range of applications, without resort to extension mechanisms.

For more detailed specifications of the PL/I language, see [IBM65], [Wei66], [Pol69], [Bat70], and [Lec68].

CHAPTER 4

APL

The APL language first appeared in 1962 in the book *A Programming Language* by K. E. Iverson (see [Ive62]). We include discussion of it here, not because of its widespread use or problem-solving applicability, but because of its dynamic power, especially in the area of array manipulation. While the language arose for the purpose of algorithm description, its implemented subset as we shall discuss it is intended for interactive use. Commands are generally interpreted and executed when specified by a terminal user, rather than compiled for later execution. This mode of execution makes it reasonable to speak of command execution times in the same realm as human response times, and APL's exploitation of this freedom from execution speed constraints is truly dramatic.

We shall not attempt to be comprehensive in our discussion of APL. Discussion of structurally uninteresting features common to the other high-level languages is omitted; such features are mentioned only as relevant to more interesting features.

The general subject area that we wish to emphasize is the extremely dynamic role of data during execution of an APL program. So far we have looked only at languages intended for compilation, and we have therefore met many language requirements for information that must be known either prior to execution or at time of block entry. In APL, such information is dynamically specifiable by executable statements in the language.

Most of our discussion centers about APL's array manipulation features, but first we mention several other dynamic features which, while perhaps less awesome in effect, are nevertheless important to the language character.

4.1 DATA TYPES

APL data are either real numeric or character string. No further distinctions are made for data within the numeric class. When used as operands of the array operators we shall examine, character strings are in most contexts treated as vectors of single characters.

A significant feature of APL is that names are not declared to have either of these type attributes. Any variable may be assigned, data of either type during execution of a program. Thus the following sequence is acceptable (← is the assignment operator):

> .
>
> .
>
> .
>
> A←'CAT'
>
> .
>
> .
>
> A←2.5

At any time, a variable contains the identification of the type of its current contents. This identification is interrogated when necessary to determine how an operation should be performed.

4.2 BRANCHING

APL statements are identifiable by line numbers; hence, integers can be used to refer to statements for purposes of branching. The branching power in APL stems from the ability to specify the integral result of any numeric expression as a branch target.

$$\rightarrow 3+(x>1)+(x>2)$$

This branch statement (→ is the branching operator) causes transfer to statement 3 if $x \leq 1$, to 4 if $1 < x \leq 2$, or to 5 if $x > 2$.

4.3 SCOPE OF NAMES

In our discussions of name scope in both ALGOL and PL/I, we have seen features of some power and complexity—features not available under the simple single-level approach in FORTRAN. But we were able to describe the complete picture in either of these languages without regard to flow of control during execution of a program; the scope of a name was determined statically at time of program creation, and was independent of execution of the program.

In APL, the picture is quite different. An APL program consists of a main body and any number of invocable subroutines and functions, structurally independent of one another. APL is similar to FORTRAN in that it has no block structure. But whereas FORTRAN names are either local to a routine or COMMON, APL has scope semantics based on calling sequences occurring during execution.

Consider the following snapshot of an APL execution:

MAIN

PROGRAM

```
    . . . X . . .

    . . . Y . . .

    . . . FUN1 4 . . . .
```

```
    ∇R←FUN1 N; X

    . . . X . . .

    . . . Y . . .

    . . . 3 FUN2 7 . . .

    ∇
```

```
    ∇M FUN2 I

    . . . X . . .

    . . . Y . . .

    ∇
```

The main program, which uses names X and Y, has called the function FUN1, passing the number 4 as an argument. FUN1 is a function accepting one parameter (N) and returning as a result the final value of R. FUN1 has declared a local variable X, but has made no declaration for Y, which is thus global in FUN1. (Note that the declaration for X does not imply its type.)

FUN1 has in turn called FUN2, passing the numbers 3 and 7 as arguments. FUN2 is a function accepting two parameters (M and I) and returning no result; it declares neither X nor Y, but uses them during execution.

X and Y are first defined in the main program when first encountered during execution (presumably that encounter serves to give values to them, not to request values of them). FUN1 has declared a new local X, so its references to X are to that new X rather than to the X in the main program. The Y in FUN1, however, since not declared, refers to the Y in the main program. In FUN2, X and Y, undeclared, are taken to refer to the X and Y of the calling routine, FUN1. X is declared in FUN1, so the X in FUN2 resolves to that declaration. The Y of FUN2 is identified with the Y of FUN1, which has resolved to the Y of the main program.

Thus the general rule for APL name resolution is to retrace the call chain, looking for the latest declaration of the name to be resolved. If no declaration is found, the name is said to be global (local to the main program). The scope of a name is totally dependent on the execution call chain, rather than on any static aspects of program structure.

4.4 ARRAYS

Here we see most strongly the dynamic beauty of the APL language; we experience the unfettered ability to expand, compress, and reshape arrays at will. We also see a generally powerful set of operators for manipulating arrays without changing their shapes.

4.4.1 VECTORS

The following command enters a vector, the most primitive of arrays, into a program. It assigns a vector of four components, the numbers 1, 2, 3, and 4, to the name A. As we shall see, the components are ordered and individually addressable by index.

$$A \leftarrow 1\ 2\ 3\ 4$$

Vectors may be operands of scalar operators, in which case a distribution of the operation is performed over the vector components.

$$1\ 2\ 3\ 4 * 2\ 3\ 4\ 5$$

$$2\ 6\ 12\ 20$$

(Our convention in the above, as in subsequent examples, is to indent the command expression, and to follow it with the less deeply indented APL system response.)

2 * 1 2 3 4

2 4 6 8

To perform the operation above, the scalar operand on the left is conceptually expanded into the vector 2 2 2 2.

4.4.2 REDUCTION

The reduction of a dyadic operator (an operator having two operands) over an array consists of the successive application of that operator to elements of the array. Suppose A is the vector 1 2 3 4, and ⊕ is a dyadic operator. Then ⊕ reduction over A is defined to be 1 ⊕ 2 ⊕ 3 ⊕ 4. Thus,

+ /A (addition reduction)

10

⌐/A (maximum reduction)

4

If A is the vector 0 1 1 0, then

∨ /A (or reduction)

1

∧ /A (and reduction)

0

A more complex example is

∨ / (1 2 3 4 = 3)

1

Execution of the comparison operator = gives the vector 0 0 1 0, on which the or reduction yields true (1).

4.4.3 SHAPE, RESHAPE

The operator ρ allows one to interrogate the shape of an array or to create an array of a specified shape.

A←1 2 3 4 5 6

ρA

6

In this example, the monadic ρ operator (having a single operand) requests the shape of A. The response indicates that A is one-dimensional of length 6.

        B←1 3 2
        (+/B) ÷ ρB
    2

The last expression gives the average value of elements of B.

        A←1 2 3 4 5 6
        2 3 ρ A
    1 2 3
    4 5 6

In the example above, the dyadic ρ operator creates an array of the shape described by its first operand (a 2 x 3 matrix) from the data given by its second operand.

        B←3 2 ρ A
        ρB
    3 2
        ρρB
    2

The shape of B is that of a 3 x 2 matrix. Hence ρB is the two-element vector 3 2, and ρρB is ρ3 2, or 2. In general ρρ yields the dimensionality (number of dimensions) of an array.

4.4.4 RAVEL, CATENATE

The comma operator (,) creates vectors from other vectors or arrays. In the following example, the monadic comma takes an array argument and ravels (unravels; it is interesting to compare dictionary definitions of these two terms) it into a vector, raveling into row-major order.

        B←3 2 ρ 1 2 3 4 5 6
        ,B
    1 2 3 4 5 6

The dyadic comma catenates two vectors into a single vector as shown below.

        1 2 3 , 4 5 6
    1 2 3 4 5 6

4.4.5 INDEX

Array indexing capabilities are generalized from those we have previously seen. Thus, in the following example, A[2;2] refers to the second element of the second row of the 2 x 3 matrix A. This is a simple index, as available in most languages.

$$A \leftarrow 2\ 3\ \rho\ 1\ 2\ 3\ 4\ 5\ 6$$
$$A[2;2]$$

5

Assume that A, below, is the same 2×3 matrix. The expression A[2;] is analogous to the PL/I expression $A(2, *)$. It yields an array cross-section.

$$A[2;]$$
4 5 6

Arbitrary subscript intersections over the dimensions of an array are allowed. We have not seen this degree of cross-sectional specification.

$$A[2;1\ 3]$$
4 6

4.4.6 INDEX GENERATION

The monadic operator i generates a vector of consecutive integers from 1 through the argument.

$$i\ 4$$
1 2 3 4
$$A \leftarrow 3\ 7\ 9$$
$$A * i\ \rho A$$
3 14 27

Suppose that we want to insert a vector B after the first N components of a vector A. We could write:

$$A \leftarrow A[i N]\ ,\ B\ ,\ A[N + (i((\rho A) - N))]$$

The dyadic i gives an index indicating where, in the first operand, the second operand occurs.

$$3\ 7\ 9\ i\ 7$$
2

The following code gives the location of the largest element of A.

```
        A←3 7 9
        A i⌈/A
3
```

4.4.7 COMPRESS, EXPAND

The compression operator / selects elements of its second operand according to whether corresponding elements of its first operand are 1 or 0.

```
        1 0 1 0 0 / 2 + i5
    3 5
```

The following example gives the elements of A that are greater than 4.

```
        A←3 7 9 2
        (A>4) / A
    7 9
```

The expansion operator \ expands its second operand according to the 1s and 0s of the first operand.

```
        1 0 1 1 0 \ 2 3 4
    2 0 3 4 0
```

4.4.8 A SORTING EXAMPLE

Now let us bring together some of the features described, and a few others, in an APL program. Suppose we have A, a vector of numbers that we want to sort into ascending order into a vector B. The statements below perform this task. The numbers preceding the statements are referred to in the discussion that follows.

```
1.      B←0ρ0
2.      →(0 = ρA) / 0
3.      MINS←A = (⌊/A)
4.      B←B , MINS / A
5.      A←(~MINS) / A
6.      →2
```

   1. B, the result vector, is initialized to a vector of length 0 (a null vector).

2. If A has no elements, then transfer is made to line 0 (a convention meaning termination). The compression operation yields either 0 (in which case the transfer is made) or a null vector (in which case no transfer is made).

3. L/A is the minimum reduction over A. It yields the minimum value in A. That value, compared for equality with A, yields a vector of 1s and 0s indicating the positions in A whose element values are that minimum. The vector is assigned to MINS.

4. A is compressed by MINS to the vector of minimal elements, and that vector is catenated onto B.

5. ~MINS reverses the 1s and 0s of MINS. Its reducing of A yields the subvector of A whose elements were not minimal. This new vector replaces A.

6. Control is passed to line 2.

The reader should now study the APL program at the end of section I (see page 61).

4.5 CONCLUSIONS

The power of the APL language has two origins: (1) its dynamic features for specifying shapes and types of data, and (2) the design of a few basic operations that, in combination, provide a myriad of functions seemingly unrelated to the individual operators. APL's power derives from its elegance, rather than from its size.

The original specification of APL is contained in [Ive62]. For more detailed specification of the implemented subset, see [Pak68], [Fal68], and [Gil70].

A Comparative Programming Example

In order to compare the features and appearances of the four languages we have discussed, we now present a program in each for solving a common problem. In each case, the method of solution is matrix multiplication. We acquire operands for the multiplication: A, having I rows and J columns; and B, having J rows and K columns. The product matrix, C has I rows and K columns. Line-by-line explanations of each solution are provided.

Each main program reads in I, J, and K and the values for elements of A and B. It then invokes a multiplication routine, MULT, which receives IP, JP, KP, AP, BP, and CP as parameters corresponding to I, J, K, A, B, and C. MULT produces its result in C, which is written out in the main program.

Recall the definition for matrix multiplication, whereby product elements are determined as follows:

$$C_{L,N} = \sum_{M=1}^{J} A_{L,M} * B_{M,N} \text{ for } \begin{array}{l} 1 \leq L \leq I \\ 1 \leq N \leq K \end{array}$$

The statements in each program are numbered for discussion purposes. The numbers are not part of the actual programs.

1. FORTRAN

```
1.    DIMENSION A(10,10),B(10,10),C(10,10)
2.    READ(9,1)I,J,K,((A(L,M),L = 1,I),M = 1,J),((B(M,N),M = 1,J),N = 1,K)
```

```
 3.          CALL MULT(I,J,K,A,B,C)
 4.          WRITE(10,2)((C(L,N),L=1,I),N=1,K)
 5.          STOP
 6.   1      FORMAT(3I10,(E16.8))
 7.   2      FORMAT(E16.8)
 8.          END
 9.          SUBROUTINE MULT(IP,JP,KP,AP,BP,CP)
10.          DIMENSION AP(IP,JP), BP(JP,KP), CP(IP,KP)
11.          DO 3 L=1,IP
12.              DO 3 N=1,KP
13.                  CP(L,N)=0
14.                  DO 3 M=1,JP
15.   3                  CP(L,N)=CP(L,N)+AP(L,M)*BP(M,N)
16.          RETURN
17.          END
```

1. The arrays must be given constant dimensions, so in this case, neither I, J, nor K can be greater than 10.
2. I, J, and K are read in, followed by the arrays, acquired in column-major order.
3. The multiplication subroutine is called.
4. The result is written out in column-major order.
5. This statement terminates the program execution.
6. This format describes the input as three integers, followed by any number of floating-point numbers.
7. The output format also describes floating-point numbers.
8. This signals the physical end of the program.
9. MULT accepts the six parameters indicated.
10. The dimensions of the array parameters can be indicated by other parameters.
11. This loop extends over rows of the result.
12. This loop extends over columns of the result.
13. Each element of the result is initialized to 0.
14. This loop extends over columns of the first matrix, rows of the second.
15. This statement, the last one in the loops, builds each result element.
16. Execution returns to the main program.
17. The subroutine is complete.

2. ALGOL

```
1.          BEGIN
2.              INTEGER I,J,K;
3.              READ(I,J,K);
4.              BEGIN
```

```
5.              REAL ARRAY A[1:I,1:J],B[1,J,1:K],C[1:I,1:K];
6.              READ(A,B);
7.              MULT(I,J,K,A,B,C);
8.              PRINT(C);
9.              PROCEDURE MULT(IP,JP,KP,AP,BP,CP);
10.                 VALUE IP,JP,KP,AP,BP;
11.                 INTEGER IP,JP,KP;
12.                 REAL ARRAY AP,BP,CP;
13.                 BEGIN
14.                     INTEGER L,M,N;
15.                     FOR L: = 1 STEP 1 UNTIL IP DO
16.                       FOR N: = 1 STEP 1 UNTIL KP DO
17.                         BEGIN
18.                             CP[L,N]: = 0;
19.                             FOR M: = 1 STEP 1 UNTIL JP DO
20.                                 CP[L,N]: = CP[L,N]+AP[L,M]＊BP[M,N]
21.                         END
22.                     END
23.             END
24.         END
```

1. This is the start of the main program.
2. The dimension variables are declared.
3. The values for these variables are read in.
4. A contained block is initiated.
5. The arrays are declared, using the values read in as bounds.
6. The arrays to be multiplied are read in. They are assumed to be in row-major order.
7. The multiplication procedure is invoked.
8. The result, array C, is written out in row-major order.
9. This starts the multiplication procedure, which accepts six parameters.
10. Only CP, the result, is received by NAME; it must be set to contain the result.
11. The dimension parameters are integers.
12. The array parameters are real. Bounds are not given with these declarations.
13. The body of the procedure starts.
14. Integers are declared for the iterations to follow.
15. This loop extends over the rows of the first matrix. The statement that is iterated extends to line 21.
16. This loop extends over the columns of the second matrix. It also extends to line 21.
17. The statement for this loop is a compound statement, bracketed by this line and line 21.
18. Each element of the result is initialized to 0.

19. This loop extends over columns of the first matrix, rows of the second.
20. This statement builds each result element.
21. This closes BEGIN on line 17.
22. This closes BEGIN on line 13 and hence PROCEDURE on line 9.
23. This closes BEGIN on line 4.
24. This closes the main program.

3. PL/I

```
 1.      P:    PROCEDURE OPTIONS (MAIN);
 2.            DECLARE (A,B,C) CONTROLLED (*,*);
 3.            GET LIST (I,J,K);
 4.            ALLOCATE A(I,J), B(J,K);
 5.            GET LIST (A,B);
 6.            CALL MULT (A,B,C);
 7.            PUT LIST (C);
 8.            END;
 9.  MULT:     PROCEDURE (AP,BP,CP);
10.            DECLARE (AP,BP,CP) CONTROLLED (*,*);
11.            ALLOCATE CP (LBOUND(AP,1):HBOUND(AP,1),
                   LBOUND(BP,2):HBOUND(BP,2));
12.  LOOP:     DO L = LBOUND(AP,1) TO HBOUND(AP,1);
13.               DO N = LBOUND(BP,2) TO HBOUND(BP,2);
14.                  CP(L,N) = SUM(AP(L,*) * BP(*,N));
15.            END LOOP;
16.            FREE AP, BP;
17.            END MULT;
```

1. The OPTIONS attribute on the PROCEDURE statement is used as required by a particular implementation. In this case, MAIN specifies to an implementation that this is the external procedure that should initially be given control.
2. A, B, and C are declared to be CONTROLLED arrays, whose bounds will be specified in ALLOCATE statements (the asterisks indicate this delay). These variables are by default FLOAT DECIMAL. The undeclared variables I, J, and K are FIXED BINARY because their initial letters are in the I–N range.
3. The values for the dimension variables are read in.
4. A and B are allocated, with the values just read in as bounds.
5. Elements of A and B are now read in. The array bounds are known, so the correct number of elements can be read into each array, in row-major order.

6. MULT is invoked. Note that C, which will contain the product of A and B, can be passed as an argument, although it has not yet been allocated. Note also that the dimensions are not passed.

7. C is written out element-by-element, again in row-major order.

8. P has no RETURN statement. When a procedure END is encountered during execution, it is taken as equivalent to both RETURN and END.

9. This is the beginning of the procedure MULT. Note that only the arrays are passed to it.

10. For AP and BP, the asterisks for bounds say to use whatever bounds the arguments have. For CP, still not allocated, bound specification is being delayed until allocation.

11. CP is finally allocated. Its first dimension has the same bounds as those of the first dimension of AP; its second dimension, the same as those of the second of BP. (LBOUND and HBOUND are built-in functions.)

12. The outer loop is set up, extending over the rows of the first matrix. This is one of many forms for PL/I loops, the most general of which is

DO variable = exp1 TO exp2 BY exp3 WHILE exp4;

13. The inner loop is initiated, extending over the columns of the second matrix.

14. AP(L, ∗) and BP(∗,N) are the Lth row of AP and the Nth row of BP, respectively. The multiplication, done element-by-element, yields the product vector; the SUM built-in function returns the sum of the elements of its array argument, in this case the dot product of the row and column.

15. The scope of a DO statement is delimited by a corresponding END. The label following END effects multiple closure; all unclosed loops and blocks between this END statement and the DO statement prefixed by that label are closed.

16. AP and BP are no longer needed, so their storage is freed.

17. A label can also be specified in the END statement of a procedure, either for multiple closure or for documentation.

4. APL

1.   I ← ☐
2.   J ← ☐
3.   K ← ☐
4.   A ← I,J ρ ☐
5.   B ← J,K ρ ☐
6.   A MULT B

```
7.      ▽CP←AP MULT BP
8.        CP←AP + . × BP
9.      ▽
```

1. The box □ indicates that input is needed. When this statement is executed, the computer requests input from the terminal. At that time, the value for dimension I must be typed in and is assigned to I.
2. J is acquired similarly.
3. K is acquired simllarly.
4. A is specified to be an array of the shape given by the vector I,J and with values requested as before. These must be typed in row-major order.
5. B is specified to be an array of the shape given by the vector J,K and with values again requested.
6. The multiplication function is invoked, and passed only A and B. The result C does not need to be passed, since APL allows functions to return array results. When returned, it will be printed out, since this command is an expression.
7. The symbol ▽ is the function header. MULT takes two parameters, AP and BP, and returns a result that will be in the local variable CP when MULT completes execution.
8. It happens that APL supports matrix multiplication directly, through a generalized inner product operation. For dyadic operators ⊕ and ⊗, A⊕.⊗B is defined by the result C, where

$$C[I;J] \;=\; \oplus/(A[I;]\otimes B[;J]) \quad \text{for} \quad \begin{array}{l} 1\leq I\leq(\rho A)[1] \\ 1\leq J\leq(\rho B)[2] \end{array}$$

9. Function MULT is ended. Encountering of ▽ during execution terminates the function.

If the inner product had not been available directly, we could have replaced lines 7, 8, and 9 by the following sequence:

```
 7.      ▽CP←AP MULT BP;L,N
 8.        L←N←0
 9.  LLAB:((ρAP)[1]<L←L+1)/0
10.  NLAB:((ρBP)[2]<N←N+1)/NOUT
11.        CP[L;N]← + /(AP[L;] × BP[;N])
12.          →NLAB
13.  NOUT:→LLAB
14.      ▽
```

7. In this case, MULT also uses local variables L and N, declared here to be local.

8. L and N are initialized to 0. The assignment N←0 gives a result 0 which is then assigned to L.

9. This sets up a loop extending over the rows of the first matrix. L is incremented by 1 and checked against that number of rows. If L is greater, transfer is to line 0, thus terminating execution of MULT.

10. This sets up a similar loop extending over the columns of the second matrix. Here the exit location is the statement labeled NOUT. Actual labels may be placed on statements and specified in transfer commands, as we have done throughout this example. Alternatively, transfers may specify line numbers.

11. This statement assigns to each element of the product matrix the addition reduction over the element-by-element product of the Lth row of AP and the Nth column of BP.

12. This ends the inner loop by transferring back to NLAB.

13. This ends the outer loop by transferring back to LLAB.

14. The function MULT is complete.

SECTION II

Basic Language Concepts

CHAPTER 5

Information Binding

A powerful characteristic of social environments is a stratification of planning for tasks to be performed. At even the most primitive level, one entity decides that a job needs to be done, and he then communicates this requirement to a second entity, who performs the task. This stratification is efficient because of its implication of specialization. One individual may be talented at decision-making, another at implementation of decisions. And the stratification is of infinite potential level, in that decision-making at one level is implementation at the next higher level.

Unfortunately, this power has an important drawback: The decisionmaker must communicate, in some symbolic way, his decision on a job to be performed. And such communication inevitably involves ambiguities, because of the generally imprecise nature of symbolic allusions. Such misunderstandings occur frequently in the communication between programmers and machines. Some programming language is their communication vehicle.

When an ALGOL programmer writes A: = 2; he is certain that the outcome will be the association of the number 2 with some name A. But less trivially, he must understand differences that result, dependent on whether A is a local variable, free variable, formal parameter by name, or formal parameter by value. In short, he must understand the machine interpretation of his symbolic use of the name A.

This chapter is devoted to analyzing various programming-language techniques for associating symbolic references with intended objects. We also begin development of a common terminology for describing such associations.

5.1 THE OBJECTS OF A PROGRAMMING LANGUAGE: LOCATION-VALUE PAIRS

We start by postulating that each object to which a programming-language program refers may be viewed as a location, with a value. Let us, for now, not view these as addresses, with scalar values. Allocation may be of arbitrary size; an arbitrary number of values may reside therein. We further postulate a hierarchy, in that for a given location, we can always ascertain its values; given a value, however, we cannot in general determine the location in which it resides.

We wish to discipline our model even more strongly, with two further assertions:

1. A value always occupies precisely one location.
2. Access to a value may be made only through its associated location.

Amidst our qualifying constraints on the objects of a programming language, we remain liberal on one particular point. We refuse to attempt definition of a value as other than a featureless landscape, to be interpreted as the accessor chooses. This disposition we derive from features currently available in languages. While we may repudiate machine-dependent synonymy as is sometimes available in FORTRAN EQUIVALENCE (one may treat the same internal representation as either fixed or floating point), we respect higher-level interpretation diversity of the type obtainable with the PL/I DEFINED attribute. In PL/I, one may write the following declarations:

```
DECLARE STRING CHARACTER(100);
DECLARE ARRAY(100) CHARACTER(1) DEFINED STRING;
```

Here one value is being declared, a group consisting of 100 characters. Viewed under the name STRING, this value is a simple character string; viewed under the name ARRAY, the value is a complex divisible aggregate of 100 single characters. This interpretation diversity is totally acceptable, and we refuse to constrain ourselves by imposing a single description upon the object in question. It should be possible to describe and use an object for multiple purposes within one program execution.

5.2 REFERENCES TO OBJECTS WITHIN PROGRAMS

Given that objects in the abstract sense described are the things that programming languages talk about, how do they relate to the symbols used in actual programs to refer to them?

5.2.1 NAMES

We shall not, at this time, develop a theory of names; rather, we resort to intuition and a few general principles. When we refer to a name, we mean the entire syntactic construct that is used to symbolize an object; thus names are not limited to what are normally thought of as identifiers. Some examples of programming-language names are:

Name	Explanation
PIG	simple name
+	simple name
a[i]	ALGOL subscripted name
NAME.LAST	PL/I qualified name
P->Q	PL/I pointer-qualified name
413	integer constant
16.40	floating-point constant
A + B	expression with operator

Our intent with this liberal view of names is to distinguish what is written as a reference from the actual mapping of that reference to an object. It does not seem useful to take the more restrictive view of a name as simply an identifier, to which other mapping information (such as sub-scripts) may be appended. That approach would be viable if the mapping information completely specified the map from name to object, but, in fact, that is seldom the case. Most of the mapping information needed is not included in the syntax of a reference.

5.2.2 VARIABLES AND CONSTANTS

Available languages have contrasting interpretations of the differences between constants and variables. In our discussions, we speak of con-stancy or variability in relative terms as execution-time phenomena relat-ing to the mapping from names to objects. Using our terminology, we can describe what some languages call constants in terms of restrictive nam-ing conventions for objects, of implicit initializations of the values of those objects, and of protection for those values by syntactic checking and copying rules. But we do not think it useful to have a model in which 3.14159 is a constant, but a name PI, initialized to that value, is a variable simply because a shorthand mnemonic is used.

In short, we subscribe to the maxim that one man's constant is another man's variable, that some data are simply more variable than others.

5.2.3 MAPPING FROM NAMES TO OBJECTS

We do not, at this time, wish to place any restrictions on the complexity of name-object mappings in our model. We assume that the mappings may be specified by arbitrarily complex algorithms, and that different portions of these algorithms may be performed at different stages of a program's progression from text through execution. We elaborate on these different times in section 5.3.

5.2.4 DECLARATIONS, DESCRIPTIONS, AND CONSTRAINTS

We would like to separate the mapping from a name to an object into two parts, meeting at what we shall call a declaration for that name. A name is always mapped first to a declaration; then it is mapped to an object.

Informally, a declaration for a name is a reference to the name that, when executed, causes a mapping to be defined from that declaration to an object; in most cases the object is brought into existence by execution of the declaration.

The declaration reference to a name varies widely among languages, both in syntactic format and in time of execution. The format may be an explicit statement of declaration of a name (ALGOL, for example), or simply its mention during execution (APL, for example). A declaration may be executed prior to execution of a program, or whenever the declaration is encountered during program flow. These possibilities are examined in more detail in section 5.3; for now we wish only to recognize the concept of a declaration.

We have made no mention of data attributes in our discussion of names. We further have refused to discuss the subject as related to objects. We have delayed our discussion of data attributes in order to be able to tie them to declarations. Since this data-attribute information is, in fact, linked to declarations, it is accessible from names (which map to declarations) but not from objects (from which we define no mappings to declarations).

We wish to distinguish two kinds of information normally thought of as data-attribute information. We designate them as *constraints* and *descriptions*. When a declaration for a name is executed, certain constraints may be placed on the types of data to be held in the object defined by that declaration. In some languages these constraints are quite severe (an ALGOL variable may hold only information of one type among real, integer, or Boolean data); in others, they are more liberal (an APL variable may in general hold either numeric or character data).

Let us assume for the moment the desirability of knowing, when a name is used, the type of data currently held in the object referred to by that name. The possibility of liberal constraints for the name implies that we cannot, in general, deduce the type of data currently held by interrogating the constraints. Thus, we need the second type of information associated with a declaration—the description of the name. This information characterizes the current contents of the object defined by the declaration.

One may at this point wonder at our mention of various "types of data," since we have repudiated the notion of descriptions attached to objects. When we say that the object of a declaration may contain only certain types of data, we are, more formally, saying that an assignment to the object of that name must be from a name whose declaration has as its description one of those types. Thus both descriptions and constraints are properties of declarations, not of objects.

5.3 BINDING TIMES FOR INFORMATION

We now discuss examples of binding of information of the types we have discussed. We recognize six bindings required:

1. name-declaration
2. declaration-declaration
3. declaration-object
4. declaration-constraints
5. declaration-description
6. location-value

By the term *binding* we mean execution of the mapping algorithm for deducing the righthand member of a pair from the left.

We consider five different times at which bindings are performed, appealing to the reader's intuition for their definitions. We are not yet ready to formalize a model for program processing, but we would like to illustrate in terms of relatively common current processes. The five times are:

1. program creation
2. linkage-edit
3. load
4. call
5. execution reference

We present our examples as entries in the following table. Each of these examples is explained in more detail in later sections; here we wish to give a feel for the variety of types and times of bindings, and for use of the terminology we have developed.

BINDINGS TIMES	Name- Declaration	Declaration- Declaration	Declaration- Object	Declaration- Constraint	Declaration- Description	Location- Value
Program Creation	ALGOL Names			All Data	ALGOL Names	Constants
Linkage Edit		FORTRAN COMMON				
Load			FORTRAN Data			
Call	APL Names	Argument- Parameter Binding	ALGOL Local Data			
Execution Reference			PL/I BASED Data		APL Names	Variables

5.3.1 NAME-DECLARATION BINDING

There are two common ways in which references to names are resolved
to declarations for those names. The first is epitomized by ALGOL, the
second by APL.

We speak of ALGOL as having a static block structure; a program is
organized at time of program creation into a hierarchical collection of
text units. Such an organization may be depicted as shown on the following page.

Text unit A contains units B and C; unit C contains unit D. Also A
indirectly contains D.

Included in the semantics of this organization is the process of
binding of names to declarations. The binding rule is:

> A name occurring in a text unit is bound to the
> declaration for that name occurring within that
> unit, if such a declaration exists; if not, the name
> is bound as though the name occurred in the con-
> taining unit.

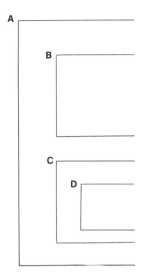

We elaborate on this binding process In later chapters. The point of immediate importance is that the blnding is made at time of program creation; it is independent of any execution characteristics of the program.

In APL, the binding rule is more dynamic, defined in terms of the execution-time sequence of calls of text units, rather than in terms of any static program structure. The rule is:

> A name occurring in a text unit is bound to the declaration for that name occurring within that unit, if such a declaration exists; if not, the name is bound as though the name occurred in the calling unit.

Note that this definition differs by only one word (*calling*) from the ALGOL definition (*containing*). But this difference is profound in effect: Binding is not done at time of program creation; it is effected only at time of call of a text unit while the program is executing.

Exercises

1. Consider an ALGOL program comprising blocks A, B, C, D, and E. Suppose the various blocks declare data with names as follows:

Block	Data
A:	x
B:	y
C:	x, y

D:	–
E:	z

Assume the program is structured as follows:

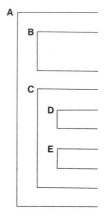

Give, for each block:

(a) the names known to it during execution

(b) the block in which each of the names was declared.

2. Consider an APL program with functions A, B, C, D, and E containing local declarations as in exercise 1. Suppose we have a call chain in which E calls D, which calls C, which calls B, which calls A. Give, for each function:

(a) the names known to it during execution

(b) the function in which each of the names was declared.

3. Consider the following PL/I program structure:

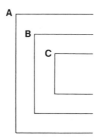

Suppose the following declarations are given in the blocks:

Block	Declaration
A	X STATIC EXTERNAL
B	X STATIC INTERNAL
	Y AUTOMATIC INTERNAL

    C   X STATIC EXTERNAL,
            Y AUTOMATIC INTERNAL

(a) How many variables have been declared in the above program?
(b) What is the name of each?

5.3.2 DECLARATION-DECLARATION BINDING

There are cases in which an intermediate mapping from one declaration
to another is required. A typical example is FORTRAN COMMON. Several
FORTRAN programs may declare a name to be COMMON. If these programs are later combined (linkage-edited) into a larger program, the
declarations are taken to refer to the same object, even though that
object has not yet been created. Conceptually, each declaration is
mapped to a newly created (at linkage-edit time) declaration that subsequently is mapped to the common object.
    Another common example of declaration-declaration binding is that
provided, at call time, between the arguments sent to a routine, and the
parameters receiving those arguments. Here a binding must be made
between each parameter declaration and the declaration of the corresponding argument. This subject is discussed further in section 5.5.

5.3.3 DECLARATION-OBJECT BINDING

Here we note three significantly different ways in which declarations
are mapped into objects.
    The first is exemplified by FORTRAN data. Objects are created
and declarations mapped to them at the time the program is loaded into
the machine and prepared for execution.
    A second, more dynamic example occurs with ALGOL local vari-
ables. The object creation and linking to a declaration is performed only
when the text unit containing the declaration is called for execution.
    Third and most dynamic is the case of PL/I based variables. With
these, the mapping from declaration to object is provided explicitly at
reference time by means of a pointer qualifier. A reference is given in the
form P–>Q, where P is a pointer and Q is a based variable. Q's declaration is mapped to an object by reference-time evaluation of the pointer
variable.

5.3.4 DECLARATION-CONSTRAINT BINDING

We have defined in our model that constraint specification accompanies
execution of a declaration. This binding is thus always determined when
a program is created.

5.3.5 DECLARATION-DESCRIPTION BINDING

In most common languages, the concept of constraints is not separated from that of descriptions. In our terms, the constraint set is so restricted that the description must always match it exactly. Thus the declaration-description binding is determined at time of program creation, as is declaration-constraint binding.

An exception to this occurs in APL, in which the general constraint is that objects may contain either character or numeric data. Any assignment to an object sets the declaration description either to character type or to numeric type. Languages of this kind, in which descriptions are modifiable dynamically, are said to have "self-describing data." The machines that execute programs in these languages are said to be "attribute-examining machines."

5.3.6 LOCATION-VALUE BINDING

In general, the two parts of an object are bound whenever an assignment is made to the object, thus changing its value. This is true of most so-called variables within languages. On the other hand, for special objects known as constants, this binding is made at time of program creation. Assignment to such objects during program execution is prohibited.

Intermediate binding times between locations and values frequently occur in high-level language processors (addresses of labels are bound at load time, those of dynamic storage areas at call time), but these sublinguistic cases need not concern us at present. The important point is that we wish to speak of the difference between constants and variables not as a qualitative one but rather as one of location-value binding time.

For more formal theories of names and their bindings to data, see [Chu41], [Chu57], and [Str66].

Exercises

4. Why is it necessary in a language to discern between the location and value components of an object?

5. Under what circumstances may either component be accessed without the other?

6. Generalize the preceding distinction to identify as many different types of access to any object as possible. In particular, discuss differences in the following varieties of access to an object named A in a PL/I program.

(a) A = 3;
(b) B = A;
(c) CALL A;
(d) ALLOCATE A;
(e) FREE A;

These distinctions may be used to restrict types of access allowed to an object referenced in a particular environment.

5.4 COMPILATION VERSUS INTERPRETATION

The evocative but nebulous terms *compilation* and *interpretation* have large amounts of associated informal semantics that we intend to disregard. When they are used in close proximity to each other in writing, however, it is usually in an attempt to contrast characteristics either of different languages or of different language processors. And the contrast is best describable in terms of information-binding times.

At a gross level, we say that a programming-language construct is compilable if its required information bindings are determinable before actual encounter of the construct during program execution. If the bindings cannot be made prior to execution-reference, we say that the construct must be interpreted.

This comparison is extended and generalized to describe entire languages. If a relatively large portion of a language's constructs are compilable, we say that the language is compilable; if not, we say that the language is interpretive.

In our preceding discussion of binding times, we pointed out that both name-declaration and declaration-description bindings were deferred longer in APL than in most languages. Thus we speak of APL as an interpretive language. PL/I is a much more compilable language in general, though our example of based variables is a case in which execution-time interpretation is required to perform the declaration-object binding.

5.5 ARGUMENT-PARAMETER BINDINGS

One of the most confusing areas dealing with information binding has been that of the association made, at call time, between arguments (actual parameters) sent to a routine, and parameters (formal parameters) declared within that routine.

Let us consider possible results (all available within ALGOL) of the following program. PL/I syntax is used for sake of communicating the example. The actual semantics peculiar to PL/I need not concern us now.

```
P:   PROCEDURE;
     DECLARE A(3), I;      /* A IS A 3-ELEMENT ARRAY */
     I = 1;                /* = IS THE ASSIGNMENT OPERATOR */
     A(1) = 2;
     A(2) = 4;
     CALL Q (A(I));        /* A(I) IS PASSED TO Q */
     Q:   PROCEDURE (B);   /* B IS THE PARAMETER NAME USED
                              FOR A(I) */
          A(1) = 3;        /* NAMES A AND I ARE INHERITED
                              FROM P */
          I = 2;
          PUT LIST (B);    /* PUT WRITES OUT THE VALUE OF B */
          END Q;
     ,END P;
```

Interpretation 1.

The result is printing of the value 2. The name-declaration and declaration-object bindings for both A(1) and A(I) have been done at program creation time and at time of entry to procedure P, respectively. The assignment to A(1) has provided a location-value binding for A(1). At time of call of Q, I is evaluated and a declaration-declaration binding for A(I) is made to the declaration for A(1). Then a new object is created identical to A(1)'s location-value pair, and a new declaration is created for this object. This declaration is passed to Q, and a declaration-declaration binding is made from B's declaration to the new declaration. The name B in Q has been bound to B's declaration at program creation time. Thus when B is written, the utlimate mapping is to the new object having the value 2. This interpretation of the binding mechanism is known as *call by value*.

Interpretation 2.

The result is 3. This differs from the first interpretation in that the declaration for A(1) is passed directly to Q; there is no copying of its object and no creation of a new declaration to pass. The result is that the assignment to A(1) within Q changes the value of the object bound to B. This interpretation is known as *call by address*.

Interpretation 3.

The result is 4. No declaration-declaration binding is made from A(I) to A(1) at time of call, so A(I) is passed unbound. Only when B is written is binding performed. At that time, I is evaluated to 2, and A(I)'s declaration is bound to that of A(2), whose value is 4. This interpretation is known as *call by name*.

One further variety of argument-parameter binding can be illustrated with a new example.

```
P:   PROCEDURE;
     DECLARE A;
     A = 1;
     CALL Q(A);
     Q:   PROCEDURE (B);
          DECLARE A, B;
          A = 2;
          PUT LIST(B);
          END Q;
     END P;
```

Note that we have declared a new A in Q, to which the name A is bound within Q. Call by value, address, or name yields the value 1. But suppose that at call time we choose not to provide name-declaration binding from the name A in the call to the declaration of A in P. Then we might say that at call time we are providing only a name-name binding from B to A. Only at time of writing of B do we bind to a declaration, and then it is to the declaration of A in Q. The result is 2. We designate this interpretation as *call by text string*.

We have presented the above examples because they illustrate common interpretations in languages today. We have not attempted to cover all possible parameter bindings. On the contrary, we have tried to give some taste of the hopelessness of any such attempt. The cases above are describable using only simple subscripted variables. Use of more complex data leads to more complicated sets of possibilities.

Exercises

7. Describe the effect of the following ALGOL program. Note that X is a call-by-name formal parameter.

```
BEGIN
    REAL ARRAY A[1:10];
    INTEGER I;
    READ(A);
    SUBR(A[I]);
    REAL PROCEDURE SUBR(X);
        NAME X;
        REAL X, S;
        BEGIN
            S: = 0;
            FOR I: = 1 STEP 1 UNTIL 10 DO
                S: = S+X
        END;
        PRINT(S)
    END
```

5.6 NAMES USED AS OBJECT VALUES

We have described a number of ways in which symbolic names within languages are related to objects they represent. But though the ways may be rich and varied, they are in general among the predefined semantics for a given language. The programmer has little explicit control over the mappings; he must understand them and program accordingly.

Of course it could not instead be required that the programmer define all these mappings; the task would be enormous and not particularly relevant to his problem. And yet, as in all endeavors governed by external discipline, there are exceptional cases where more freedom for individual decision is required. The programmer must, on occasion, have the ability to provide the mappings from names to objects at execution time. He must also be able to change those mappings as dynamically as he desires.

The subject area that we are approaching, at least in an abstract sense, is usually known as *list processing*. This area is involved with manipulation of data having either or both of two characteristics:

> 1. The internal structure and description of individual data objects is highly variable during execution.
>
> 2. The ordering of a collection of data objects is likewise highly variable.

Let us contrast these characteristics with those of arrays, as they exist in FORTRAN, ALGOL, and PL/I. An array has two significant characteristics:

> 1. All elements have identical structure and description.
>
> 2. An array defines a static ordering of its elements. That ordering, and the number of elements, are not variable during execution.

Structures, as they exist in PL/I, have a different set of characteristics:

> 1. Elements may have different structuring and description.
>
> 2. Elements are not ordered, but the number of elements is not variable during execution.

The execution-time variability requirements not provided for by arrays or structures can be met by providing the ability to have names as object values. We have not discussed internal content or structure of what we have called values, but we have tacitly assumed that when a name is referenced, the name is mapped eventually to a value, at which time the symbolic resolution is completed.

In the case of a name occurring as an object value, either of two resolution interpretations may be desirable:

1. The name occurring as an object value is the complete resolution of the reference.

2. The name occurring as an object value must itself be resolved to provide the complete resolution of the reference. This interpretation provides for indirect addressing of data.

The interpretation provided for a given reference may depend on the particular operator with which the reference occurs as an operand. A computational operator, requiring numeric data, may be defined to continue resolution of its operand references through a total chain of indirection. The target operand of an assignment operator would not, however, be resolved in this manner.

Because some operators do not by definition resolve indirection chains for certain operands, we suggest a pair of operators for providing further resolution explicitly:

→(name) provides resolution of a single level of indirection, returning the object named by the simple resolution of the given name.

⇒(name) provides complete resolution of an indirection chain, returning the first object in the chain started by the given name that is not itself a name.

Suppose that we are involved in an application in which we must create an aggregate of objects, order them in some way, and frequently modify the internal structures of those objects. What sort of structural model do we need to carry out this process?

Obviously, neither arrays nor structures, as we have described them above, are adequate. We need a picture in which elements may grow or shrink, ordering can be changed, and the number of elements can vary.

Assume that we are at a stage in processing in which we have n elements, ordered in some fashion as shown on the following page. Each N_i denotes a name that maps to an object with two value parts, each of which is itself a name. The first of the latter names is that of the current succeeding element (according to the current ordering); the second is that of the object represented by the current element. This separation of the elements from one another and from their identifying objects allows us to modify their sizes and structures without destroying our overall picture.

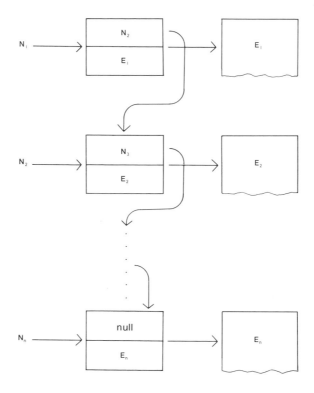

Now suppose that we create a new element of our aggregate and decide that it should be the second element in the ordering; the current second element should become the third; and so on. Let us call our new element N_{n+1}. We establish the following:

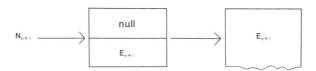

There remains the requirement to update our ordering. This involves two modifications:

      1. The first value part of N_{n+1} must be set to the name N_2.

      2. The first value part of N_1 must be set to the name N_{n+1}.

This completes our update.

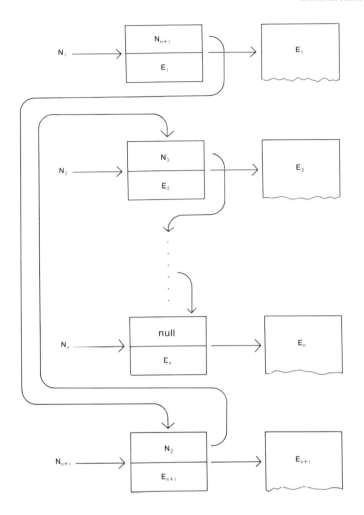

We have used names as values here for two purposes: (1) to provide separability of the elements and thus allow their modification, and (2) to impose ordering upon the elements. We shall for now regard these as primary uses for objects with name values. We have already seen their use in PL/I in chapter 3, and we return to the subjects of list processing and name data in chapters 16 and 17. For further discussion of list handling, see [Fos67], [Mad67], and [Han69].

Exercises

8. Describe the requirements of deletion of an element from a list.

5.7 SHARING OF OBJECTS AMONG DECLARATIONS

We have described functions for binding names to declarations; declarations to declarations, objects, constraints, and descriptions; and locations to values. We postulate now that our protocol does not admit the inverses of these functions, and that in some cases such inverses would be describable only as multiple-valued relations.

A case of particular interest is the relation of objects to declarations. Consider a possible sharing of a single object among different declarations. We have already mentioned the PL/I DEFINED attribute as permitting such use, and we have emphasized that descriptions are to be tied to declarations rather than to objects. It should be clear, then, that our motivation for allowing sharing of objects is to permit different interpretations to be placed upon an object, depending on the declaration from which it is referenced.

This feature is different from that provided by declaration-declaration maps as mentioned previously. Under the latter, a name reference might be mapped through any number of intermediate declarations, but those declarations serve only as linkages to the final declaration, to which descriptions and constraints are tied. Through object sharing, different sets of descriptions and constraints can be associated with the same object.

5.8 SUMMARY

In this chapter we have begun our excursion into programming-language semantics. We have developed the foundations of a terminology for talking about language constructs, a terminology that we shall expand and detail further as we progress beyond the level of generalities into particular language features. We have suggested that understanding of information bindings is a critical step toward development or comprehension of any language, and we have tried to indicate some of the profound effects that information bindings can have on semantics of program execution.

Exercises

9. The terms *syntax* and *semantics* are used loosely to differentiate form and content of a language. The former term is used to describe the grammatical aspects of a language, while the latter deals with the effect of execution of language constructs. How might this distinction be explained in terms of information binding times?

CHAPTER 6

Arithmetic

The arithmetic features defined within programming languages tend to be flavored by the underlying characteristics of their host machines. This is a natural result of the need, in deference to efficiency, to use each machine's computational capabilities as directly as possible.

In most languages, arithmetic semantics are given in a quasi-machine-independent fashion, with numerous footnotes and asterisks providing the bridge to actual hardware characteristics. The primary problem is, of course, the finite bounds on accuracy and representation reflected in all machines, contrasted with the luxuries of unbounded precision enjoyed within more pure mathematics.

We shall organize our discussion of arithmetic in terms of the language attempts to mimic the number-theoretic concepts of the discipline.

6.1 NUMBER DOMAINS

We look first at the classes of numeric data recognized in programming languages. Some of these may be explicitly declared in a particular language, while others may be recognized only implicitly in certain contexts. Some may not even be expressible in certain languages.

6.1.1 NATURAL NUMBERS

No prominent programming language recognizes the set of natural numbers (the positive integers) as an explicit data type. There are, however, numerous language examples, both semantic and syntactic, of contexts requiring such data. We list a few such examples—syntactic ones in which positive integer constants must occur, and semantic ones in which expressions may be specified, but evaluation must be to a positive integer.

Syntactic

FORTRAN, APL statement labels
FORTRAN array dimensions
PL/I precisions

Semantic

FORTRAN DO values
ALGOL SWITCH subscripts
FORTRAN subscripts
most array sizes

In general, we intuitively associate uses of natural numbers with cases in which one is specifying the number of occurrences of some construct, or is ordinally indexing some structure (e.g., mentioning the nth item in a list).

6.1.2 NONNEGATIVE INTEGERS

This domain (the natural numbers and zero) is also reflected in programming languages only through restrictions on wider domains, not through an explicit data type. Examples of occurrence of this domain follow.

Syntactic

FORTRAN, PL/I field widths in format specifications

Semantic

APL array sizes
PL/I string lengths

Occurrences of 0 in such contexts usually indicate degenerate constructs with no occurrences. Usually, such specification via the constant 0 is of little programming use, but the arising of constructs such as null strings during execution can be very common and useful.

6.1.3 INTEGERS 0 AND 1

This domain, again usually occurring only as a language restriction, is most often used to represent the Boolean truth values false and true, respectively. Thus operands of operators such as NOT, AND, OR, IMPLIES, and IF, may be required to evaluate to integer values 0 and 1. The logical representation of truth values as integers often allows convenient use of such values as operands of subsequent arithmetic operators, such as in an APL branch:

$$3+(A>1)+(A>2)$$

This statement causes a transfer to statement 3, 4, or 5, depending on whether $A \leq 1$, $1 < A \leq 2$, or $A > 2$, respectively.

6.1.4 INTEGERS

Here we find the most restrictive number domain directly represented in programming languages, and in their underlying machines. We need not dwell on the multitude of programming contexts in which integer results are required. In such contexts, evaluation to a noninteger causes either an error, as is usual in FORTRAN, or an appropriate conversion to integer, as in PL/I. Such conversions usually involve either truncation or rounding to the nearest integer. The point of interest is the linguistic effect of recognizing integers as an explicit data type, as is the case in FORTRAN and ALGOL, but is not the case in PL/I and APL.

It is not obvious that there need be any far-reaching effect of the choice of declarable data types of a language; what clearly does have such effect is the set of data types required for use in various contexts, and the conversions provided to satisfy those requirements. As we have already seen, the declarable and required data types within a language are generally not identical.

But, in fact, the choice of declarable types in a language is important, because of the tendency to keep the declarable data types closed under the available operations. Thus, for example, FORTRAN integer division is defined to yield the greatest integer of the rational quotient as an integer result; PL/I fixed-point division yields a fixed-point result.

This mania for closure stems in part from the aesthetics of the concept with regard to modularity—someone should be able to work solely with data of type X, not worrying about types Y and Z. It rises also from similar characteristics of most underlying machines. Different hardware registers are used for operations on different types of data, with the closure property preserved.

Awkward situations may arise when a language differentiates data types more strictly than does its host machine. If one is translating FORTRAN into a machine language that represents and uses all numeric data identically, the compiler must actually generate extra code to reflect accurately the FORTRAN integer division rules.

6.1.5 RATIONAL NUMBERS

Few languages explicitly recognize rational numbers as a data type. Of those we have looked at, only PL/I can make any claims in that direction, and those claims are rather weak. PL/I FIXED data, with scale factors specified, can be used accurately to hold rational quantities whose denominators are powers either of 2 (FIXED BINARY) or of 10 (FIXED DECIMAL). Rational numbers with any other denominators can only be approximated with FIXED data.

Languages that recognize and truly implement rational data are discussed in [Bon64], [Sam67], and [Hal71]. Such languages are used in algebraic symbol manipulation, and availability of rationals is necessary for work with rational functions. Rational data are represented by a pair of integers giving the numerator and denominator, in that order. Arithmetic operations are carried out exactly. Thus, for example, (A,B) + (C,D) = (AD + BC, BD).

6.1.6 REALS

All languages must use finite rational approximations for irrational quantities; we cannot speak of any language as working computationally with the total real number spectrum. The best a language can do is permit the user to specify, as an additional operand of an operation, the finite precision for the result of that operation. To do so can be feasible and useful for operators implemented either as convergent series sums or as successive approximations.

PL/I provides what outwardly appears to be this sort of feature in a number of built-in functions that accept desired result precisions as operands. Close scrutiny reveals, however, that such specification merely causes the operation to be performed in the normal way and then expanded to the desired precision—the computation is not carried out with that precision.

The linguistic impact of real numbers in ALGOL, and of floating-point ones in FORTRAN and PL/I, is simply that they have a wider range of assumable values than integers do, and they may take on nonintegral values. They are carried internally as a characteristic-mantissa pair, allowing for representation of greater magnitudes than is possible otherwise.

6.1.7 COMPLEX NUMBERS

FORTRAN, PL/I, and several other languages allow the direct use of complex numbers. Arithmetic operations are performed on such quantities according to mathematical rules. Thus, for example, in PL/I,

$$(3+2i)*(1-i) = 5-i$$

6.1.8 DEWEY DECIMAL NUMBERS

We digress for a moment to a topic outside the realm of number theory. JOSS ([Mar67]) is a language designed for interactive use at the terminal. Statements are entered with at least a two-part label indicating primarily program part, and secondarily part step. Thus the statement

2.3 SET X = 0

is interpreted as the third step of the second part of the program being constructed. Statements need not be entered in order of intended execution; their labels provide the desired ordering property.

Suppose that, after entering the above statement, the JOSS user enters the following transfer statement:

2.4 TO STEP 1.7 IF Y = 3

Further suppose that he suddenly realizes he has left out a critical incrementing of Y to be done prior to the test of its value. He simply types

2.3.1 Y = Y + 1

This statement is assembled into the proper relative position. The depth of such index nesting is unbounded in JOSS.

Exercises

1. In what ways might the automatic-ordering characteristic of Dewey Decimal numbers be generally useful as a feature of a programming language?

6.2 NUMBER BASES

Assembly languages have always allowed, or even required, numeric quantities to be expressed to nondecimal number bases. Common bases have been 2 (binary), 8 (octal), and 16 (hexadecimal), with the choice made in accordance with natural underlying machine storage unit sizes (bits, bytes, words).

High-level languages have in general required numeric expression in base 10, or decimal form. PL/I went a step further, in deference primarily to assembly-language programmers accustomed to thinking in binary, and provided for base 2 specifications, both as variable attributes and in designation of constants. Thus the PL/I programmer may write the constant 101B to represent the decimal integer 5.

APL has generalized the features for specification in different bases with the two operators ENCODE ($\top$) and DECODE ($\bot$). DECODE gives the value of its second operand evaluated in a number system with bases given by its first operand.

$$24\ 60\ 60 \bot 2\ 5\ 17$$
$$7517$$

This gives the number of seconds in 2 hours, 5 minutes, and 17 seconds:

$$7517\ =\ (17 \times 60^0) + (5 \times 60^1) + (2 \times 60^2).$$

Note that the first member of the base vector, here indicating the number of hours in a day, is irrelevant.

$$(3\rho 8) \bot 4\ 2\ 7$$
$$279$$

This gives the decimal value of 427:

$$279\ =\ (7 \times 8^0) + (2 \times 8^1) + (4 \times 8^2).$$

ENCODE gives the representation of its second operand expressed in the base given by the first operand.

$$(4\rho 2) \top 13$$
$$1\ 1\ 0\ 1$$

This gives the base 2 representation of the decimal integer 13.

While numbers may be translated among bases by these operators, values are in all other uses assumed to be in base 10.

$$(4\rho 2) \top 13\ +\ (4\rho 2) \top 6$$
$$1\ 2\ 1\ 1$$

The value is that of 1 1 0 1 + 0 1 1 0 as a decimal vector sum, rather than the binary sum, which would be 1 10 1 1. Note that results of ENCODE are vectors, not numbers.

A related APL operator supporting number bases is LOGARITHM
(❋), which evaluates the logarithm of its second operand to the base of
the first.

$$(4\rho10) ❋ 1\ 10\ 100\ 1000$$
$$0\ 1\ 2\ 3$$

Exercises

2. Suppose a language has the requirement to convert values between
   representations in a pair of number bases, m and n. For integers, there
   need be no loss of accuracy, but for fractions, exact conversions may
   be impossible.

   (a) Describe general algorithms for converting both integer and frac-
       tional values between number bases m and n.
   (b) In what cases does the fractional conversion yield an exact replica
       of the original value in a finite representation?

6.3 ARITHMETIC OPERATORS

The repertoire of arithmetic operators and built-in functions is rather
consistent among programming languages. We shall list a fairly comprehensive set taken from a number of them. Together, these operators
form a powerful set of features for arithmetic manipulation.

Operator	Operands	Result	
ADD	A, B	$A + B$	
SUBTRACT	A, B	$A - B$	
MULTIPLY	A, B	$A \times B$	
DIVIDE	A, B	$A \div B$	
NEGATE	A	$-A$	
POWER	A, B	A^B	
EQ	A, B	$A = B$	These operators,
NE	A, B	$A \neq B$	the relationals,
LT	A, B	$A < B$	are also avail-
GT	A, B	$A > B$	able for other
LE	A, B	$A \leq B$	than arithmetic
GE	A, B	$A \geq B$	data.
SIN	A	$\sin(A)$	
COS	A	$\cos(A)$	
TAN	A	$\tan(A)$	
ARCSIN	A	$\arcsin(A)$	
ARCCOS	A	$\arccos(A)$	
ARCTAN	A	$\arctan(A)$	

SINH	A	sinh(A)
COSH	A	cosh(A)
TANH	A	tanh(A)
ARCSINH	A	arcsinh(A)
ARCCOSH	A	arccosh(A)
ARCTANH	A	arctanh(A)
LN	A	$\log_e A$
EXP	A	e^A
MAX	A, B	$A \geq B \Rightarrow A$
		$A < B \Rightarrow B$
MIN	A, B	$A \geq B \Rightarrow B$
		$A < B \Rightarrow A$
ABS	A	$A \geq 0 \Rightarrow A$
		$A < 0 \Rightarrow -A$
SIGN	A	$A > 0 \Rightarrow 1$
		$A = 0 \Rightarrow 0$
		$A < 0 \Rightarrow -1$
RECIPROCAL	A	$1 \div A$
FACTORIAL	A	$\Gamma(A + 1)$
MODULUS	A	integer R, $0 \leq R < B$
		$\ni \exists$ integer $Q \ni A = Q \times B + R$
FLOOR	A	largest integer $I \ni I \leq A$
CEILING	A	smallest integer $I \ni A \leq I$
TRUNC	A	$A \geq 0 \Rightarrow$ FLOOR(A)
		$A < 0 \Rightarrow$ CEILING(A)

The above set is not all that one might envision, but it provides a rich nucleus on which more sophisticated operators can be built.

6.4 PRECISIONS OF ARITHMETIC RESULTS

We pointed out in chapter 3 that PL/I assumes all arithmetic values to be exact, rather than rounded on the last digit. This assumption is generally made in languages. Successive operations tend to increase, rather than decrease, the numbers of digits required to express the precisions of their operands. With this assumption, let us look at the most common arithmetic operators and investigate result precisions as functions of operand precisions. If the reader is confused by our use of the term *precision*, let him instead think of significant digits as the subject at hand. Terminology aside, what we really are investigating is the number of digit positions required to hold the result of an operation. The case we consider is that of scaled integers.

We speak of a quantity's precision and scale as the pair (p,s), where p represents the number of significant digits and s the number of those to the right of the decimal point. We assume real decimal quantities throughout, and operands A(p1,s1) and B(p2,s2). We denote precision and scale of results by p and s, respectively.

Addition, Subtraction: $p = 1 + \text{MAX}(p1\text{-}s1, p2\text{-}s2) + \text{MAX}(s1, s2)$
$s = \text{MAX}(s1, s2)$

Space must be allowed for the longer integer plus the longer fraction + 1 in case the addition carries beyond a power of 10.

Example:

$$
\begin{array}{rl}
93.8 & (3,1) \\
+ \quad 8.275 & (4,3) \\
\hline
102.075 & (6,3)
\end{array}
$$

$p = 1 + \text{MAX}(2,1) + \text{MAX}(1,3) = 6$
$s = \text{MAX}(1,3) = 3$

Multiplication:

$p = p1 + p2$
$s = s1 + s2$

Example:

$$
\begin{array}{rl}
9.73 & (3,2) \\
\times \quad 2.4 & (2,1) \\
\hline
23.352 & (5,3)
\end{array}
$$

Division: Having observed the inadequacy of any finite precision, we work under the rule that we always allow enough space for the integral portion of the result and allot the remaining portion of the result area (up to M, the total digit maximum allowed on our machine) to fractional digits.

$p = M$
$s = M - p1 + s1 - s2$

Example:

$$
\begin{array}{rl}
82.7 & (3,1) \\
\div \quad 3. & (1,0) \\
\hline
27.566\ldots & (M, M\text{-}2)
\end{array}
$$

Much freedom is given to systems that process data according to such rules. Clearly the precision-scale pair implied for a quantity need not be reflected directly in its internal representation. These must be exact only when values are displayed to the programmer. At other times, it is sufficient that at least enough digits be carried to give a precision no less than that implied.

In PL/I, where precisions are paid greatest homage, a compiler can always discern the precision needed for a result (recall our example of character strings in section 3.3. The ramifications of weakening this ability via variable precisions could be disastrous in view of most machines' ignorance on the matter. Target code might have to include precision tests prior to selection of either single-precision or double-precision operators. The effects of this interpretation could well render a language inefficient to the point of infeasibility in a compiler environment.

Exercises

3. For the operators ADD, SUBTRACT, MULTIPLY, and DIVIDE, give precision rules for results in the following cases:

   (a) rational operands
   (b) complex operands with integer real and imaginary parts
   (omit DIVIDE)

4. Our precision rules for division can cause problems in some cases.

   (a) Use the rules for addition and division to find the precision and scale of the result obtained by evaluating the expression 25 + 1/3.

   (b) What changes to our precision rules can you suggest to relieve any problems that you encountered?

6.5 ARITHMETIC EXCEPTIONS

Let us look briefly at the exceptional conditions that might arise during execution of any of our set of arithmetic operators. We distinguish two varieties of such conditions:

> **Domain Errors:** An operand of some operator lies outside of the domain required for it by that operator.

> **Range Errors:** The operands of an operator are individually within their domains, but the attempt to perform the operation on the set of them is abortive.

An example of a domain error is occurrence of the value 0 as the second operand of DIVIDE. We identify two range errors, OVERFLOW and UNDER-FLOW, which may occur if the mathematical result of an operation is either too large or too small in magnitude to be representable on the particular target machine. (It is a moot point as to whether, for example, the attempt to evaluate TAN(π/2) is a domain or OVERFLOW error.)

In chapter 14 we look in detail at exception handling. We propose a minimal adequate set of exception-handling features—yet a larger set than is now available in any language. Our current aim is only to identify those exceptions parochial to arithmetic operators.

Exercises

5. Enumerate the set of domain errors associated with the operator set of section 6.3. Note that a number of the arithmetic operators should not allow COMPLEX operands.

6.6 OPERATOR PRECEDENCE

The subject of operator precedence is not peculiar to arithmetic, and we examine it in detail in appendix 1. We mention it now because of its recurring significance in arithmetic, where complex hierarchies of operators and operands are commonplace.

Most informal language descriptions speak of operator precedence in terms of when suboperations of an expression are evaluated. Let us assume a language with binary infix operators + (lowest precedence), × (middle), and ↑ (highest). Then in the expression A + B × C, it is said that B × C is evaluated first because × has higher precedence than +. The quoted rule is usually that within an expression, operations are performed in order of precedence (highest to lowest). But this rule is uselessly restrictive and, in fact, never followed by language processors. In the expression A × B + C ↑ D, it is not essential that the ↑ be executed prior to the ×. It is critical only that the × and ↑, in any order or in parallel, be executed prior to the +.

We propose a rather more general semantics associated with operator precedence:

> The specification of operator precedence within a language allows determination, for any operator appearing within an expression, of the set of operands of that operator. The only sequencing rule is the evident one that execution of an operator must come later than evaluation of all its operands.

We give now a standard arithmetic operator precedence table, applicable with minor deviations to most high-level languages.

Precedence	Operators
Lowest	Relationals (EQ, LE, etc.)
	ADD, SUBTRACT
	MULTIPLY, DIVIDE
	POWER
	NEGATE
Highest	Built-in functions

Most languages differentiate syntactically between operators and built-in functions by enclosing the operand set of the latter in parentheses, thus forcing their highest precedence.

A further specification must be made to be able to determine the operands of an operator. If we write A − B + C, it might be interpreted either as (A − B) + C or as A − (B + C). Hence, we must associate, with each precedence level, an associativity direction, left-to-right or right-to-left, so that we can resolve unambiguously, expressions involving sequences of equal precedence operators. Within most languages, this association is left-to-right, though an exception occurs in PL/I exponentiation, where A ∗∗ B ∗∗ C is interpreted as A ∗∗ (B ∗∗ C). This exception was made in deference to mathematical notation, where A^{B^C} is interpreted as $A^{(B^C)}$.

Exercises

6. Consider a language with three binary operators: + (ADD), × (MULTIPLY), and ↑ (POWER). Suppose that + is of lowest precedence and ↑ of highest. Assume also that + and ↑ are left-to-right associative, while × is right-to-left associative. Parenthesize the following expressions to indicate operator-operand associations accordingly.

   (a) A+B+C
   (b) A+B × C↑D
   (c) A+B/C+D
   (d) A×B + C×D
   (e) A↑B × C×D

We can now give a general three-part rule for determining operands of an operator in a language making use of operator precedence and assuming left-to-right associativity. This rule is relevant only to expressions involving unary prefix and binary infix operators.

■ The operand of a unary prefix operator is the text to its right up to the first binary infix operator having equal or lower precedence.

■ The first operand of a binary infix operator is the text to its left following the last operator having lower precedence.

■ The second operand of a binary infix operator is the text to its right up to the first operator having equal or lower precedence.

Now that we have glibly characterized what we have repeatedly referred to as "most languages," let us consider an important exception. APL has no operator precedence rules—or, in terms of our previous model, we can say that all operators have equal precedence, and right-to-left association governs that single precedence level. Thus A × B + C = D × E ρ F is interpreted as A × (B + (C = (D × (EρF)))). Contrasting examples of left-to-right associativity with no precedence levels are common among macro assembly languages.

Exercises

7. Discuss the merits of the following three human-factors claims:

   (a) Left-to-right associativity (with no precedence) is most natural because things are done in the order in which they are written.
   (b) Right-to-left associativity (with no precedence) is most natural because things can be written in order of importance (leftmost operators characterize the expression, while rightmost ones simply give details on the operands).
   (c) Having different precedences is most natural because of its algebraic heritage (e.g., a + b^{c}d is naturally interpreted as (a + ((b↑c) × d)).

8. How would our rule for determining the operands of an operator differ if we were assuming right-to-left associativity?

CHAPTER 7

String Handling

There is a point of view, as espoused within APL, that the notion of strings is an unnecessary one, duplicated and dwarfed by vectors. And indeed at a level of description insensitive to context of use, this is indisputable. We can describe the inherent characteristics of a string as an ordered collection of elements, individually addressable as the first, the second, and so forth. And these characteristics are just as easily describable in terms of a vector of elements with lower bound 1.

We choose nevertheless to separate the concepts of *string* and *vector*, because of what we view as desirably rather different properties exhibited by the two when under the influence of a number of operators. In this chapter we investigate a simple set of string operators adequate for most unsophisticated uses of strings, and we contrast the effects of these operators when used in this manner with their effects when used with vectors.

Features adequate for specialized string manipulation are not introduced in this chapter. Such study is deferred until chapter 17, where we look at SNOBOL as an example of a language heavily oriented toward string manipulation.

Our discussion centers on strings of characters because of their strong intuitive connection; however, the string concept might be applied to any other variety of scalar data (PL/I recognizes strings of bits as well as of characters). Utility of the concept is probably highest with character data, and most languages recognize no other kinds of strings—there is, however, no theoretical requirement for linking the two.

7.1 A MODEL FOR STRING HANDLING

We now develop a set of features adequate for general string-manipulation needs within a language.

7.1.1 CHARACTER-STRING ATTRIBUTES

We start by observing two string characteristics that are independent of any context in which a string is used: (1) current length of string and (2) variability of string length. The first of these indicates, at any time, the number of characters currently residing within the string. The second implies a dichotomization of strings into those whose lengths are frozen at creation time, and those whose lengths may vary dynamically. The latter are reflections of most text undergoing creation or modification, while the former reflect the imposition of fixed-format environments on text disposition (e.g., each line of text in a book contains sixty characters).

We might introduce a third string characteristic relevant only in the case of variable-length strings, that being the pair of lengths bounding the variability (a line of text may contain up to sixty characters); but utility of this concept seems marginal. It is present in PL/I, but its motivation was from implementation, not linguistic, sources. We choose to describe a black and white world in which strings are either of constant lengths or of arbitrarily variable lengths.

7.1.2 STRING OPERATIONS

As a prototypal area for driving our discussion of string operations, we look at some basic requirements of any text creation and editing facility. Primitive needs include the following, each of which is identified by a number and discussed more fully below.

1. Create a string of text.
2. Concatenate two strings to form a new string.
3. Extract a portion of a string.
4. Search within a string for a given substring.
5. Identify a string.
6. Interrogate the length of a string.
7. Delete a substring or replace it with another substring.
8. Insert a string within another string at a specified point.

1. the first of these requirements is satisfied by the ability to write character data, and to allow its retention in variables. Let us use enclosing single quotes to denote a string of characters. Let us also agree to the

convention that an embedded quote must be represented by two successive quotes.

Representation	String Value
'Ab.x4'	Ab.x4
'7D'','	7D',
''''''	' '

2. Concatenation requires a binary operator CAT, which creates the concatenation of its arguments.

CAT('SUN','DRY') = 'SUNDRY'

3. Extraction is accomplished by an operator SUBSTRING(A,B,C). A is the source string, B is an integer indicating the starting index of the desired substring, and C is an integer indicating its length. Thus if A is the string 'ALIBI', then

SUBSTRING(A,2,3) = 'LIB'

4. For searching, we define an operator INDEX, which returns the starting index of the leftmost substring of its first argument that matches its second argument.

INDEX('BANANA','AN') = 2

We use the convention that 0 is returned if the search fails.

5. We identify strings by means of the relational operators EQ and NE, either of which returns the truth or falseness of a comparison as an integer, 1 or 0.

EQ('KNICK','KNACK') = 0

We use the convention that if compared strings are of different lengths, the result is as though the shorter string had been extended on the right with blanks to match the longer one in length. Thus

EQ('KNICK','KNICK ') = 1

We can expand our comparison feature to include all of the relational operators, by first defining a character collating sequence, and then defining comparison as yielding lexical ordering, as in a dictionary—on the basis of successive left-to-right character comparisons.

6. The operator LENGTH returns the length of its argument string.

LENGTH('YEAR') = 4

7,8. We now consider several more interesting operations, involving changes to strings rather than simply interrogation or creation. And we encounter our first need to differentiate between fixed-length and variable-length strings. We look first at operators provided for variable-length strings. Then we investigate their possible adaptation to fixed-length strings.

Substring replacement might be provided by a statement naming the source string, its substring to be replaced, and the replacement string. But we already have SUBSTRING, an operator for providing the first two of these operands, so why not just assign the replacement string to that referent?

SUBSTRING(X,3,3)←'RAT';

If X = 'BEWARE' before execution, then X = 'BERATE' afterwards.

This approach is all right as long as we are careful in our definition of SUBSTRING. We cannot afford here, as we could before, to have the SUBSTRING operator create the given substring as a result. If it did so, we would be assigning to a created result string, and not affecting the source string. Thus we must define SUBSTRING as returning addressability to the desired portion of the source string, not as creating a result whose value is that desired substring. PL/I denotes such functions as *pseudo-variables*; we refer to them as *selection operators*—they select and return addressability to data.

The most common selection operator in most languages appears as subscription into an array. If, in FORTRAN, one executes A(3) = 4, the effect is to assign the value 4 to A(3), not to assign 4 to a new result created by executing A(3).

So we effect substring replacement by assigning the replacement string to a substring of some source string.

Substring deletion is easily accomplished as a degenerate case of replacement, where the replacement string is null (we denote the null string by''). Thus, if X = 'BEWARE', the statement

SUBSTRING(X,3,3)←'';

leaves X = 'BEE'.

Substring insertion can be introduced with a convention regarding length specification of 0 with the SUBSTRING operator. When the value of a substring is referred to in this way, the result is a null string. Simple selection via SUBSTRING also addresses a null string, but the address of that null string is important. If X = 'BEE', then

SUBSTRING(X,2,0)←'MUS';

ensures X = 'BEMUSE'. We define SUBSTRING(S,n,0) to identify the null string following the nth character of S. We allow the convention that SUBSTRING(S,0,0) identifies the null string preceding the first character of S. Thus if X = 'NIGN', then

SUBSTRING(X,0,0)←'BE';

ensures X = 'BENIGN'.

All of our above examples have dealt with variable-length strings. We have assumed that the substring of a variable-length string is itself a variable-length string; assignment to it may change its length. Now let us look at the preceding features in the case of fixed-length strings.

For fixed-length strings, let us say that a substring of a fixed-length string is itself a fixed-length string. We further make two convenient definitions for assignment to a fixed-length string: (1) if the source string is shorter than the target, right padding with blanks occurs; and (2) if the source is longer, right truncation occurs. Thus if x is fixed-length of length 3, then

X←'AB';

yields X = 'AB ', and

X←'DIET';

yields X = 'DIE'.

With these conventions, we look at replacement, deletion, and insertion in the fixed-length case. As in the variable-length case, replacement occurs only if the replacement string and the identified source substring are of equal length, If x is of length 6 and has the value 'BEWARE', then

SUBSTRING(X,3,3)←'FOR';

leaves X = 'BEFORE',

SUBSTRING(X,3,3)←'IG';

leaves X = 'BEIG E', and

SUBSTRING(X,3,3)←'FUDDLE';

leaves X = 'BEFUDE'.

Note in the fixed-length case that the statement

SUBSTRING(S1,n,0)←s2;

has no effect on s1. Thus insertion is meaningless for fixed-length strings.

Deletion is simply the replacement of deleted characters by blanks. If X = ,HIDE,' then

SUBSTRING(X,2,2)←'';

leaves X = 'H E'.

Exercises

1. Use the operators that we have defined to perform the following actions:

    (a) Insert a given string at the end of a variable-length string.
    (b) Delete the last character of a string.
    (c) Delete the leftmost occurrence of a given substring in a variable-length string.

7.2 STRING HANDLING IN PL/I

Now let us compare the string-handling facilities of PL/I and APL against those defined. We first look at PL/I, which admits a string data type.

PL/I has, syntactically, a set of features almost identical to the ones that we have described, but there are two significant semantic differences. The first is that a variable-length (VARYING) string must be declared with a maximum length. Attempts to extend the string beyond this length result in right truncation. The reason for this restriction is purely an implementation one: Specification of the maximum length allows an implementation to allocate that length of space for the string, with assurance of its sufficiency.

The second PL/I difference is very restrictive. Selection of a substring of any string, whether fixed or variable, is defined to identify a fixed-length string, so the replacement, deletion, and insertion features are of no more use than in our fixed-length case. The following table compares our features with PL/I requirements to do the same. We assume initially a variable-length string x with the value 'BELIE'.

Our Model	PL/I
SUBSTRING(x,3,2)←'SIEG';	x = SUBSTR(x,1,2)‖'SIEG' ‖SUBSTR(x,5,1);
SUBSTRING(x,3,2)←'T';	x = SUBSTR(x,1,2)‖'T' ‖SUBSTR(x,5,1);
SUBSTRING(x,3,2)←'';	x = SUBSTR(x,1,2) ‖SUBSTR(x,5,1);
SUBSTRING(x,5,0)‹ 'VE';	x = x‖'VE';

The PL/I examples are verbose, and, unfortunately, an implementation disadvantage lies in the opacity of intent hidden within that verbosity. In each case the initial string is dissected and then reassembled with minor changes. Our examples emphasize only the changes. The PL/I cases emphasize the dissection, which tends to be obeyed beyond the call of duty by any nondiscriminating implementation. In the first case, for example, all that is needed is to replace 'LI' in the source string by 'SIEG'. The PL/I rendition indicates, however, that three intermediate strings are to be created, then concatenated together, then assigned to x. This may cause generation of much redundant manipulation of the data.

7.3 STRING HANDLING IN APL

We now look at APL's string features, which are interesting because of APL's lack of distinction between vectors and strings. APL's syntax allows strings to be written just as we have done, enclosed in quotes. But we must remember that a string so written is considered to be a vector of individual characters, and that all APL vectors are variable-length.

Our SUBSTRING operator is neatly available in APL through subscripting. If x = 'CHARACTERS', our construct

SUBSTRING(x,5,3)

identifying the string 'ACT', can be written simply as

x[5 6 7]

Subscription is a selection process in APL, so one may use such a construct as a target of an assignment.

Our concatenation is directly available in APL with the comma. Thus,

CAT('CATE','NATE')

is expressed in APL as

'CATE','NATE'

Our LENGTH operator is analogous to the ρ operator of APL.

The first problem encountered in APL is the same as one that occurs in PL/I. The subscription operator, used to select a substring, is considered to be fixed-length in the same way that SUBSTR is in PL/I. This makes the replacement, insertion, and deletion operators as unwieldy as their PL/I equivalents. In fact, there is an additional problem in that APL does not support truncation and padding conventions. Lengths of operands must in general match exactly.

It is in the area of searching and comparing that APL's failure to recognize strings is most evident. In our model, the result of the comparison EQ('KNICK','KNACK') is the value 0, indicating falseness of the comparison. But in APL, the following occurs:

'KNICK' = 'KNACK'
1 1 0 1 1

The strings are considered to be vectors. The result is a vector of their common length, with individual elements representing values of the individual character comparisons. The effect of a single answer can be acquired only by something like the following, for equality comparison of strings A and B:

$$\wedge / A = B$$

Other ordering comparisons, for which we use lexical ordering, are also difficult to express in APL.

Searching, as we have defined it with the INDEX operator, again creates a problem. In our model, the result of INDEX ('SHOEHORN','HORN') is 5. But in APL, using the apparently analogous operator ι, we obtain a different result:

'SHOEHORN' ι 'HORN'
2 3 7 8

Indexing of a vector by a vector yields the vector of indices resulting from indexing the first vector with each element, in turn, of the latter. Searching is difficult in APL.

Exercises

2. Define APL operators to provide the following features:

(a) lexical comparison of strings
(b) an INDEX operator defined for searching within a string

7.4 STRINGS VERSUS VECTORS

One should by now begin to sense the not-so-subtle semantic distinction between strings and vectors, as we intuit them, and as operators view them. Vectors can be viewed as a very nonprimitive programmatic concept. Their use in the context of many operators is no more than shorthand notation for an expanded iteration over the elements on which the operators perform their duties. If we write A $\oplus$ B, where A and B are ten-element vectors and $\oplus$ is some scalar operator, we have just used a shorthand to avoid the tedious but equivalent enumeration:

$$A(1) \oplus B(1)$$
$$A(2) \oplus B(2)$$
.
.
.
$$A(10) \oplus B(10)$$

We speak of the operator $\oplus$ as being *distributed* over the elements of Its vector operands. And this phenomenon of distribution is the critical characteristic that should semantically distinguish vectors from strings. If we write C $\oplus$ D, where C and D are strings, we are not using a syntactic shorthand. We neither want nor expect distribution to occur. We are expressing an operation to be performed on strings as units, not on their individual elements.

The distinction can be clarified by an example from PL/I, which, as we have indicated, recognizes both strings and vectors. One can in fact have vectors whose elements are strings. We might declare three-element vectors for holding first names, last names, and whole names, and execute the following code:

```
DECLARE (FIRSTNAME,LASTNAME)(3) CHARACTER(10) VARYING,
        WHOLENAME(3) CHARACTER(20) VARYING;
FIRSTNAME(1)  =  'JOHN ';
FIRSTNAME(2)  =  'MARY ';
FIRSTNAME(3)  =  'FRED ';
LASTNAME(1)  =  'JONES';
LASTNAME(2)  =  'SMITH';
LASTNAME(3)  =  'BLACK';
```

The first-name and last-name vectors are initialized with character strings representing names. We can now execute the following statement:

```
WHOLENAME  =  FIRSTNAME∥LASTNAME;
```

The effect of this concatenation and assignment is the assignment of values to elements of WHOLENAME. WHOLENAME(1) is 'JOHN JONES', WHOLE-NAME(2) is 'MARY SMITH', and WHOLENAME(3) is 'FRED BLACK'.

The concatenation operator ‖ is recognized as a string operator in PL/I, not as a vector operator. Yet its operands are vectors in our example so distribution occurs. The statement above is equivalent to the following sequence:

$$
\begin{aligned}
\text{WHOLENAME(1)} &= \text{FIRSTNAME(1)}\|\text{LASTNAME(1)};\\
\text{WHOLENAME(2)} &= \text{FIRSTNAME(2)}\|\text{LASTNAME(2)};\\
\text{WHOLENAME(3)} &= \text{FIRSTNAME(3)}\|\text{LASTNAME(3)};
\end{aligned}
$$

Beyond this, however, distribution over individual characters of the strings does not occur. The fact that they are strings rather than vectors stops the distribution at this level.

So we are choosing very consciously to distinguish between strings and vectors, and to consider strings at an intermediate level of data complexity. They are not scalar in the way that numbers are, since they can be dissected. Yet they are not aggregations in the way that vectors are, and we do not choose to consider them as data structures. This difference has motivated our devoting a special chapter to strings, flanked on the one hand by arithmetic scalars, and on the other by data structures, of which our contrasted vectors are probably the simplest example.

CHAPTER 8

Data Structures

In this chapter we examine not only the several varieties of data structures directly available in languages, but also a number of other structures of general descriptive utility. These latter structures often are simulated in programs written in languages possessing only arrays as data structures. In languages possessing list-processing features, they can be built in a more straightforward manner.

In chapter 16 we examine list processing as a mechanism for complex data-structure manipulation. Here we look, not at techniques for building structures, but at the logical properties possessed by a number of such structures.

8.1 PRIMITIVE DATA STRUCTURES WITHIN LANGUAGES

In this first section we look at the structural characteristics directly specifiable within languages, and at the attendant operations available on such structures as a natural result of their structural characteristics.

8.1.1 VECTORS

By far the most common language construct for aggregation and structuring of data is the vector. If we view a vector as simply an ordered set of data items, we can identify only two inherent properties:

1. Reference to the vector itself may be used to indicate reference to all of its elements.

2. Reference to an element may be given as a reference pair; the first value identifies the vector, and the second a position according to the ordering of the vector.

Languages do, in fact, reflect these properties, but three other properties also have been commonly adopted. The first two of them may be viewed as liberties, the third as a restriction.

First, and most significant, is the ability to defer evaluation of position references until reference is made to a vector element. While name-declaration and declaration-object bindings for vectors may be rather static, the binding to an element of a vector object is performed only at reference time via the operation of subscription. Thus in the reference A[I], the A and the I may be totally bound to objects very early, but the value of I, used to index within the vector A, is accessed only when the reference is made. We can intuitively view this common feature as a primitive dynamic naming capability; it is this late binding that makes vectors such a powerful language construct.

The second, and lesser, liberty provided in languages is the ability to specify a vector index set starting at other than 1 and extending to the number of elements in the vector. One may, in ALGOL, declare a vector A[−4:2], indicating an ordered set of seven elements, from which the nth element is retrievable by the index value n-5.

The restriction placed on vectors by most languages is that of homogeneity: All elements of a vector must be similar in type. One is pressed to find useful linguistic rationale for this constraint. We may suppose it enforces a sort of programming discipline, and we admit that similarity is weakly implied when one is using the calculated subscript capability. If one is performing some known operation on an element to be determined only at point of use, then the set of elements to which resolution might lead must have a significant degree of homogeneity simply because of their candidacies for use with the operator.

But the above rationale is more of an observation on how data are used than a reasonable excuse for requiring homogeneity. When we look at the issue pragmatically, we see the conventional homogeneity restriction as motivated by implementation, rather than by language considerations.

In pure implementation terms, a desirable vector characteristic is size consistency among elements. If such elements are stored contiguously, the location of the nth one can be found easily, as base address + (n * element size). Note that this restriction is less severe than that of identical data type, since various types of data may require similar amounts of storage. But at this point we see the arguments of machine independence arising: A language should not reflect in its specification the amounts of physical storage required for its various types of data on some particular machine. Thus we reach the further restriction of homogeneity at the language data-type level.

We observe now the vector characteristic mentioned in chapter 7: distribution. There are, of course, many operations on vectors that are not distributed across elements. We have seen a number of these in APL. Perhaps the simplest example is ρ, which is an array (including vector) operator, not a scalar operator. Many other operators, however, such as those listed in chapter 5, are not aggregate operators; they are defined only for operands that are single quantities. But a very natural and useful domain extension for such operators is to vector operands, as we have seen commonly both in APL and PL/I. The effect of specifying a scalar operator with vector operands of the same length (or with mixed scalar and vector operands) is, as we have seen, to distribute the operation over the corresponding pairs of vector elements.

Two reasonable alternatives arise regarding how this distribution is to be effected. The first is to specify that the operation be carried out sequentially along the vector elements, from first to last. This interpretation is that reluctantly specified in PL/I because of the difficulties involved in adhering to the alternative. The alternative is the specification that the distribution be performed as though in parallel among all operand sets. This approach is used in APL. We saw in chapter 3 a typical example of the difference in our failure to normalize a vector A by the statement A = A/A(1).

During the PL/I development that led to the iterative sequential interpretation of distribution, all difficulties centered around situations in which there might be interplay between different parts of the distributed operation. The example above is a simple case of this, where one of the divisions affects the divisor used in the others. The difficulties both of describing parallelism in detail, and those of supporting that description with cumbersome simulations, proved overwhelming, and the other interpretation was adopted instead.

APL, on the other hand, adopted the parallelism approach very satisfactorily. This is because of the marked contrast between PL/I and APL, in regard to possible varieties of unexpected interplay resulting from side-effects of operations. PL/I operations in general have unlimited ability to result indirectly in changes to data not supposedly involved (as through the interrupt-handling features), while APL has much tighter controls over such possibilities. Adequate simulation of parallelism depends heavily on being able to see all possible operation side-effects.

Exercises

1. Describe an implementation technique to simulate parallelism in array operations. You may assume that operations have no side effects (the only data accessed or modified during an operation are the operands of the operator).

8.1.2 ARRAYS

We have described vectors as the simplest and most common data structure in programming languages. Now we extend that picture to an almost
equally common structure, the array. Usually, languages define vectors as
special cases of arrays, but we shall proceed in the other direction by
defining arrays as special cases of vectors—we choose this direction because of the relative simplicity of vectors as the basic structural building
block. It may seem unusual to the reader that one may speak of either a
vector or an array as a special case of the other; we shall attempt to clarify
this point as we go.

Let us start with the following set of array definitions:

1. An array of dimensionality 1 (a one–dimensional array) is a
   vector whose elements are scalars.

2. An array of dimensionality $n>1$ (an n-dimensional array) is
   a vector whose elements are (n-1)-dimensional arrays.

Suppose that we stop with these definitions. Then clearly we have encom-
passed the intuitive concept of an array as it exists in various languages.
But our definition also admits structures that are not classified as arrays
in most programming languages. For example, we think of a matrix as a
two-dimensional array, represented by rows and columns when we depict
it graphically. Thus we might picture a 3 × 4 array as follows:

```
9   7    6    12
2   4   10     8
5   3    1    11
```

But what about the following picture?

```
9   7    6
2   4   10   8
5   3
```

This is not a structure describable in languages as a two-dimensional
array, because the rows are of different lengths (or we might say because
the columns are of different lengths). Yet in terms of our above definition,
it is a two-dimensional array, according to either of two derivations:

■ It is a three-element vector. The first element, call it v1, is a
   vector of three elements, $v1(1)=9$, $v1(2)=7$, $v1(3)=6$. The
   second element, v2, is a vector of four elements, $v2(1)=2$,
   $v2(2)=4$, $v2(3)=10$, $v2(4)=8$. The third element, v3, is a
   vector of two elements, $v3(1)=5$, $v3(2)=3$.

■ It is a four-element vector. v1 and v2 are three-element vectors, $v1(1) = 9$, $v1(2) = 2$, $v1(3) = 5$, $v2(1) = 7$, $v2(2) = 4$, $v2(3) = 3$. v3 is a two-element vector, $v3(1) = 6$, $v3(2) = 10$. v4 is a vector with indexing starting at 2 rather than 1 as in the other cases, and it has only one element, $v4(2) = 8$.

So we need to tighten our set of definitions somewhat to bring it into closer accord with the usual array concept. We do this by extending our second definition, so that it appears as follows:

> 2. An array of dimensionality $n > 1$ (an n-dimensional array) is a vector whose elements are (n-1)-dimensional arrays with identical index sets.

Now our above derivations fail. In the first derivation, the index set of v1 is (1,2,3); that of v2 is (1,2,3,4); and that of v3 is (1,2). In the second, the index set of v1 and v2 is (1,2,3); that of v3 is (1,2); and that of v4 is (2). Our definition now is adequate for defining arrays in terms of vectors, but we need several more definitions and some terminology to complete the picture.

First, we admit that we used arbitrary names v1, v2, and so on, above, to denote the various vector elements. We should have used our formal subscript notation, for example, v(1) and v(2). Then we could write v(1)(1), v(1)(2), and so on, to obtain the various elements of the element vectors of v. More generally, we could address some scalar nested within an n-dimensional array v as $v(i_1)(i_2)...(i_n)$ or, if we use conventional notation, as $v(i_1,i_2,...,i_n)$.

Next, we want to be able to speak of certain characteristics of the mth dimension of an n-dimensional array and to describe the shape of an array in terms of such characteristics.

We say that the mth dimension, $m > 1$, of an n-dimensional array A is the (m-1)-dimensional array B defined by $B(i_1,i_2,...,i_{m-1}) = A(i_1,i_2,...,i_{m-1})$ for all i_j's within their respective index sets. The first dimension of an array A is A itself.

We now define the lower bound (LB) of the mth dimension of A to be LB(A,m), the common starting index for elements of B; and the upper bound (UB) to be UB(A,m), the common finishing index for elements of B. We also conveniently define dimension size to be $DS(A,m) = UB(A,m) - LB(A,m) + 1$.

Now we can completely describe the shape of an array by specifying the bounds of its dimensions.

An array as we have developed it is identical structurally to an array as often defined in languages. Such definition usually is in terms of coordinates within n-dimensional spaces, and a vector then emerges as a particular space of one dimension. The characteristics of vectors and arrays turn out to be identical to ours in theory, though there is a difference of emphasis. Our approach emphasizes a hierarchy—vectors of vectors of vectors..., involving a simple building block. The alternate approach emphasizes a single level of containment—an array contains scalar elements—but a sophisticated building block.

Our approach engenders references to certain subportions of an array; for example, if A is a 3 × 2 matrix, then A(2) naturally identifies the second row of A. The other approach leads to special syntactic notations—A(2,∗) in PL/I or A[2;] in APL. For some subportions, however, we are not better off; for example, to refer to the second column of A, we must use a notational means similar to the A(∗,2) of PL/I or A[;2] of APL.

We shall not go further into operators available with arrays, because all are shorthand conveniences; we have looked at a plentiful set available in APL. We should mention one operator, however, which is natural to the structure of an array. All languages that recognize arrays use this operator implicitly, but it is seldom available to the programmer. This operator is the RAVEL operator as we defined it in chapter 4. Many contexts of array-use require a defined linearization of an array, a canonical mapping of its scalar components onto a vector. This requirement is encountered during sequential distribution of an operator over an array or, similarly, during transmission of an array to or from any one-dimensional medium (e.g., a tape, printer, or terminal).

Since we have defined arrays in terms of vectors, which are already linearized, we need note only the recursive nature of distribution. If we have an operator $\oplus$ acting on a 2 × 3 matrix, then sequential distribution says that $\oplus$A is evaluated as $\oplus$A(1) followed by $\oplus$A(2). Since A(1) is itself a vector, $\oplus$A(1) is evaluated, with subdistribution, as $\oplus$A(1,1), then $\oplus$A(1,2), then $\oplus$A(1,3). Then $\oplus$A(2) is evaluated as $\oplus$A(2,1), $\oplus$A(2,2), $\oplus$A(2,3).

The above ordering is often adopted within languages. It is known as *row-major ordering*, a terminology that has arisen as a generalization from matrices. The row-major linearization of an n-dimensional array A is given by the sequence dictated by our distribution rules on arrays. So we define that for an array A, RAVEL(A) yields a vector of scalars, the linearization of the scalar components of A.

Exercises

2. Suppose that we have an n-dimensional array A with lower dimension bounds $L_1, L_2, ..., L_n$ and upper dimension bounds $U_1, U_2, ..., U_n$. Give a formula indicating which element of the ravel of A is represented by $A(i_1, i_2, ..., i_n)$.

8.1.3 TREES

We have covered the defining characteristics of vectors and arrays. We turn now to contrast these with another common structure type, the tree.

A tree, like a vector, is a collection of data items, which we shall designate its *components*. Reference to the tree itself can be used to indicate reference to its set of components. And there the similarity between trees and vectors ends.

The first significant difference between trees and vectors is that the components of a tree are not ordered, and therefore are not accessible by an index into the tree. Instead each component is given a name, which must be distinct from names of other components of the same tree. A reference to a tree component appears as a reference pair naming the containing tree and the component within that tree. This means of reference, coupled with the general inability in languages to calculate names (as opposed to indices), begets less flexible addressing features for trees than for vectors.

A second important difference is that trees need not be homogeneous. Whereas a vector is limited to containing a single type of scalar element (or, in our model, also vectors ultimately containing as scalar components only that type), a tree may contain any collection of scalars of any type, arrays, or trees (known in such a case as subtrees). And we now appropriately expand the domain of array elements to include trees. In such a case, all the array elements must be of identical shape. We shall elaborate on this point in a moment.

One further point is implicit in the preceding discussion but needs emphasis. While our model introduced the concept of hierarchy into our discussion of arrays, the hierarchies were very restricted—recall the tightening of our array definition to require identical index sets. Here we have arrived at the ability to build an arbitrary hierarchy, with no necessary similarity among components of an involved tree.

Let us tie together all of these points with an example, taken from PL/I. We consider the following PL/I declaration:

```
DECLARE 1 A,
          2 B(2,3),
            3 C FIXED,
            3 D,
              4 E FLOAT,
              4 F(4) BIT(2),
          2 K CHARACTER(3),
          2 L FLOAT;
```

A is being declared as a tree (a root tree because it is contained in no other tree) with three components (those items with level numbers of 2). The second and third of these components are simple scalars: a character string and a floating-point number. But A's first component is a 2×3 array named B, and each element $B(i_1,i_2)$ of B is itself a tree. In particular, each $B(i_1,i_2)$ has two components, named C and D. C is a fixed-point number. D is a tree with two components, E (a floating-point number) and F (a four-element vector of bit strings).

Let us reiterate the above description pictorially to clarify the relations among the data.

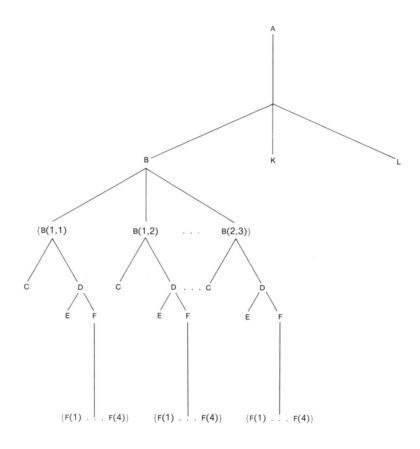

Now let us look at each name and the set of data items named by it.

A names the overall tree.

B names an array of six elements.

C names a scalar within each element of B. Therefore there are
six (2 × 3) different c's.

D names a tree within each element of B, so there are also
six D's.

E names a scalar within each D, so six E's are identified.

F names a four-element vector within each D. Therefore twenty-four (4 × 6) F's are identified.

K names a scalar within A, so only one K is identified.

L names a scalar within A, so only one L is identified.

How can we refer to items within this data complex? We said that a tree component reference is made with a pair of names, the containing tree and the component. We shall indicate this by separating the names by a period, and thus, for example, refer to A.B to obtain the array B in A, or to A.K to obtain the character-string K. A.B(2,1) identifies the appropriate tree element of B. A.B(2,1).C identifies the fixed-point scalar component of that element of B. A.B(2,1).D.F(3) identifies the third bit string within the array F within the structure D within that element of B in A.

We observed that there is a D within each element of the 2 × 3 array B. Therefore we can think of D itself as a 2 × 3 array, and we can write A.B.D to refer to that array. Similarly A.B.D.F refers to the total 2 × 3 × 4 array F. We see here a powerful feature for structural expression provided by interplay of the two types of structures described.

Now let us consider in what contexts tree names can be used, and with what effect. Our observation that tree components are unordered is an overstatement; it is true in regard to component reference capabilities, but not under distribution, which occurs with trees as well as with arrays. For example, consider two trees:

```
1 A,            1 F,
  2 B,            2 G,
    3 C,            3 H,
    3 D,            3 J,
  2 E             2 K
```

We can unite these trees under a scalar operator ⊕ (such as assignment) and write A ⊕ F. The effect is a distribution over the components (there must be the same number in A and F) to obtain

```
B ⊕ G
E ⊕ K
```

A second-level distribution over B ⊕ G yields

```
C ⊕ H
D ⊕ J
```

The components are considered, for distribution, to have a natural ordering according to the order of their syntactic specification.

Now we look at a feature that is natural to trees but not to vectors. Suppose that we have the following simple trees:

```
1 EMPLOYMENT_RECORD,        1 PERSONAL_RECORD,
  2 NAME CHAR(20),            2 ADDRESS CHAR(30),
  2 POSITION FIXED,           2 FAMILY_SIZE FIXED,
  2 YEARS FIXED,              2 NAME CHAR(20),
  2 SALARY FIXED,             2 AGE FIXED
  2 AGE FIXED
```

Here we have two dissimilar trees with two commonly named components, NAME and AGE. For an operator $\oplus$, we can specify that the indicated operation be performed on all identically named components of the trees:

```
EMPLOYMENT_RECORD ⊕ PERSONAL_RECORD, CORRESPONDING;
```

The effect here is as though we had written the following:

```
EMPLOYMENT_RECORD.NAME ⊕ PERSONAL_RECORD.NAME;
EMPLOYMENT_RECORD.AGE ⊕ PERSONAL_RECORD.AGE;
```

With this feature, we are taking full advantage of the individual names given for tree components by providing for selective distribution of an operator over identically named components. Note that there is no requirement for any type of structural similarity between the trees named with the operator.

There is at this point every reason to wonder why we have identified two types of aggregates, rather than proposing a single mechanism uniting the good qualities of each. The answer lies in implementation considerations. While we will not go into details of techniques used for each, we shall try to characterize the implementation issues that have dictated the various combinations of characteristics of vectors and trees.

Two characteristics are critical: homogeneity and dynamic naming. Dynamic naming, as available with vectors, implies some mechanism for evaluating references and finding the appropriate component for an aggregate. As long as the aggregate is homogeneous, both in length of scalar elements and in the sense of the identical index set, this mechanism can be very efficient, and no unbearable overhead results at time of reference to an array component. Heterogeneity would necessitate a mechanism that was much more complicated and time-consuming.

On the other hand, heterogeneity is acceptable if dynamic naming is not allowed; this is the case with trees. Component references can be resolved satisfactorily at time of program compilation, so no overhead is incurred at reference time. This difference is the single most important implementation reason for having both arrays and trees. From a purely linguistic point of view, we might easily introduce an aggregate potentially heterogeneous, with arbitrary hierarchy, and with dynamically indexable or nameable components. But significant problems would confront those involved in supporting our language with compilers.

Exercises

3. The rules given in the preceding text for naming a subportion of a tree require that all containing trees be named. This strict requirement allows subtrees of different trees to be named identically. Thus one might declare two trees as shown below and be able to refer to either A.B or X.B.

```
1 A,          1 X,
  2 B,          2 B,
  2 C           2 D
```

Our rules require that reference to D also be given as X.D, which in this case is clearly unnecessary. Define a less stringent rule that requires only as much name qualification as is necessary to relieve ambiguity. The rule should define when a given reference is valid, and if valid, to what data it refers.

4. Consider the following array of trees:

```
1 A (10),
  2 B,
  2 C (5,2),
    3 D (6),
    3 E,
  2 F
```

   (a) Describe the collection of data represented by each name above.
   (b) What is the total number of scalars identified by the above declaration?

5. The trees that we have discussed through our PL/I examples are fixed trees; their structures cannot vary during execution. Describe a set of operators adequate for building trees in a more dynamic environment. These operators should allow creating a tree, inserting a tree as a subtree at some location in another tree, and modifying the structure of some portion of a tree. Since the tree structures are dynamic, you should also provide operators to interrogate the current shape of a tree.

8.2 OTHER DATA STRUCTURES

We have examined the most common data structures directly specifiable in programming languages. We turn now to a collection of structures commonly used in programming applications but not directly available in most languages. When structures such as we shall describe are required in some application, the usual tool for their simulation is the vector or array. The structures involve the necessity for one data item to be able to name (point to) other data items. And such identifications must be alterable easily during execution. The usual technique for giving this facility is to use, as data items, integers interpreted as subscripts identifying array elements. This technique is applied because, as we pointed out earlier, the array subscript provides the nearest thing to a dynamic naming ability in most languages.

Each of the structures that we look at involves ordered collections of data items, so the operations that we have defined for vectors are reasonable also for these structures. But as we shall see, the natural set of access operations inherent to each structure may vary somewhat from the indexing features used with vectors.

8.2.1 FORWARD-LINKED LISTS

The first and simplest structure that we shall consider is an ordered collection of data items in which each item contains not only some value, but also the identification of the next item of the collection. A *cursor* is used to identify the last-accessed list item. We can depict such a structure, a forward-linked list, as follows:

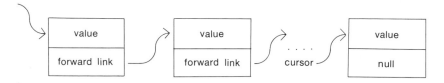

We introduce two operators for use with a forward-linked list:

INITIALIZE(listname,data item) puts a first item into the list.

EMPTY(listname) returns a truth value in accordance with whether the list has any elements.

We next observe three operators natural to interrogation and access within this structure:

START(listname) returns the first data item of the list. A cursor is set to identify this item.

NEXT(listname) returns the data item identified by the item currently indicated by the cursor for the list.

LAST(listname) returns a truth value indicating whether the item indicated by the list's cursor identifies a subsequent list item.

This set of operators clearly suggests an operative mode in which the list's elements are stepped through sequentially from first to last. This is indeed the usual way that such lists are used. It is easy to use the operators to perform the more vector-like operation of indexing; indexing cannot, however, be considered an operation natural to the structure, which has no implications of locations of elements relative to one another.

Two other operators are useful and natural to modification of this structure.

INSERT(listname,data item) inserts the data item into the list at the position following the item indicated by the cursor. Implementation support of this operator involves setting the identification field of the item indicated by the cursor to the new item, and setting that field of the new item to identify the item previously identified by the former item.

DELETE(listname) deletes the item identified by the item indicated by the cursor from the list. That latter item is set to identify the item previously identified by the deleted item

These last two operators indicate the use of a forward-linked list structure in implementing strings as we described them in chapter 6, with their powers of insertion and deletion. The most impressive power gained with any structure in which logical ordering is imposed independent of physical locale is the relative ease of insertion, deletion, and other reordering operations.

8.2.2 BIDIRECTIONAL-LINKED LISTS

Suppose that we sophisticate our previous lists by adding a field to each data item that identifies the item's predecessor in the list. What new features become natural to the structure?

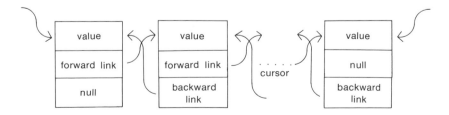

We have already established that the START operator returns the first item of a list. Now we also have occasion to use the **END operator** which returns the last list item. END is valuable because we are able to step backward through the list with the **PRIOR operator**, analogous to NEXT but moving us in the other direction. We complete this part of the picture with the **FIRST operator**, which tells whether or not we are at the start of the list.

And now what about our INSERT and DELETE operators of before? We defined DELETE without defending its obviously awkward semantics—deletion, not of the named item, but of the next item. The reason for that definition was the requirement to update the identification field of the deleted item's predecessor. How were we to find that predecessor if the operator named the item to be deleted? Another cursor would be required. Furthermore, with our old definition, another operator would be required to delete the first list item (but in that case there would be no predecessor to update).

Now the problem of locating an item's predecessor is solved. We can modify DELETE for our bidirectional-linked list so that the item indicated by the cursor is deleted. Its predecessor must have the successor field updated, and its successor must have the predecessor field updated, but these updates are easily accomplished, because all necessary items are available.

For insertion, a natural extension is to add an **INSERTPRIOR operator**, which inserts an item before, rather than after, the indicated item. This completes our set of operators for bidirectional-linked lists.

Note that, with these lists, natural operations are no longer limited to first-to-last sequencing, or even to last-to-first. Any variety of sequencing that involves stepping from an item to either of its neighbors is readily accomplished.

Exercises

6. Describe implementations of the substring replacement feature of chapter 7, under the following approaches:

   (a) Use of forward-linked lists to hold string elements
   (b) Use of bidirectional-linked lists to hold string elements.

   In doing so, be sure to specify the attendant operations that should be available on each.

8.2.3 CIRCULAR LISTS

We introduce a minor modification into our forward-linked lists, whereby the last item identifies the first as its successor, rather than being special in identifying nothing.

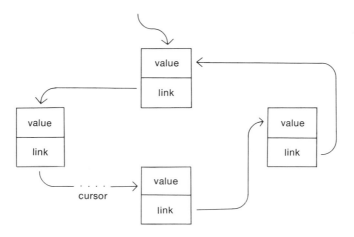

We now eliminate the LAST operator, but we introduce a **SIZE operator**, which returns the current number of elements in the list. Our old set of natural operators remains valid. Support of the PRIOR operator is also feasible, though not apt to be efficient. It can be obtained as a sequence of NEXT operators of length SIZE(listname)-1. We have thus made possible support of all the operators for bidirectional-linked lists, while retaining the structural simplicity of forward-linked lists.

8.2.4 QUEUES, STACKS

A *queue* is a list of data items for which insertions are always made at one end and deletions at the other. A queue is often spoken of as a first-in first-out (FIFO) list in recognition of the progress of an item through the list.

Only three primitive operators are required here, as long as it is appropriate to view the list as a black box. Under some relaxed circumstances, other interrogation operations relating to list contents may be of use, but under strict discipline, we recognize only the following:

> **ENQUEUE(queuename,data item)** appends the data item to the start (insertion end) of the queue.

> **DEQUEUE(queuename)** returns the item at the end (deletion end) of the queue and deletes that item from the queue, thus effectively bringing its predecessor element to the end of the queue.

> **EMPTY(queuename)** returns a truth value depending on whether or not the queue contains any elements.

A *stack*, also known as a last-in first-out (LIFO) list, operates like a queue except that deletions are made from the same end of the list as insertions. Thus only one end of the list, called the top of the stack, is addressable. Our three analogous operators are:

> **PUSH(stackname,data item)** places the data item onto the top of the stack, thus pushing down the other stack elements.

> **POP(stackname)** returns the item at the top of the stack and deletes that item from the stack, popping up the rest of the stack elements and thus bringing its predecessor back to the top of the stack.

> **EMPTY(stackname)** is as for a queue.

We look at some representative uses of these structures in chapter 13 and appendix 1.

Exercises

7. Suppose that we wish to simulate the existence of a queue in an environment in which we have available only two stacks. Describe how the stacks can be used to support the queue operations.

8.2.5 GRAPHS, RINGS

We have already discussed trees as an explicit type of data aggregate commonly available within languages. We now look briefly at two generalizations of this hierarchical kind of structuring. The structures introduced here are less restrictive than trees in any of three ways:

> 1. An item may be a component of more than one structure.
> 2. Components of a structure may be ordered in the linked-list sense.
> 3. A structure name takes on a value (and identifies components as well).

If we generalize with items 1 and 3 above, we define a *graph* such as the one on the next page.

Each item has a value and may identify a set of components. A given item, such as F or G above, may be a component of any number of containing items of the graph. The graph is *directed*, because each link has an identifiable head and tail; it is *rooted*, because there is a single item, A, that is a component of no other item. We can further characterize the graph as being *connected* (any two items have at least one common predecessor, i.e., a common item back up the containment chain), and as being *noncircular* (no item precedes itself).

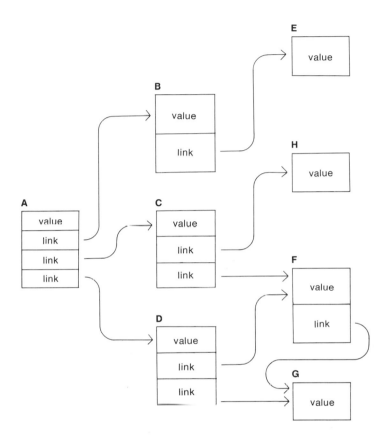

There is a clear analogy here with the mathematical concept of a relation. If we view the items in our graph as members of a set S, the graph can be described as a partial ordering relation (P) on S × S. S has a least element under P (A), and P is transitive, noncommutative, and nonreflexive.

This kind of structure is ideal for describing such relations as genealogical trees, where the containment criterion is parenthood. It is generally useful in describing structures involving containment of a non-hierarchical nature (i.e., structures in which an item may be contained within more than one other item).

We first describe *rings* as generalizations of structures by virtue of our properties 2 and 3. In their most general form, they also have property 1. We depict a ring as a hierarchical structure in which the set of components of an item are themselves linked as a circular list.

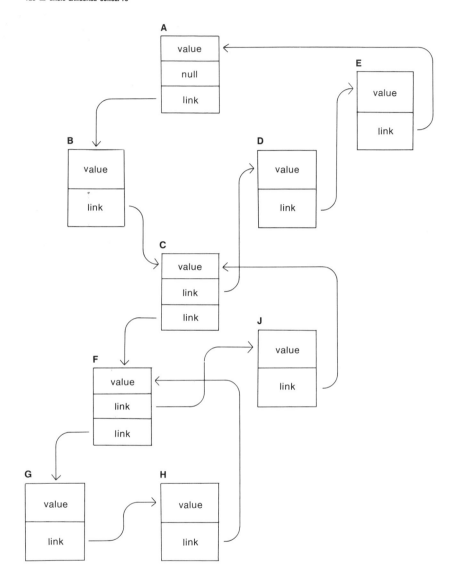

Each item has a potential of three fields, giving (1) a value for that item, (2) an identification of its successor within the item of which it is a component (or if it is the last component, identification of its containing item), and (3) an identification of the first of its components. This generalization gives values to items having components, and provides for ordering of those components via circular lists. We may, as we said, further generalize to allow each item to be a component of more than one other item.

Rings as fully generalized are a very general, very powerful data structure for describing data relations. They are used heavily in support of problems embodying the most severe requirements for complex structural relations among data. [Cod70] gives a useful approach to the problem of representing data relationships in a complex environment of data and users.

Further studies of the variety of data structures can be found in [Knu68], [Har71], [Ear71], [Cod70], and [Flo70].

Exercises

8. A number of trees exist, describing people by name, age, and sex. Such a tree can be declared as follows:

```
1 PERSON,
  2 NAME,
  2 AGE,
  2 SEX
```

We would like to be able to relate reasily the members of the following classes: (a) all men, (b) men over forty years old, and (c) women named Clovis.

Describe a generalized ring structure linking all people together, but also providing linkages among the subclasses specified.

CHAPTER 9

Data Storage and Mapping

Techniques for formal description of programming-language syntax have been exploited for a number of years (see appendix I), but use of formalism for describing semantics is more recent ([Fel68], [Fel66], and [Neu71]). A formal semantic description of some language is derived by definition of an abstract (or perhaps real) machine that interprets programs written in that language. This usual approach embodies the recognition that an infallible way of discovering how a given program will execute is, in fact, to execute it.

An integral part of any such abstract machine description is the postulation of an abstract storage into which language data elements are mapped. For it is, after all, conceptually no easier to execute a program on an abstract machine lacking abstract storage than on a real machine lacking real storage. A program tends to have little semantics at all until executed by some machine. This is not to say that the machine must be given and defined as any particular real hardware machine, but it must at least be emulatable on real machines. This is the only useful meaning of the over-used term *machine-independent*.

In this chapter we develop the rudiments of a storage model adequate for hosting the storage-sensitive features of prominent high-level languages. We separate our discussion into two major areas. The first of these relates to temporal characteristics of our store associated with support of the PL/I storage classes, ALGOL OWN data, APL local and global data, and so on. The second area concerns the storage requirements for support of language phenomena involving relative locations of separate data items (FORTRAN EQUIVALENCE, PL/I DEFINED, and the like).

9.1 STORAGE PERSISTENCE CHARACTERISTICS

We speak of storage as that medium consisting of locations as described in chapter 5. The persistence of a unit of storage (a location) is the time during which a declaration-object binding is in effect, with the object of that binding having that location component.

Our discussion here is necessarily related to that of control structures as we study them in chapter 10, but the relation is a general enough one that we can get along with a minimum of control concepts.

Ironically, the most essential and intuitively simple control concept that we need is also the concept that is metalinguistic to most language descriptions: execution of a program. This seemingly strange omission is due to language description without aid of an interpreting machine. A program tends to consist of a number of procedures, blocks, functions, subroutines, library routines, and the like. Each of these types of element is discussed in isolation, but the means (linkage editing, loading, and so forth) by which all are gathered together and executed seems to be outside the language description jurisdiction. In PL/I, for example, the language does not even specify in what block execution begins when a program is run. Such specification is given, instead, by each implementation of the language.

Nevertheless, the most common declaration-object binding is that which extends over an entire program execution. It is this persistence that governs all FORTRAN data, APL global data, PL/I STATIC data, and OWN data in ALGOL.

A number of amusing contortions have been used in attempts to describe this variety of data in ALGOL and PL/I, both of which admit to no more global an execution unit than the external block. One interesting invention was PL/I's concept of an ephemeral "dotted block." The terminology arose from the depiction of a PL/I program as collections of nested blocks.

On page 131, the figure on the left might have been used graphically to describe the structure of a PL/I program consisting of external procedures A, E, and G. But now suppose that X, a STATIC variable, is declared within D. Then the effect, in terms of storage persistence, was given in terms of more amenably treated AUTOMATIC variables by picturing a conceptual block Q, containing A, E, and G.

Once Q is admitted, it is possible to describe X by saying that its persistence is as though X had been declared as a normal AUTOMATIC variable in block Q. Thus Q was used to circumvent the notion of an entire program as a lingual construct.

So our most common variety of declaration-object binding is that which extends over an entire program execution. At time of termination of that execution, the binding is permanently severed, and the object is destroyed. We say that the storage for the object persists no longer.

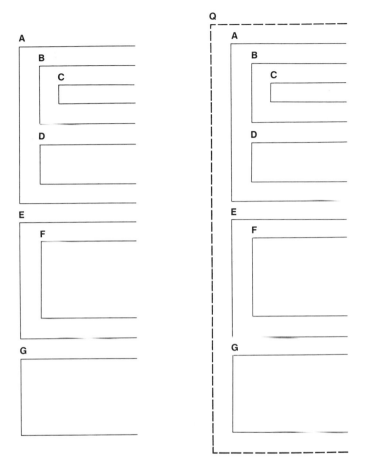

To describe the second common unit of storage persistence, we must again resort to use of an intuitive concept, which we shall designate a *module*. It corresponds to the smallest executable units of code in the various languages: an ALGOL or PL/I block or procedure; an APL main routine or function; a FORTRAN main routine, function, or subroutine.

The unit of data storage persistence indicated here is an instance of execution, which we shall call an *activation*, of that module. The declaration-object binding is established at time of call of the module, and it is severed at time of return from the module activation resulting from the call. This persistence unit does not occur in FORTRAN, but it is common as the local data of ALGOL and APL, and the AUTOMATIC data of PL/I.

These two persistence units, the program execution and the module activation, are sufficient to describe nearly all declaration-object bindings of languages. We should, however, mention three other secondary varieties of storage persistence—secondary in that one is so stylized that it need not be considered a general phenomenon, and the other two are rightfully considered metalinguistic.

The first variety of importance is epitomized by CONTROLLED and BASED data in PL/I. Here, persistence is not automatically related to any execution control disciplines; instead it is directly at the discretion of the programmer, who uses explicit ALLOCATE and FREE statements to create and destroy the storage and the bindings of declarations to objects.

Second, we note a persistence not directly specifiable in languages but often simulated in language implementation compilers. This persistence is that of a single statement execution, and it is used primarily for holding temporary results during expression evaluation. Assume that the following assignment statement is executed:

$$A \leftarrow (B\text{-}C) + (D\text{-}E) + (F\text{-}G);$$

It is likely that one or even two subtraction results will, in the generated machine code, have to be stored temporarily before use. A compiler will have laid out an area for temporaries, and will allocate part of that area for each temporary and generate code to store it there. Upon statement completion, the allocated area will be freed for subsequent use.

Finally, we expand our earlier observation that program termination signals destruction of all objects associated with the program. That comment is true in the sense put forth there, but it is a little strong in connotation if one wishes to think of executing programs and retaining results generated by them. Of course, this retention is a normal result of program execution, but it is best described, not as a persistence of binding or of storage in the linguistic sense, but rather as a copying of the value component of an object onto some metalinguistic medium. If a later program, or person, wishes to use that value, he must reestablish a declaration-object binding for naming it, and a location-value binding, via something like a READ statement, for reacquiring its value. So we can talk about a persistence of values in storage beyond a single program execution, but we must do so in a realm external to that of programming languages, for which even that single program is usually considered too global to define.

Exercises

1. Consider an ALGOL program comprising blocks A, B, C, D, and E. Suppose the various blocks declare data with the following storage requirements:

Block	Units of storage
A	50

B	40
C	30
D	20
E	10

Assume the program is structured as follows:

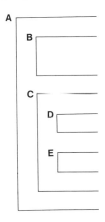

Assume the following execution sequence:

1. A is entered.
2. A calls B.
3. B calls C.
4. C calls D.

5. D returns.
6. C calls E.
7. E calls E.

How much storage for declared data is required immediately following each of these steps?

2. Consider the following PL/I structure, with declarations as indicated:

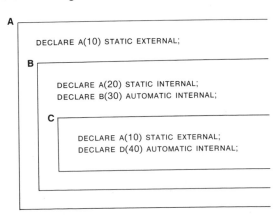

Assume the following execution sequence:

1. A is entered.
2. A calls B.
3. B calls C.
4. C calls C.

How much storage for declared data is required immediately following each step (assume one unit of storage per array element)?

9.2 LOCATION RELATIONSHIPS

As long as a unique correspondence is maintained in a language between declarations and locations, a simple view of storage is adequate. No relationships among locations need be specified. Even if we allow the kind of storage sharing provided by PL/I CELL's, we need not significantly complicate the picture. While multiple declarations may be mapped to the same location, they are mapped to distinct objects, whose location components happen to be identical. If names A and B are both specified in cell C, we cannot store under the name A and subsequently retrieve under the name B. The object represented by A differs from that represented by B.

Our first complication arises when a language includes features for allowing different declarations to be mapped to the same object. Consider a case of FORTRAN EQUIVALENCE:

DIMENSION A(10,10), B(100)
EQUIVALENCE (A(1,1), B(1))

Implicit in this kind of remapping is an assumption of a canonical single-dimensional ordering to any array, under which B(I) relates to the Ith member of A according to this ordering. The storage locations for elements of A comprise an ordered vector, so that the equivalence gives the desired results. Here, we have the first implication of a linearly ordered storage, a vector of locations for objects.

At this level of remapping, PL/I does a more adequate job of camouflaging storage characteristics by having the programmer specify required mappings. This specification is necessary unless the aggregates to be overlaid are identical in characteristics, in which case a one-to-one mapping is used.

DECLARE A(10,6), B(10,6) DEFINED A;

Here A and B are of identical shape, so the obvious mapping of A(I,J) to B(I,J) is assumed. But a remapping such as the above FORTRAN example must be specified explicitly by a programmer-provided mapping function.

DECLARE B(100), A(10,10) DEFINED B(10∗(1SUB-1) + 2SUB);

There is no assumption of a one-dimensional ordered storage in which A and B reside.

This kind of remapping in PL/I is called *correspondence defining*, and it always involves a mapping from element to element. Its characteristics are independent of any underlying storage model. But as we look further into PL/I defining, we encounter more problems. The language allows a conceptually different kind of remapping called *overlay defining* in which, as the term indicates, an underlying store is essential for describing the facilities.

Overlay defining provides for remapping of strings (bit or character) or of arrays or structures consisting solely of such strings. Simple cases pose no threat to a storage-free model.

DECLARE A CHARACTER(10), B CHARACTER(10) DEFINED A;

DECLARE 1 A,
        2 B CHARACTER(3),
        2 C CHARACTER(4);
DECLARE 1 X DEFINED A,
        2 Y CHARACTER(3),
        2 Z CHARACTER(4);

The correspondence mappings above are obvious and involve no implications of storage characteristics. But possibilities are not limited to simple kinds of defining.

DECLARE A(20) CHARACTER(3), B(5,4) CHARACTER(3) DEFINED A;

What we have here strongly resembles our FORTRAN example, with a mapping between aggregates of different shapes. This case brings us right back to the notion of a linearly ordered store (linearization is in row-major order). The reasons for allowing such remapping only with strings should become clearer in a moment.

We look at a further step in defining that is qualitatively very different from anything encountered earlier.

DECLARE A(5,4) CHARACTER(3), B CHARACTER(60) DEFINED A;

The correspondence here, perhaps less intuitive than in previous cases, is given by

$$A(I,J) = SUBSTR(B,5 ∗ (I-1) + J,3)$$

Note that in this case we are no longer defining a correspondence between scalar data items; the single item B is composed of the combination of all twenty items in A.

So we are saying at this point that we can redefine any aggregate of strings as a single string. The aggregate resides in a linearized store containing in order the strings for each of the elements. But even more is being implied. The ordering between elements is the same variety of ordering as that between characters of a string, since we have defined B to encompass all of A. Transition from the last character of one string within A to the first character of the next is no more difficult than moving between characters of the same string.

While the reader puzzles over this last point, let us give several other examples and then return to the point in more detail.

```
DECLARE 1 A,
        2 B CHARACTER(4),
        2 C CHARACTER(8);
DECLARE D CHARACTER(6) DEFINED A POSITION(3);
```

D is the string starting at position 3 in the linearization of A (the third character of B), and extending through the fourth character of C.

```
DECLARE A(2,3) CHARACTER(5),
        B(3,4) CHARACTER(2) DEFINED A POSITION(7);
```

The linearization of A is a thirty-character string. That of B is a twenty-four-character string beginning at the seventh character of A's linearization: SUBSTR(A(1,2),2,1).

Now let us return to our perhaps overly cryptic observation on linearization governing elements and that governing characters within a string element. We have presented the PL/I features as more liberal than they actually are. There are several restrictions on the use of overlay defining, such as:

■ An aggregate base on which an item is defined must have the attribute UNALIGNED.

■ A base for defining cannot be an array cross-section.

■ A base cannot be an array within an array of structures.

■ A base cannot be a procedure parameter.

Recall the PL/I aggregate attributes ALIGNED and UNALIGNED. For the most part, their language impact is negligible, and they are described instead as optimization attributes: Access to ALIGNED data is faster than to UNALIGNED data, but ALIGNED data consumes more storage space. The attributes are important, however, in implementation.

Assume, for example, that one declares a structure of bit strings to be ALIGNED. Then each bit string may be aligned starting on a storage boundary convenient for its access via machine instructions; the successive strings need not be placed contiguously, each starting on the bit following the end of the previous string. This contiguity must be adhered to, however, if the aggregate is UNALIGNED.

We know that a bit string occupies a sequence of consecutive storage bits. We need to realize that an aggregate of strings is governed by this ordering of contiguity only if it is declared to be UNALIGNED.

Thus we see the implementation motivation for the first restriction. The others are related. Restrictions 2 and 3 prevent defining on a portion of an aggregate that has potential for consisting of discontiguous elements (although the aggregate itself may be UNALIGNED). If, for example, we have the declaration

DECLARE B(3,5) BIT(4) UNALIGNED;

then the cross-section B(∗,I) consists of discontiguous bit strings. Note that B(I,∗) would be contiguous, but this too is disallowed as a base, to simplify the rule.

Similarly, if we have

DECLARE 1 A(10) UNALIGNED,
       2 B BIT(3),
       2 C BIT(4);

both B and C are arrays of discontiguous bit strings.

The restriction against parameters is, of course, to prevent defining on a parameter whose corresponding argument might be such a discontiguous aggregate.

In short, the PL/I picture with regard to overlay defining is a complicated one, fraught with rules and restrictions which on the language surface appear quite arbitrary and unmotivated. The rules could be given more clearly if the language admitted of a storage model and described the defining phenomena in terms of it. We have already introduced such a model as a linearly ordered sequence of elements, and we now see in addition the need to speak of two different types of ordering, simple linearity and contiguous linearity. The latter comes into play when one is defining new objects as overlapped portions of several base objects.

In the case of PL/I, the required storage model has even more characteristics than we have described so far. Recall the built-in function UNSPEC, which is used to obtain the internal representation of an object. While it is true that the value of the result is undefined in PL/I, its format is defined: UNSPEC results in a bit-string representation. So the basic unit of information in a PL/I storage model must be the bit, onto strings of which all other objects are mapped in an undefined way.

Most other languages need not go to this descriptive extreme in their storage models; they can be content to describe the basic units of the storage as receptacles for any type of data defined within the particular language. PL/I must pay the price of further definition because it allows access to internal representations.

Exercises

3. PL/I does not allow defining on a variable-length string because the language chooses to hide the implementation of such strings by fixed-length allocations. But suppose that a language had truly variable-length strings, and the attendant operations described in chapter 7, through which lengths could be changed. The storage model for that language would then also admit expansion and shrinkage to accommodate length changes. But how would one define the effect of shrinkage or expansion on data overlaying variable-length strings? What if the data is variable-length? Or should such overlaying be precluded?

9.3 SUMMARY

In this chapter, we have attempted to defend the necessity for languages to include in their semantic descriptions a storage model in terms of which to describe various language phenomena. Storage is not simply an implementation issue to be shunned in linguistic discussions.

We have identified the following characteristics of a much-needed storage model.

■ A storage consists of a collection of receptacles for objects. Each receptacle has one of four persistences: the program execution; the module activation; indefinite, to be controlled manually; or the statement execution.

■ Storage receptacles are linearly ordered.

■ Two varieties of linear orderings exist, simple and contiguous.

These three characteristics form a basis for a storage model adequate for underlying most programming languages. This basis should be sufficient for most new language descriptions. In the particular case of PL/I, we have seen a further characteristic: The basic receptacle of information is the bit, in terms of which data must be definable. We choose to leave this characteristic to PL/I, rather than insist that it be a general storage model requirement.

CHAPTER 10

Basic Control Structures

We now concern ourselves with the execution of various programmatic units within languages. We look at the types of control flow within each unit, and at the features available for transfer of control between units. Data communication between units is discussed only briefly; this aspect of communication is covered in chapter 11.

Emphasis is as usual on features directly available within languages, but we shall on occasion mention also some programmatic control techniques requiring simulation within most languages. We limit coverage in this chapter to elementary types of control taking place in the context of a single execution process. More sophisticated contexts involving exceptions, monitoring, and multiprocessing are covered in chapters 14 and 15.

10.1 EXECUTION UNITS

In our discussion of storage persistence in chapter 9, we identified three units of execution: the program, the module, and the statement. In this section we elaborate on those and other units of execution found within common languages. We work from outside toward inside, by describing first more global units, and subsequently those smaller units of which they are composed.

10.1.1 THE PROGRAM

A program is the most global unit of execution that we shall consider. It is autonomous in that its execution is not linguistically dependent on previous program executions, nor does it influence succeeding program executions. Such dependencies do, of course, exist through the planning of the programmer and through external data dependency occurring during data input, but no bonds are created through the language of the program.

We accept the program execution as occurring by undefined means, and we observe that in no language-defined manner does it pass on an execution result to any other execution unit. The program is thus our axiomatic building block; all subsequently discussed execution units can be defined on the basis of their roles within a program execution.

10.1.2 THE EXTERNAL MODULE

We now move down a level to look at the executable units that comprise a program. In FORTRAN, for example, a program consists of a main routine, any number of functions and subroutines, and usually a number of routines (built-in functions) contained in a rather general subroutine library. Other languages have analogous units, which we choose to characterize generally as external modules. We also postulate that within a program, one of its external modules is somehow distinguishable (syntactically or positionally, for example) as the initial external module of the program. It is the module to be invoked when a program execution is begun.

An external module enjoys an autonomy less than that of a program, but greater than that of other units we shall study. To describe its dependencies, we must introduce the concept of linkage-editing as the means by which a collection of external modules are bound together into a program. We define linkage-editing as meeting two critical needs:

1. An external module may contain a statement requesting execution of another external module within the executing program. Linkage-editing provides the association of this request with the desired module.

2. A module may specify that certain of its named data are to be identified with similarly specified data in other external modules of a program. Linkage-editing provides the linkings of references to such data.

The above linking processes represent the two particular areas in which an external module is dependent upon other program modules for its execution. A simple example from FORTRAN illustrates each:

```
.
.
COMMON A
.
.
CALL JOE
.
.
```

The COMMON statement specifies that the name A within this routine is to be identified with all other A's that have been specified in COMMON statements in other program modules. CALL JOE requests execution of subroutine JOE, which presumably will have been link-edited into the program in which this routine is executing.

Other execution dependencies of external modules, such as data dependencies resulting from input or from parameter reception, are again metalinguistic. But the sharing of data and modules among modules of a program is the limit of language dependency of a module for its execution. In implementation terms, one can recognize the external module as the unit of compilation, if one is working with a compiled language. Of course, this compilation is incomplete in that it defers declaration-declaration bindings of the declarations of the shared symbols we have mentioned.

10.1.3 THE INTERNAL MODULE

Internal modules are illustrated by the nested blocks and procedures of ALGOL and PL/I, and by statement functions in FORTRAN. Internal modules are similar to external modules with one large exception: Whereas data sharing among external modules occurs by explicit module specification resolved at linkage-editing time, the more basic name-declaration bindings of an internal module involve examination of other modules. For now we characterize an internal module as having always a single containing module (internal or external). Name-declaration binding for any name occurring but not declared within the internal module is dependent upon its containing module. So execution of an internal module is dependent upon its containing module for necessary bindings. We return to this subject in more detail in chapter 11.

10.1.4 THE STATEMENT

For the moment, we pass over statements as an intuitive concept, with obvious embodiments in most languages as the units taken together to form a module. We observe their heavy dependency on modules for name-declaration bindings. In section 10.2 we elaborate on their characteristics in terms of control communication.

10.1.5 THE EXPRESSION

Once again we appeal to intuition, as we describe the expression as the most basic execution unit. An expression consists either of a single data element, or of an operator and a set of one or more operands, each of which is itself an expression. In the next section, we characterize expressions more rigorously in terms of control communication.

10.2 CONTROL COMMUNICATION BETWEEN EXECUTION UNITS

We have tried thus far to give only an intuitive feel for the kinds of execution units prevalent in languages. We shall now be more explicit by characterizing them in terms of how control passes between pairs of them. We defer until chapter 11 most of our discussion of the environmental prerequisites for one unit to call another, and concentrate only on the communication protocols in effect when such communication occurs.

10.2.1 SEQUENTIAL VERSUS REQUEST CONTROL FLOW

Two important kinds of control communication may occur between execution units: *sequential control flow* and *request control flow*. The former is in effect when a unit completes execution and transfers control to a subsequent unit. The most obvious example is the control flow between statements, or between adjacent blocks in an ALGOL or PL/I program. We can identify two varieties of transfer of this kind: (1) that where the transfer target is implicit within language semantics (usually by physical ordering), and (2) that where it is specified by the programmer, as with a GO TO statement identifying a target statement.

One critical characteristic marks the execution of units participating in this type of control: They do not yield results. They may perform arbitrarily sophisticated acts, with far-reaching consequences, but upon completion they do not return a value resulting from their execution.

Request control flow occurs when an executing unit requests that some other unit perform a task for him. The understanding here is that the requestor has not completed his execution, but wishes to relinquish control temporarily to the second unit. The second unit is then to execute completely, while the first waits. Control is to be returned eventually to the first unit so that execution of that unit can continue.

This protocol includes the option of the invoked unit returning a result to the requestor. The result case is exemplified by a function reference within an expression (or even a simple reference to a subexpression); the no-result case is exemplified by a CALL statement.

Two other options are present in this kind of control communication: (1) the requestor may specify the point in the invoked unit at which he wishes execution to commence (as in the PL/I ENTRY statement), and (2) he and the invoked unit may agree upon the point to which control is to be returned upon completion of that unit (label parameters in ALGOL).

10.2.2 SUMMARY OF CONTROL FLOW THROUGH PROGRAMS, MODULES, STATEMENTS, AND EXPRESSIONS

Let us look at each of our defined execution units and see which protocols may govern its execution. We can do so by following through the table below with examples from the languages we have looked at. Note that internal and external modules are identical in terms of the protocols discussed. We explore their differences in terms of autonomy (already mentioned) and availability for execution in chapter 11.

PROTOCOL / UNIT	Sequential	Request	Result	No result	Variable entry	Variable exit
Program				*		
External module	*	*	*	*	*	*
Internal module	*	*	*	*	*	*
Statement	*			*		*
Expression		*	*			

We view a program as being invoked neither sequentially nor by request but, as we have said, in a manner undefined within languages; it has no result. Its entry point cannot be said to be variable since we don't define how it is entered, and we similarly refrain from defining its point of return.

Modules may have any of the properties shown. They may be executed sequentially (BEGIN...END blocks) or by request (procedure blocks); they may or may not return results (functions versus subroutines); they may have variable entry points if invoked by request (PL/I ENTRY statement); and they may have variable points of return (ALGOL label parameters or PL/I generalized GO TO out of a block).

Statements are executed sequentially and never return a result. They are always entered similarly, and return is variable (sometimes the next statement; sometimes elsewhere, as is usually the case, for example, when the statement is GO TO).

An expression is always invoked by request, either of its containing statement or (if it is itself a subexpression) of the expression of which it is an operand. It always yields a result, and both entry and return points are fixed.

10.2.3 CONDITIONAL SEQUENTIAL CONTROL FLOW

We saw in ALGOL a very powerful and general capability for conditional specification. In its simplest form, which is common to many languages, the conditional governs statement execution.

> IF condition THEN statement1 ELSE statement2;

In ALGOL, the capability for conditional specification is also available below this—at the expression level.

> V1: = IF condition THEN exp1 ELSE exp2;

Furthermore, the ability to nest such conditionals provides for multiple conditional specifications.

> IF cond1 THEN
> > IF cond2 THEN spec1 ELSE spec2
> ELSE IF cond3 THEN spec3 ELSE spec4;

The above logic can be represented in flowchart form as shown on the following page. This kind of specification logic is usually considered in the realm of control flow. Nevertheless it is important to realize that conditionals represent a specialized kind of variable. In ALGOL we write

> GO TO IF condition THEN label1 ELSE label2;

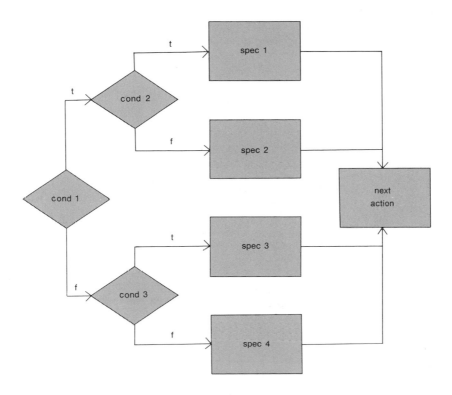

whereas in PL/I, to set up similar logic, we write

GO TO label variable;

where the label variable has as its value either label1 or label2.

The ALGOL case is considered a form of conditional control flow; the PL/I one is not, though in the eyes of a compiler it is the most difficult kind of conditional to handle. In general, the domain of possible target labels is not known prior to execution of a PL/I program.

10.2.4 ITERATION

A somewhat more complicated form of implicit conditional is available with iterative features present in most languages. The features usually represent little more than a shorthand notation, but we mention a general iterative statement because of the frequency of use of the function provided.

Suppose, within some language lacking a direct iterative capability, we wish to search a ten-element vector v for an element with the value 7. We wish to exit from the search with an index variable I telling us the first element (if any) having the value 7. Our code might resemble the following sequence:

```
        I←1;
LAB:    IF V(I) = 7 THEN GO TO OUT;
        I←I + 1;
        IF I≤10 THEN GO TO LAB;
OUT:    next statement
```

Exit will be made from the search above with I having either the index of the element with value 7 if such an element exists, or the failure value 11 if no element has the value 7.

This example illustrates a typical general algorithmic technique. The technique is useful when a sequence of statements is to be executed repeatedly until either some exit condition is met or a maximal number of iterations has occurred. The following critical tasks are being done:

1. A counter variable (I) is initialized.
2. A test is made.
3. The counter variable is updated.
4. The counter variable is compared with a terminal value.
5. Control is conditionally returned to the top of the loop (step 2).

Generally, any sequence of statements may be executed between steps 2 and 3 above, though for our simple search, none was required.

This iterative capability may be provided directly by a statement of the form

```
DO variable←exp1 TO exp2 BY exp3 WHILE condition;
    [statement1 . . . statementn]
END;
```

The statement sequence from statement 1 through statementn is to be executed repeatedly, subject to two criteria. First, whenever the condition is not met, the execution of the sequence is terminated (the condition is checked prior to each execution of the sequence). Second, we look at the counter variable. It is initialized to exp1 prior to the first execution sequence. After each sequence, it is incremented by exp3 and then checked against exp2. If the counter is greater than exp2 (for exp3≥0) or less than exp2 (for exp3<0), the sequence is terminated.

Using the above format, our search example can be specified as follows:

```
DO I←1 TO 10 BY 1 WHILE V(I)≠7;
END;
```

We can introduce several obvious shorthand extensions involving default assumptions, but one extension is more than a shorthand. If the TO clause is omitted, the test of the counter variable is not performed, and termination results only from failure of the condition.

This explanation, while hopefully providing a good general feel for the features of DO, is nevertheless fraught with ambiguities that are resolved in a number of different ways in the various languages having a similar statement. Differences in interpretation revolve around the following:

1. What if the counter variable is updated by some statement of the sequence? Is this allowed?

2. How should the first-time problem be handled, for example, should the statement sequence below be executed at all?

```
DO I←1 TO 0 BY 1;
statement1
    .
    .
    .
statementn
END;
```

3. How often are the various expressions executed? This question is critical if their values are modified by statements within the sequence.

A definitive resolution of these questions involves specifying a precise expansion of the DO statement into more primitive statements such as we used in our search example. We refrain from doing this and choose instead to leave such an expansion to the reader. The reader should look carefully at the following examples and assure himself that his expansion provides acceptable renderings of them.

```
1.    DO I←1 TO 0 BY 1;
      .
      .
      .
      END;
2.    J←2;
      DO I←1 TO 0 BY J;
      .
      .
      .
      END;
3.    J←-1;
      DO I←1 TO 0 BY J;
```

```
           .
           .
       J←2;
           .
           .
       END;
  4.   DO I←1 TO 0 BY 2;
           .
           .
       I←-3;
           .
           .
       END;
  5.   DO I←J TO K BY L;
           .
           .
       J←J + 3;
       K←K-7;
       L←L + 6;
           .
           .
       END;
  6.   DO I←I + 1 BY I + 2;
           .
           .
       END;
```

Exercises

1. Define several expansions of the general DO statement. Expansions may vary in where the out-of-range test is made and in whether various expressions (exp1,exp2,...,expn) are evaluated only prior to the iteration, once per iteration, or on each reference within each iteration. They may vary also in where the value of the control variable is used.

2. Check each expansion defined in response to exercise 1 against the sample loops given in this text, and select the expansion most appropriate for all of them.

3. Defend the choice that you made in response to exercise 2.

10.3 A DIVERSION

We digress for a moment to look at an issue involving the simplest of all language features for control flow, the GO TO.

A prominent school of thought ([Dij68(March)]) contends that use of the GO TO statement is the bane of a large number of programs, and that languages would be better as algorithm-expression vehicles if the GO TO statement were eliminated from their repertoires. The school contends that GO TO serves as a confusing crutch, allowing deferral of program decisions that should be made immediately, rather than put off until some indefinite later point in code.

Let us postulate a language containing a CALL statement and some variety of iterative capability such as we have described, but with no other feature for sequencing except by statement ordering. It can be shown in theory that any program written in that language augmented by the GO TO can be equivalently reformulated without occurrences of GO TO.

Perhaps the reader is impressed by this claim, but it should be viewed as programmatically irrelevant, even if mathematically interesting. What we are after is clarity of thought and algorithm, and, in fact, some reformulations of intricately entwined masses of GO TO's can become even more hopelessly entwined. Reformulation is in general not useful at the coding level.

Although it may sound as though we are dismissing programming without GO TO's, this is not the case. Rather, we are trying to dismiss the notion that suddenly running off and recoding all one's programs to delete GO TO's according to theoretic rewriting rules results in better, clearer programs. The opposite is often the case. Avoiding GO TO's as a valuable programming discipline must be approached at the level of initial algorithm formulation, not as a reprogramming game. At this former level, it is surprisingly attractive and (after the programmer has overcome initial traumas in becoming accustomed to the new way of thinking) a boon to lucid and easily readable programs.

We do propose a statement, to be made available for convenience in a language without GO TO's. The statement provides a very limited and highly disciplined temporary branching capability. We designate it the CASE statement and recommend that it have the general form

CASE expression OF statement1...statementn END;

The expression is evaluated to an integer index into the collection of statements, and the appropriate one is executed. Control is then transfered to the statement following the CASE-statement END.

This statement is simply a useful generalization of the more common

IF condition THEN statement1 ELSE statement2;

which can be used in the same way as CASE if enough nestings of IF's are included.

We can identify four positive benefits of programming without GO TO's:

1. The programmer is forced to discipline his thought processes, to formulate his logic according to an appropriate structure.

2. The programmer finds himself looking for similarities rather than differences in subportions of his problem. Rather than simply generating conditional branches to many program locations to handle a number of cases, he is encouraged to handle them together, perhaps with additional use of variables serving as parameters to differentiate the cases.

3. The reader or inheritor of a program has a much easier time following program logic if he can read the program sequentially rather than with constant page-flipping through the program listing.

4. A compiler for a language without GO TO's has a relatively easy time of characterizing all flow paths through a program. This allows for much broader code optimization possibilities than would otherwise be the case.

The last of these reasons is a useful byproduct of excluding GO TO's, but it is not a motivation for doing so. We are, after all, dedicated by this time in computer evolution to aiding the user rather than the implementor.

For further discussion of basic control structures, see [Fis70].

Exercises

4. Give a translation of our CASE statement in terms of only IF's and GO TO's as control features. The result of this translation is a control complex seen frequently in programs using many GO TO's.

5. Undertake formulation of a significant programming problem, as a structured program without GO TO's. Feel free to use other features that we have described, in particular DO and CASE. With some languages, it may be necessary to translate unavailable constructs into sequences involving GO TO's as a means of running the program. But formulation of the program should be free of GO TO's.

CHAPTER 11

Execution Environments

In chapter 10 we looked at the ways in which various execution units communicate with one another, but we concentrated mainly on control protocols, delaying our discussion of data communication between units until now. In this chapter we look at data communication. The units of primary concern to us are internal and external modules. The data communicated to a module is in general the same as that communicated to subunits of the module during its execution.

We investigate primarily the data passed to an execution unit from its invoker, but we also look at the data it passes back to that invoker upon completion. As prerequisite for these discussions, we first look at the concept of invocability, the environmental criteria that must be satisfied in order for a module to be available for invocation.

11.1 INVOCABILITY CRITERIA

Two kinds of execution requirements must be met in order for a module to be available for invocation. The first of these is the obvious requirement that some name that resolves to the object representing the desired module be available to the invoker—one must be able to refer to a module in order to request its execution. Second, because of the various ways in which modules inherit information, there are requirements for activity of modules from which such inheritance is to derive.

11.1.1 MODULE REFERABILITY

In a brief review of data-scope rules as they relate to modules in block-structured languages such as PL/I and ALGOL, two principles stand out:

1. An ALGOL or PL/I procedure name is INTERNAL, in the PL/I sense, if the module is internal. Otherwise the name is EXTERNAL.

2. The name of an internal module is considered to be declared within its containing module.

In languages that are not block-structured, such as FORTRAN and APL, all modules are external.

We adopt our previous scope rules from ALGOL and PL/I, and note some examples of cases in which modules can be referenced by name and others in which they cannot.

Case 1:

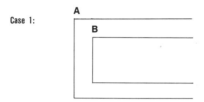

Module B is referable from module A. In general, an internal module is always referable from its containing module. In this same case, A is referable from B if either (1) B contains no declaration of the name A, and thus has no contained module named A, or (2) B contains a declaration of the name A with the attribute EXTERNAL. This declaration would resolve to the external module A.

Case 2:

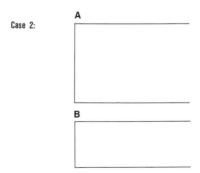

A is referable from B under the same criteria as in case 1. Similarly B is referable from A. We generalize to say that in a program with no duplicate names, all EXTERNAL modules are everywhere referable.

Case 3:

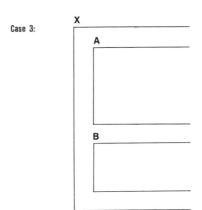

A and B are referable from each other if and only if neither has any declaration of the name of the other. In a block-structured language, brother
modules (two modules with the same containing parent module) may refer
to each other if neither has a declaration of the other's name.

Case 4:

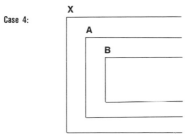

A is always referable from X, as in case 1. B is similarly always referable
from A. A is referable from B if and only if B contains no declaration of
the name A. X is referable from B if either (1) B has an EXTERNAL declaration for X, or (2) neither A nor B has an INTERNAL declaration for X.

Case 5:

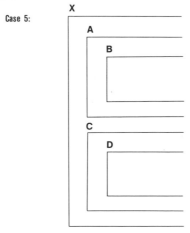

Here is a general picture. We need not elaborate on the cases already covered, but we look at the new possibilities. A is referable from D if and only if neither C nor D contains any declaration for the name A (similarly C is referable from B). But D is under no circumstance referable from A or B; its name is not known within A or B.

Let us coalesce these cases into a single general rule, using male genealogical terminology. A module A is the father of module B if A contains B. In case 1 above, A is the father of B. Modules A and B are brothers if they have the same father. An ancestor of a module A is any of A's father, A's grandfather, A's great grandfather, and so on. A private ancestor of A is an ancestor of A which is not an ancestor of B. Additional terms follow from these. Our rule is the following:

> Module B is referable by its name from module A if and only if the following conditions hold:
>
> ■ If B is internal, then B's father must be either A or an ancestor of A.
>
> ■ If B is internal and not A's son, then neither A nor any private ancestor of A can contain a declaration of the name B.
>
> ■ If B is external, and if either A or any private ancestor of A has a declaration of the name B, then the youngest generation of such modules must specify that declaration EXTERNAL.

11.1.2 ACTIVITY REQUIREMENTS FOR MODULE INVOCABILITY

Our above requirements for referring to a module revolved solely around the pedantics of where its name was available. But we do not wish this arbitrary constraint to define the concept of invocability. In this section we see that a module may be potentially invocable at some execution point, even though its name may not be known.

Let us agree upon some terminology. An *activation* of a module is an instance of execution of the module. We say that a module is active at some time if there is at that time a current activation of the module. An activation of a module is said to exist from time of invocation of that module until time of its final termination. Thus a module may be active though not currently executing, if it has invoked some other module and is waiting for the latter's activation completion.

Recall our rules of data-declaration inheritance from ALGOL and PL/I for internal modules. An undeclared name in an internal module was resolved to a declaration in the parent block, if such a declaration existed

there; or to the grandparent block; and so forth. But we know also for
ALGOL local data and PL/I AUTOMATIC data, that the objects exist only
during an activation of the declaring module. And clearly we cannot resolve undeclared data to declarations for which no objects exist. Therefore we establish the following rule for invocability of an internal module:

> An internal module is invocable only if its parent
> module is active.

This rule is more interesting than the one developed in the preceding section, for here we are describing a logical restriction less arbitrary in nature
than our previous rule related to referability.

How do our two rules relate to each other? As we shall now discover, our invocability rule admits a larger class of modules than does
our referability rule; hence the terminology "only if" was used above
rather than "if and only if."

Consider the following block structure:

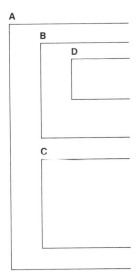

Case 5 in the last section, and our rule following, precluded the possibility of C invoking D. We said that D is never referable by C.

Yet suppose we have a calling sequence in which A calls B, which in
turn calls C. While C is executing, B is still active. According to our invocability rule, D should be invocable, if C could refer to it. Here we have
a case for which our rules do not match.

We suggest a descriptive model employing our somewhat broader
second rule but with the phrase "if and only if," rather than "only if."

Furthermore, we wish to retain the name scope rules implied in the earlier referability rule. To have the best of these two worlds, we postulate a feature primitively available in PL/I, but not generally available in any language we have studied. We wish to allow variables accepting data of type module.

PL/I has this feature only in the form of parameters. In our example above, we could have executed the following PL/I sequence:

```
A: PROCEDURE;    B: PROCEDURE;       C: PROCEDURE(P);
   .                .                   DECLARE P ENTRY;
   .                .                   .
   CALL B;          CALL C(D);          .
   .                .                   CALL P;
   .                .                   .
   END;             D: PROCEDURE;       .
                       .                END;
                       .
                    END;

                    .

                    .

                 END;
```

Here A calls B. B calls C, passing as a parameter its internal procedure D. C then calls D via its parameter name P. This invocation is legal and actually works, since D at time of its call has the appropriate environment (activity of B) available to it.

A more general feature permitting variables to accept module values is desirable. Then we could accomplish the above as follows:

```
A: PROCEDURE;              B: PROCEDURE;       C: PROCEDURE;
   DECLARE PV PROCVAR;        .                   .
   .                          .                   .
   .                          PV = D;             CALL PV;
   CALL B;                    .                   .
   .                          .                   .
   .                          CALL C;             END;
   END;                       .

                              .

                              D: PROCEDURE;
                                 .

                                 .

                                 END;

                              .

                              .

                           END;
```

We see here only the simplest cases of the use of module variables. In chapter 13 we discover complex implications of their use when, in a recursive situation, there exist multiple activations of the same module simultaneously. We hope, at this point, to have motivated the concept as a natural way of supporting our simple logical invocability rule. A module should be invocable, even if not referable by name, at any time that its parent is active. Module variables make this possible.

Exercises

1. We saw that a module might be invocable even if not referable by name. This was possible if certain activity requirements were met. Show that if a module is referable by name, those activity requirements are satisfied, and hence the module is invocable.

11.2 AN EXECUTION MODEL

We can now identify three kinds of data residing in a module: (1) declared data local to that module, (2) data undeclared within that module and resolved to a declaration in some other module, and (3) explicit parameters passed to the module.

We can also identify formally three kinds of units that we have lumped together informally with the term *module*:

> 1. A *module* is a unit of text, examples of which we have seen in various languages. It is not executable, because it has no inherent resolutions for undeclared symbols.

> 2. An *invocation* is an executable unit. It has two components: a module, and a reference to an activation (see 3 below), through which undeclared data are to be resolved.

> 3. An *activation* is the representation of the execution of an invocation. It has five components: an invocation, a dictionary of declaration-object resolutions for its declared data, a location counter indicating the current point of execution of the invocation, a resolution table for parameters, which we shall not specify more precisely now, and an identification of its calling activation.

Let us then model a point of execution of a program as follows on the next page.

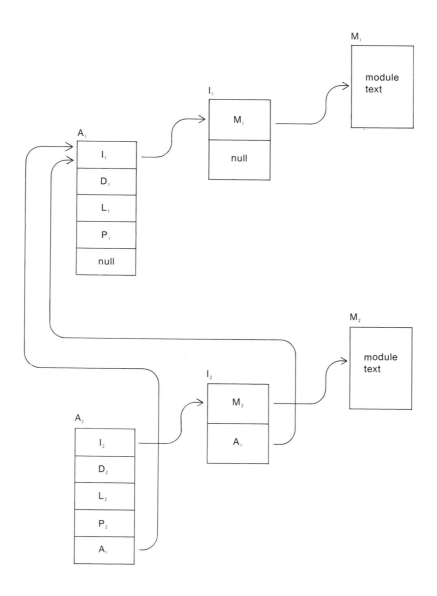

The program was entered with activation A_1, consisting of invocation I_1, dictionary D_1, location counter L_1, a null parameter resolution table P_1, and indication of the calling activation. I_1 identifies module M_1 but identifies no activation for resolution of undeclared symbols of M_1.

A_1 has called A_2, which has similar components, but identifies A_1 as its caller. I_2 identifies A_1 as the source for resolving (through D_1) undeclared symbols of M_2. This case of resolution through the caller models APL; it also models ALGOL and PL/I cases in which a procedure calls a procedure nested within it.

In terms of this model, let us look at some aspects of the languages that we have studied to see how and when various bindings can be made.

We observe that our model usually will need some sort of conceptual first activation containing the declarations for PL/I EXTERNAL, FORTRAN COMMON, APL global, and similar data with program-wide scope. We choose not to dwell on these in detail, but to look at the more normal kinds of data scopes.

We need say little of the *module*. All of its characteristics are determined at the time of its creation. But let us suppose now that we have a program involving a collection of modules $M_1...M_n$. The program involves, during execution, an indefinite number of *invocations* per module, and an indefinite number of *activations* per invocation. Suppose we define for our model, at compile-time, the set of modules and some large collection of invocations and activations, initially without component parts. When can we fill in the various components of these data?

Suppose we have in practice allotted sufficient invocations and activations so that we can dedicate some quantity K_i of invocations to each module M_i, and some quantity L_j of activations to each invocation I_j. Then we can initialize the module components of our activations at time of compilation.

Now consider the activation component of an invocation—the component identifying the resolver of undeclared data. For FORTRAN that component is nonexistent or, if we wish to consider COMMON data as undeclared, then it is the artificial activation containing declarations of COMMON data. For APL we can do nothing; we simply have no knowledge, at time of program creation, of resolution for undeclared symbols. But now consider PL/I and ALGOL internal module invocations. While we cannot determine totally the activations to be identified by these invocations, we can limit the choice drastically. The activation identified by an internal module invocation must be one of the activations identifying, through its invocation, the parent module of this module. So we can fill in to our invocations for our module, arbitrary identifications of the activations that we have allocated to the parent module. Those activations are, of course, not yet complete, having only an invocation identification and perhaps, if we wish, a dictionary component with unresolved mappings.

We can do no more until we begin to execute our program. We start to execute in an external module by taking an activation identifying the current module, building its dictionary of mappings as we create objects for its data, and updating its location counter as we proceed (presumably the first activation takes no parameters).

We now come to a CALL statement (or any such execution request) requesting execution of some module. What must we do to update our model?

First, we must choose an activation to link to our current one. It must be an activation identifying through its invocation the module called. For APL this requirement is sufficient. The new activation's identified invocation is set to name our first activation as its symbol resolver (resolution via the call chain). For PL/I or ALGOL, with which more initialization has been done, we must be more selective. We must choose an activation whose identified invocation names the latest activation in our chain resolving to the parent module of the module to be invoked. This provides for the possibility of recursive calls, which result in more than one chain activation identifying the same module.

A series of pictures can be used to clarify our discussion above. Suppose that a program has the following block structure:

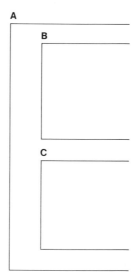

We allocate our data as follows:

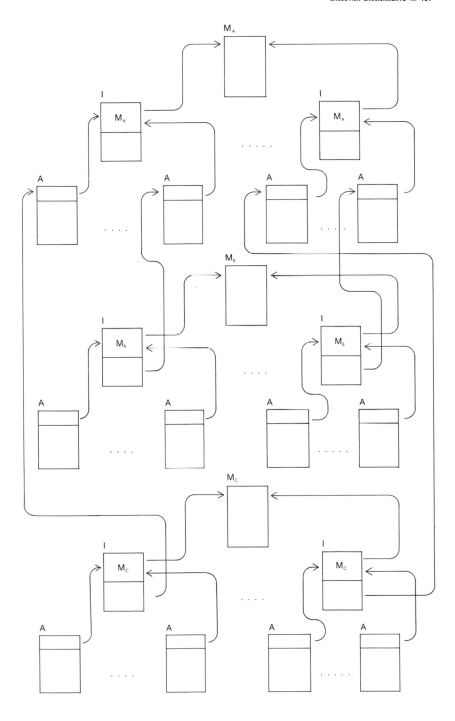

We begin executing A with activation A_1.

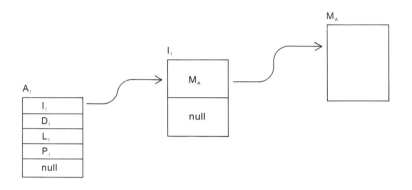

Now A calls B, and we expand our model as follows:

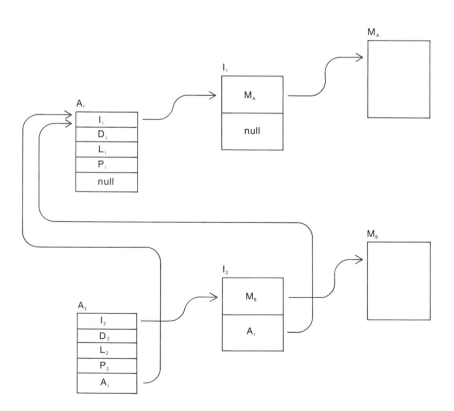

Now B calls C.

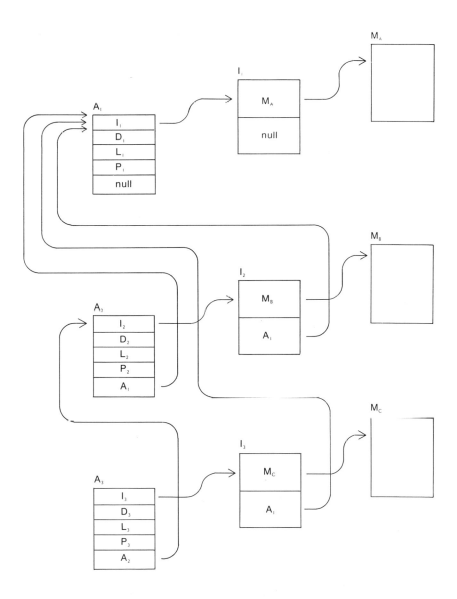

At time of a call, a new activation is added to a chain of activations, and its dictionary, location counter, and parameter resolution table are set. In APL it is necessary additionally to set the activation component of the invocation identified by the new activation to identify the calling activation.

We will not go into further detail on the subject of parameter communication, which we looked at in chapter 5. But we should discuss briefly the actions that occur upon completion of an activation.

Generally, we think of an activation as terminating by a return to the calling activation, at the point in the latter just beyond the call. A value (in most languages, required to be scalar) may be returned for use by the caller. BEGIN...END blocks in PL/I and ALGOL cannot return results. This restriction may not appear to be significant, but, as we shall see when we discuss language extensibility (chapter 18), it impedes the definition of user-defined operators as expansions into blocks.

The point of return from a module need not be as simple as our common case. Suppose that, in some activation, we execute the statement GO TO X. Further suppose that x resolves ultimately to a label of a statement contained in an activation that precedes this activation by several levels in the call chain. The effect is to return successively from each intervening activation, terminating all activations further down the call chain than the one in which the label occurs. Thus a GO TO in one block may cause control to resume in any active block, and may cause termination of any number of intervening blocks. We shall treat this subject in more detail when we discuss recursion (chapter 13).

Exercises

2. Use our execution model to describe the execution sequence involving the module variable PV of section 11.1. In particular, describe the effect of the assignment of D to PV.

11.3 SUMMARY

We have described the basic characteristics of an execution model designed in a common way to describe the control flow, and the data communication flow, among program modules in various languages. Our model is broader than any language that we have studied, in that it allows the possibility of data resolution via any chain of prior activations. The actual protocols of individual languages are more restrictive.

Exercises

3. The execution model given in this chapter is more general than required for either block-structured languages or APL-like languages. This generality derives primarily from the fact that the activation component of an invocation is in no way limited to identifying particular activations. Describe the resolution characteristics of a language designed to require the total power of the execution model.

CHAPTER 12

Input/Output

The treatment of input and output in programming languages has been a very inelegant part of high-level language evolution. A gross characterization of the problem is that I/O facilities have tended to reflect linguistically irrelevant characteristics of storage devices rather than aspects logically significant within hosting languages. An equally gross defense of this situation is that, in general, devices have been extremely inflexible in their communicative powers—one speaks to a storage device in precisely its own hardware-oriented terms, or not at all. The sacrifice resulting from software translation of high-level specifications into device-dependent commands is one of often intolerable inefficiencies.

We shall discuss two problem levels in this area:

1. Those language requirements for I/O that are seemingly device-oriented rather than problem-oriented;

2. Those cases in which languages require use of I/O to perform functions that logically are no different than those provided by assignment statements—cases that rightfully seem not to belong to the realm of I/O.

In a less critical vein, we also look at input/output as a set of linguistic needs, and at the language (not device) requirements for support of these needs.

12.1 FILE CHARACTERISTICS

Let us first scan a typical set of specifications used to direct transmission of data to/from some storage device. We do this without regard to language aspects; those we subsequently examine, and then we note the functional intersection of the two points of view of I/O.

We use the term *file* to denote a basic repository for data storage, and we use the term *record* to denote the smallest unit of storage available on a file. These terms tend to comprise the interface between a high-level language description of I/O, and the hardware-oriented specification which then describes files in terms of physical data sets residing on physical devices.

12.1.1 FILE IDENTIFICATION

An obvious requirement for data transmission to/from a file is an identification, in some fashion, of the file involved. Such identification may occur in any of a number of ways, which individually are not of interest to us.

12.1.2 FILE PREPARATION

Normally, certain preliminary operations are necessary to ready a file for data transmission, and certain cleanup operations are needed when transmission is complete. We refer generically to these requirements as opening and closing of the file, respectively. We speak of a file as being open from the time it is opened until the time it is closed. Again we are not concerned with the specifics, which vary widely in accordance with equipment in use and system requirements.

12.1.3 TRANSMISSION MODE

Files vary in their versatility for direction of transmission, but typically one must specify when opening a file whether it is to be used for input (reading records), output (writing records), or update (changing records). This specification limits the transmission possibilities during the ensuing open period for the file—one cannot, for example, write records onto a file opened for input only.

12.1.4 FILE DISPOSITION

One must specify for a file what is to become of its data when the file is closed. Is the file to be retained (a file being used for permanent storage), or can it be destroyed (a scratch file used for holding data temporarily during execution of a program)? We speak of such alternatives as the file disposition.

12.1.5 FILE ORGANIZATION AND ACCESSIBILITY

Three basic kinds of record organization are found in files: *sequential, direct,* and *keyed*. Each imposes certain requirements that affect how records within a file are accessed.

Records are linearly ordered within a sequential file and must be read or written sequentially, backward or forward, according to that order. A magnetic tape is a common example of a physical medium upon which only sequential files can be defined.

Records are in no implied order in a direct file. Each is accessed by referring to its location within the file.

Records in a keyed file are self-identifying by a key (name). Access to such a record is done by specifying its name. This causes a search of the file for the record so named. Ordinarily a keyed file is organized in an ordered fashion determined by some linearization of keys, so the file can also be treated as a sequential file. Thus, for example, one might access the file as a keyed file to read the record with a certain key; then one might proceed to read sequentially the records following it in order of key value.

Exercises

1. While languages do not include sequential or keyed organization of internal aggregates, it is often useful to simulate aggregates of these kinds.

   (a) Describe how one might use common aggregates and access techniques described in chapter 8 to simulate sequential aggregates and accesses to them.
   (b) Repeat (a) above, but for keyed aggregates.

12.1.6 RECORD SIZE

A file may be specified to contain records of either fixed-length or variable-length. In the former case, a length is given, and access to records is facilitated by the homogeneity. In the latter case, we subdivide further into two cases, depending on who is responsible for remembering the length of a given record and, if necessary, using that information in locating other records of the file. This housekeeping task may be provided automatically by the system; that is, the system may append a length field to each record that is written and use the information later when the record is read (though this field is not usually given to the program causing the record to be read). Alternatively, the length may be remembered and used by the application program to locate other records relative to that one.

12.1.7 RECORD BLOCKING

Efficiency considerations may dictate that records on a file be grouped into blocks; in this case the physical transmission unit is an entire block, rather than just a record (though this fact is hidden from the programmer). If input records are blocked, or if output records are to be blocked, then a block size (number of records per block) must be specified for the file.

12.1.8 BUFFERING

Normally, data is not transmitted directly between a file and the storage area reserved for it; rather, it passes through an intermediate storage area called a *buffer*. Use of buffers provides several types of efficiency relating to overlapping I/O work with program work, and to deferring actual I/O transmission until a significant amount of data can be transmitted. Details need not concern us, as again this aspect of I/O does not show through directly to the programmer except as efficiency considerations. We note only that a file may make use of, or even require, buffers for its transmission, in which case one may specify the storage areas to be used by that file as buffer areas.

12.1.9 SPACE REQUIREMENTS

A required amount of record space, with perhaps some overflow provisions, must be specified for many files to be written. This specification ensures that the system allocates sufficient space on the output medium to hold all the information written.

12.2 LANGUAGE I/O CHARACTERISTICS

The programmer whose requirements for storage media involve only reading from cards or a standard system input tape, and writing onto a printer, often need not worry about device considerations. Standard defaults may satisfy his needs. But when his demands go further, he often must describe his device I/O requirements in some detail, including many of the specifications above. He may have to do this explicitly as part of the language that he is using, or indirectly via control information appended to his program. Either way the responsibility is his.

It is useful now to look at the language specifications that have linguistic significance with respect to I/O, and then to compare those with the set of device characteristics that we have scanned.

12.2.1 STORAGE

Let us first separate two aspects of I/O that are functionally dissimilar, though, unfortunately, presented identically within languages. One is storage; the other is message transmission.

We indicated in chapter 10 the obvious necessity to retain data between program executions. At the same time, we recognized the linguistic autonomy of a program: It is the largest unit of execution, the largest unit over which reference names have validity, the largest unit over which program data storage persists.

To retain data across programs, I/O is used to write the data onto a file and later read it in to computer storage for use by a subsequent program, having remembered the identification of the file and the locations of data on it. What is happening here is functionally no different than, within a program, storing some data and later using it. The only difference is that in the I/O case, techniques other than language (human memory, tape serial numbers, disk unit identifications, and the like) are used to assure retrieving of the data that was stored. Why then, with the evident functional similarity, is the one case given by simple assignment statements, but the other by I/O?

We recognize that if simple assignment is to be used for holding data across programs, some conventions must exist to provide for names more global than the program; current metalinguistic techniques for identifying files must be absorbed into language. But what of all the other device characteristics that we mentioned? What place have these in a feature for assignments and storage persistence valid across programs?

There are, of course, loose analogies between some of our file specifications and some characteristics of language stores and assignments.

If we view a file as a data aggregate, and records as its elements, then file identification corresponds to naming of the aggregate. The transmission mode specification sounds rather like the choice between storing and retrieving. Disposition relates to storage persistence characteristics. Sequential files have no direct language analog, though their property of ordering corresponds to vectors, and the sequential processing to loops through those vectors. Direct files are similar to one-level trees in which components are named directly. And keyed-file access corresponds to search algorithms within languages; however, keyed aggregates are not directly available.

Record-size specification relates generally to the homogeneity properties of aggregates, and space requirements are, of course, reflected at allocation time for language aggregates. Other characteristics such as blocking, buffering, and opening and closing haven't even remote language analogs.

Our argument is simply that, from the point of view of language, there is no reason that storage across programs should be treated differently from storage within a program—assignments of values to named locations should suffice, provided that some extensions are provided for global naming.

The counter argument, as we have indicated, is one of efficiency; translation from such logical assignment into physical I/O can be very inconvenient because of device idiosyncrasies.

For additional discussion of the structuring of data on files, the reader should refer to [Lef69] and [Flo70].

12.2.2 MESSAGE TRANSMISSION

We have tried to write off storage I/O by the claim that it belongs, not in the realm of I/O, but in that of assignment, name scope, and storage persistence. In deference to common usage of the terms *input* and *output*, however, we shall discuss what we view logically as I/O under the term *message transmission*.

How does message transmission differ functionally from storage I/O? We identify three qualitative differences:

1. Message transmission involves data entering or leaving a computing system; origin or target of the transmission is some external being (say, a human, sensor device, or other system). There is no retention of data.

2. Data items transmitted within messages must be in a display form suitable for comprehension by the target (if written) or the source (if read).

3. Since messages are displayed information, formatting features must be available to provide not only comprehensible individual data items, but also a suitable display format for the data.

None of these characteristics holds for stored data (either within a program or across programs). So we may usefully view message transmission as a separate area with its own set of language requirements.

We limit our discussion of messages to the simple but usual case of printed text: a sequence of pages ordered front to back, each containing a sequence of lines ordered top to bottom, each containing a sequence of characters or blanks ordered left to right. We omit consideration of audio and video message transmission, and of analog transmission in general. These areas are not yet well represented within programming languages.

12.2.2.1 SIMPLE MESSAGES

We look first at simple transmission cases in which the aim is to read values into some data items or, in a straightforward way, to display such values as an output message. We assume that display formatting is of no concern to the programmer—he wishes only to transmit values associated with program data names. We leave undefined the ways in which values of different kinds may be represented within character sets; this subject is primarily a matter of syntactic design.

Two ways of transmitting values and associating them with names can be identified. They are analogous to our referencing alternatives of naming and indexing.

We speak first of *transmission by order*. A language command specifies by names a collection of items to be transmitted, and the message medium contains a list of ordered values, separated from one another in some arbitrary fashion (a sequence of blanks, for example). Association between values on the medium and names in the specification, whether in input or output, follows from the ordering of the names: The first name is associated with the first value, second with second, and so forth. The values are in no sense self-identifying; their association with names is only discoverable through the program transmission command.

Second, we identify *transmission by name*. Here the programmer indicates with an appropriate command that he wishes transmission (input or output) to occur. He may specify a collection of data names. If specified, this collection delineates the candidates for transmission, but it is not imperative in the case of input.

Under this mode of transmission, the message medium contains a delineated list of values, each of which is self-identifying by an attached character-string name. For output, these are the data indicated in the named collection; if no such collection is given, they are all data known at this point in the program. For input, the situation is more interesting. Assignment is made to each program datum having the following characteristics:

1. Its name is known at this point in the program.

2. If a collection of names is given with the input command, its name is among those given.

3. A value on the message medium is self-identified by the name of this datum.

When these three conditions are satisfied, the value as noted in condition 3 is assigned to the named datum identified with it.

Note that in this case no ordering is used to direct the association between names and values. Such freedom is possible because of the self-identification of the values.

12.2.2.2 FORMATTED MESSAGES

Now we look at cases in which the programmer desires more explicit control over his display formats for output. He may need this control in three areas: representation of data, inclusion of literals, and positioning of information.

In our simple cases, we disregarded the representation for data types, assuming only that, for any type of data, some obvious character-string form to indicate its value must be available. But now that simplicity is no longer sufficient, particularly for numeric data, which may have multiple representations.

The primary representational choice for numeric data is whether a value is represented directly as a signed scaled integer, or by use of a mantissa and exponent. Beyond this, choices exist as to how many digits are shown to the right and left of the decimal point, whether unused digit positions are represented by zeroes or blanks, and, perhaps, what number base is used for the representation.

Even more sophistication may be required for applications such as check printing, where integrity is important. A dollar sign preceding a value, with no intervening blanks, regardless of the number of digits, may be desired. This kind of case leads to introduction of a floating format character that appears in a representation at a position determined only after the value that it appears with has been calculated. PL/I offers many such features via PICTURE formats; hence, the programmer can exercise extensive control over representation.

Inclusion of literals is the ability for the programmer to intersperse, with data, literal character strings (punctuation, headings, data explanations, and the like).

Finally, for an output specification involving transmission of named data values and of literals, the programmer must have the power to position information, relative to columns within lines within pages of his transmission file. As a preliminary step, he must be able to initialize his output medium to contain a given number of lines per page, a given number of columns per line, and a certain set of margin specifications (perhaps also a set of tab positions). These settings are, of course, similar to those established when using a normal typewriter.

A simple set of positioning format specifications follows:

- ■ skip n columns
- ■ skip to nth column
- ■ skip to next tab
- ■ skip n lines
- ■ skip to nth line
- ■ start new line
- ■ start new page

Further degrees of power allow specification of headings, footings, page numberings, multiple spacing, not splitting information across pages, and a host of sophistications found in application languages geared to text formatting.

Note that in all these features for message transmission, we are hard-pressed to find useful analogs with our earlier set of file characteristics. We have defined message files to be sequential, with fixed-length single-character records, and with transmission mode determined dynamically by the transmission command; otherwise there are really no similarities.

While storage I/O features were argued to be logically subsumed by normal assignment, for message transmission this is certainly not the case. Features here provide formatting controls that are not available with assignment statements.

Exercises

2. Consider messages emerging as pictures on a two-dimensional grid, rather than as streams of characters. Assume that the grid has identifiable x and y coordinate positions. Limiting the pictures to containing only straight lines, circles, or arcs of circles, define a set of formatting features adequate for drawing pictures on the grid.

12.3 CONCLUSIONS

We have briefly examined I/O, both from the standpoint of a storage feature, and from that of a message transmission feature. We have argued that the former requirement is more palatably handled by normal assignment, though the latter is not. In any event, neither aspect of I/O relates closely to the requirements for file description that programmers must fulfill in addition to specifying their problem-oriented needs. Remedy of this difficult problem, involving both linguists and storage engineers, is critical to progress in usability of languages, particularly for those not versed in storage device characteristics.

Sophisticated data-formatting features, extending from simple messages to graphic display, are given in [IBM65], [Kul68], [Ber69], and [Hir70].

SECTION III

Specialized Language Concepts

CHAPTER 13

Recursion

By now the reader unfamiliar with recursion as a technique of both definition and programming should be rather curious. We have repeatedly passed over the subject, in its relation to other topics, with only reference to this chapter. Now we examine recursion in greater depth, looking first at its intuitive characteristics and some occasions of its use, and later at a more formal characterization based on our execution model.

13.1 INTUITIVE NOTIONS

The term *recursion* may evoke any of a number of associations, some useful in a programming context, others extremely misleading. If one sees the term with no prior exposure, he may go to an English dictionary. In Webster's (abridged) he will fail to find *recursion* and so will look under *recur* to find

> **4**: to occur again after an interval **syn** see RETURN

He will look just below to *recurrent* and see

> **2**: returning from time to time **syn** see INTERMITTENT

These associations are precisely what we must dispel in beginning to understand recursion as a programming-language feature. The above definitions bring to mind, in particular, iteration—DO loops and FOR loops—with which we shall sharply contrast recursion.

A second, useful introduction to recursion might be through mathematical induction, used to define functions on the natural numbers. The technique is axiomatic to development of arithmetic and to all recursive function theory. Some examples follow:

Example 1: Calculation of Factorials
We have looked at this simple example before. For an integer n≥1, we define

$$\text{FACTORIAL(n)} \equiv \text{ IF } n{<}3 \text{ THEN } n \text{ ELSE } n*\text{FACTORIAL(n-1)}$$

We construct a recursive module to calculate it, say,

```
MODULE FACTORIAL(N);
    RETURN(IF N<3 THEN N ELSE N*FACTORIAL(N-1));
END FACTORIAL;
```

Example 2: Towers of Hanoi Puzzle
A number of hollow discs, ordered by diameter, reside on one of three pegs. The problem is to move all discs onto peg A, with order preserved. A single move consists of taking the top disc from any peg and placing it on a larger disc on another peg. How many moves are required?

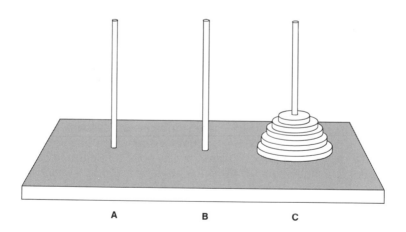

A	B	C

We solve the problem inductively by noting that when the number of discs (n) is 1, the number of moves (HANOI(n)) is 1. For n>1, we first move the top n-1 discs to peg B; this requires HANOI(n-1) moves. Then we move the bottom disc to peg C, then the set of discs from peg B to peg C (another HANOI(n-1) moves). Thus we define

$$\text{HANOI(n)} \equiv \text{IF } n = 1 \text{ THEN } 1 \text{ ELSE } 2*\text{HANOI(n-1)}+1$$

or in module form

```
MODULE HANOI(N);
    RETURN(IF N = 1 THEN 1 ELSE 2*HANOI(N-1) + 1);
END HANOI;
```

Example 3: Fibonacci Series

This number series has as its first two terms, 0 and 1. Each succeeding term is obtained as the sum of the two preceding terms. Thus the series proceeds

0 1 1 2 3 5 8 13 21 ... ...

We define the nth term by

FIBONACCI(n) ≡ IF n<3 THEN n-1 ELSE FIBONACCI(n-1) + FIBONACCI(n-2))

or with the module

```
MODULE FIBONACCI(N);
    RETURN(IF N<3 THEN N-1 ELSE FIBONACCI(N-1)
            + FIBONACCI(N-2));
END FIBONACCI;
```

Example 4: General Case

We generalize our recursive module to the following:

```
MODULE RECURSION;
    declaration of local data (V)
    calculation1 involving local data (V)
    IF condition THEN CALL RECURSION;
    calculation2 involving local data (V)
    RETURN;
END RECURSION;
```

Here we are defining a module with some local data. We symbolize the data as a single datum called v. Some calculations precede and follow a conditional call on RECURSION, and then RECURSION returns. (RECURSION may accept parameters and may return a result.)

This generalization encompasses the preceding cases and another common one: A module is written to perform analysis on a construct, for example, translation of a sentence into its diagrammed form. That analysis may involve analysis of a subconstruct by the same technique, for example, a clause within the sentence. This analysis can be accomplished by an analyzing module that calls itself to perform analysis of the subconstruct.

So, intuitively, we define recursion as the act of a module calling itself to do work.

13.2 GUIDELINES FOR USE OF RECURSION

One may by now appreciate recursion as a vehicle for expressing definitions or algorithms. And indeed the general conciseness of recursive specifications tempts one to go out of his way to use recursion in programming. Unfortunately this may be a grave error. In most languages allowing recursive use of modules, severe time and space overheads may result if recursion is used. While details of implementation problems need not concern us, we consider the primary problem of ensuring that data used in one instance of a module is not destroyed by recursive calls producing other instances of the module

There are languages whose processor design eliminates the problems of recursion, usually at the cost of generally slow execution (e.g., LISP, described in chapter 16). In most general-purpose languages, the efficiency tradeoffs of recursion are easily noticeable. Fortunately, recursion is never required for expressing an algorithm, so long as the language being used has features for providing effectively infinite-sized vectors of data (via vectors as in APL, BASED or CONTROLLED data as in PL/I, or sequential input/output as in most languages). Recursion is really only a coding technique; its effects may be obtained in other ways.

Let us look at our recursive examples above and see how each might be coded without recursion.

1. Calculation of Factorials

```
MODULE FACTORIAL(N);
    RESULT←1;
    DO I←2 TO N;
        RESULT←I * RESULT;
    END;
    RETURN(RESULT);
END FACTORIAL;
```

2. Towers of Hanoi Puzzle

```
MODULE HANOI(N);
    RESULT←1;
    DO I←2 TO N;
        RESULT←2 * RESULT + 1;
    END;
    RETURN(RESULT);
END HANOI;
```

3. **Fibonacci Series**

```
MODULE FIBONACCI(N);
    IF N<3 THEN RETURN(N-1);
    RESULT←1;
    LASTRES←1;
    DO I←3 TO N;
        TEMP←RESULT;
        RESULT←RESULT + LASTRES;
        LASTRES←TEMP;
    END;
    RETURN(RESULT);
END FIBONACCI;
```

4. **General Case**

```
MODULE RECURSION;
    DECLARE V VECTOR;
    DO COUNT←1 BY 1 WHILE condition;
        calculation1 involving V(COUNT);
    END;
    DO COUNT← COUNT 1 BY -1 WHILE COUNT>0;
        calculation2 involving V(COUNT);
    END;
END RECURSION;
```

Each of these translations has an obvious similarity to its recursive counterpart, and all of them employ iteration as a substitute for recursion. But whereas the first two examples are about as easily expressed iteratively as recursively, some minor complexity has entered the third, and the fourth has become quite complicated. What differences in the examples have caused this progressive loss of simplicity?

The answer lies in the degree of use of local data in the original recursive examples. In the first two cases, the only local datum required for each invocation of the module is the result of its calling for another invocation ($n*$FACT(n-1) and $2*$HANOI(n-1) + 1, respectively). And since these quantities are returned immediately without further processing, we do not even need local names temporarily, to assign their values.

The third example is similar but has one added complication. We use as local data the results of two successive invocations. These results are then added to give the current invocation result. This means that in our iterative rendition, we must house each result (LASTRES) while we calculate the next. And in calculating the next, we must not lose the current value (RESULT), so we must also store it locally (TEMP).

Finally, in our last example, we encounter the general problem of substituting iteration for recursion when explicit local data is declared and used both prior and subsequent to a recursive call. We must, for all such local data, use vectors of indefinite length up to the possible number of levels of recursion. We also must maintain a counter containing the current recursion level (and, hence, the appropriate vector component to use to simulate the local data).

These complications disappear if all of the local data use precedes the recursive call (if, in the recursive example, calculation2 is absent). Then we can get away with the following:

```
MODULE RECURSION;
    DECLARE V;
    DO WHILE condition;
        calculation1
    END;
END RECURSION;
```

In practice, however, this seldom occurs, since the expression returned by an invocation usually involves values of local data.

So we see a tradeoff in the use of recursion. For simple functions involving little use of local data, an iterative expansion is usually about as concise as, and more efficient than, the recursive expansion. As local data requirements increase, however, the unwieldy iterative renditions become less and less attractive, from standpoints of both brevity and efficiency. Quantification of this tradeoff depends on implementation and language nuances that we shall not investigate.

13.3 RELATION OF RECURSION TO STACKS

We can also consider the use of stacks, as discussed in chapter 8, as an alternative to recursion. Let us suppose we can declare the v of our general example as a LIFO stack, and then recode example 4 accordingly.

```
MODULE RECURSION;
    DECLARE V STACK;
    DO WHILE condition;
        PUSH(V,any value);
        calculation1 involving v
    END;
    DO WHILE ~EMPTY(V);
        calculation2 involving v
        POP(V);
    END;
END RECURSION;
```

We can use stacks here because of the discipline provided by recursion. In our expansion approach to this general case, we were always either adding to the end of a vector, using the last element, or effectively deleting the last element. These operations are precisely the set available for LIFO stacks. Such stacks are, in fact, used frequently to translate high-level languages with recursion into lower-level ones lacking it.

13.4 RECURSION AND THE EXECUTION MODEL

So far we have approached recursion from a totally intuitive viewpoint, using such phraseology as "a module calling itself." Let us now be more formal and look at recursion in terms of our execution model.

Suppose that, at some point during execution, our model includes the following call chain:

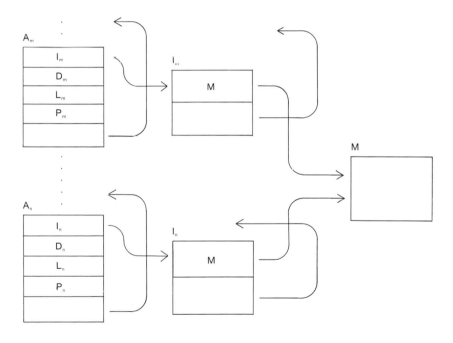

We have within our call chain two activations, A_m and (more recently) A_n. Each is general in its componentry, with the exception that the respective invocations I_m and I_n, as identified by the activations, both name as their first components the module M. We say that module M has been used recursively, since two activations in the current call chain identify, through their invocations, the module M.

Note that it is not significant whether A_n is in fact A_{m+1}. In all of our examples above, the recursion was immediate, but it may well be that activations intervene prior to the recursive call.

There is an interesting practical difference, with regard to recursion, between APL-like languages and block-structured languages, with early name-declaration binding. For APL, our above constraint of module identification is the only noteworthy characteristic of a recursive situation. In ALGOL, however, we can nearly always say more, in terms of the resolution of symbols that are not local to a particular block.

We claim that in ALGOL or PL/I, it is nearly always the case for a recursive module, that the invocations identified by its activations are identical not only in their first components (naming the module) but also in their second components (naming the activation to use for other than local (global) symbol resolution). Suppose, for example, we have the following block structure:

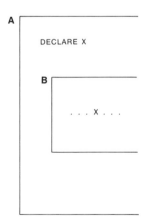

Now assume that A calls B, which recursively calls itself. Then our execution picture looks as shown on the next page. We observe that I_2 and I_3 are identical in content. Each identifies M_B as the module and A_1 as the resolver for global data (the name X).

Our general claim is that for a block-structured language, nearly always, all invocations named by activations of a recursive module are identical.

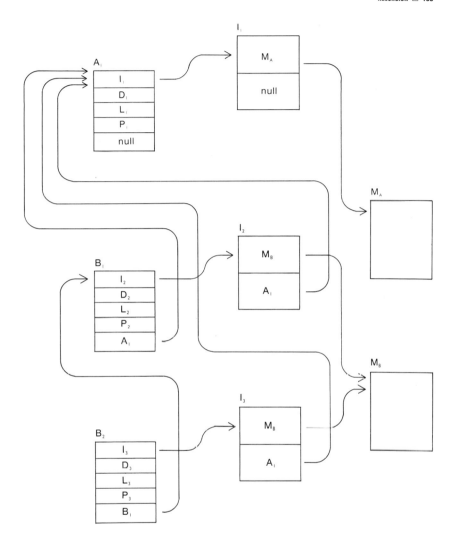

Exercises

1. Why is it not always the case that invocations of a recursive module have the same activation for global symbol resolution? (Hint: Suppose that, in the example above, A calls B, which then calls A, which in turn calls B.)

13.5 TWO COMPLEX EFFECTS OF RECURSION

In chapter 11 we looked at the effects of allowing labels and modules to be considered data types. Now we make those definitions more precise to handle recursive contexts.

Let us consider the following program segments. In each segment, R is nested within Q, which is nested within P.

```
1.    MODULE P;
          DECLARE MV MODULEVARIABLE;
          I←1;
          CALL Q;
          MODULE Q;
             DECLARE X;
             X←I;
             IF I = 1 THEN DO;
                MV←R;
                I←2;
                CALL Q;
             END;
             CALL MV;
                .

                .
             MODULE R;
                WRITE(X);
             END R;
          END Q;
      END P;


2.    MODULE P;
          DECLARE LV LABELVARIABLE;
          I←1;
          CALL Q;
             .

             .
          MODULE Q;
             DECLARE X;
             X←I;
             IF I = 1 THEN DO;
                LV←LCON;
                I←2;
                CALL Q;
             END;
             CALL R;
```

```
LCON:    WRITE(X);
         MODULE R;
             GO TO LV;
         END R;
     END Q;
   END P;
```

In each example, what is the printed value of X? 1 or 2? Let us trace each example.

In the first case, we enter Q with I = 1, having a global module variable MV. We declare X to be local and set it to 1. Since I = 1, we assign to MV the module R, bump I, and call Q recursively. This new activation of Q assigns 2 to its new X and then calls MV, whose value is the module R. In R we write X. But to which X are we referring, that of Q's first activation (1), or that of its second (2)?

In the second case, all is similar except that we have declared a label variable, and, in our first activation of Q, have assigned to it a label identifying a statement in Q. After the recursive call of Q, we call R, which executes a GO TO LV. But is transfer back to the first activation of Q, where X = 1, or to the second, where X = 2?

We favor the interpretation shared by the analogous constructs of PL/I and ALGOL: The value is 1 in both cases. Reference is to the X of the first activation of Q and thus, in the second case, transfer is to the label of that first activation.

Module and label data identify a module and a label of that module, respectively. In addition, each identifies the activation used to resolve that module's global data. In other words, each identifies an invocation, rather than just a module.

So in case 1 above, MV is given the invocation value, R, consisting of (1) the module R, and (2) the activation of Q used to resolve that R's data, namely, the current activation of Q. Thus when we finally call MV, we call an invocation that uses the first activation of Q to resolve X.

Similarly in case 2, LCON, and thus LV after the assignment, identifies the first activation of Q. So GO TO LV terminates the R activation and the second activation of Q. Subsequent reference to X is therefore to that X belonging to the first activation of Q.

These examples may seem to contain painfully complicated programming, but questions such as those raised above must be answerable in a language that is to be well-defined. One can argue reasonably that questions involving remote language use can be resolved quite arbitrarily; it is irresponsible to argue that they need not be resolved at all.

Further discussion of recursion as a programming technique can be found in [Bar68].

CHAPTER 14

Execution Monitoring

In this chapter we look at several concepts in execution control. These concepts are somewhat more sophisticated than the basic ideas presented in chapter 10. We discuss structures of importance in an execution environment of supervisors and their employed workers, in which the supervisor may interrupt the worker's progress, for various reasons, at times of certain prescribed actions by that worker. We develop a set of features that are not tied closely to any existing language; they are often similar to features built into software systems via cumbersome language tools.

14.1 LOCAL EXCEPTIONS

First let us consider the simplest kind of monitoring feature, the ability within a module to specify the action to be performed if some abnormal event, which we designate an *exception*, occurs during execution. The exception may be overflow, subscript out of range, reference to an undefined value, and so on—the set of possibilities is highly specific to the language being defined. To speak of this feature as monitoring is perhaps slightly misleading or overstating; it is really just a way to allow the possibility of some recovery (fail-soft, if not fail-safe) from potentially disastrous events that otherwise might necessitate termination of execution of the program.

We look upon exceptions as characteristic of particular operators within a language; for example, overflow is a characteristic of arithmetic operators but not of any other operators. So in defining a language that recognizes exceptions, we must define, for each operator, the set of exceptions that may be caused by its execution. We also must define the circumstances that cause that exception to be raised. Finally, we must define, for each exception, the default system action to be taken if that exception arises and the containing module has no specification for it.

Now suppose these preliminaries have been defined in some fashion. What features should the user be given to override the various (probably simplistic and fatal) default specifications?

In this discussion we intentionally avoid the common distinctions among modules, statements, and operators. They are semantically identical, in taking a set of operands and doing something to them, perhaps returning a result as an operand to some pending operator. A module is simply an operator constructed by the user of language, rather than built-in to the basic operator set of the language. A statement is a built-in operator, peculiar in that it does not return a result.

We use simple language here in suggesting that an execution consists of an operator, PROGRAM, calling in some fashion for execution of its operands, and using the results of those executions in some way. Generally, the operands are also operators that execute similarly, giving us a picture of execution as a tree, with operator names at the nonterminal nodes which then identify their operands. The manner in which a particular operator requests execution of its operands and uses their results is totally specific to that operator.

We might have, for example, a simple program, consisting of a single module A:

```
MODULE A;
    X←Y + Z;
    RETURN;
END A;
```

We could depict this module with the tree as it is shown on the following page.

Here the PROGRAM operator has a single operand, since there is only one module involved. The MODULE operator has two operands, one for each executable statement. The statement operator ← has two operands, target and source. The source is the + operator with operands Y and Z. RETURN has no operands, since A returns no result.

The main point of this picture is that we can look at any operator except PROGRAM as an operand of some other operator. And we are using a very simplistic terminology that recognizes only operators and data (terminal nodes) as language components.

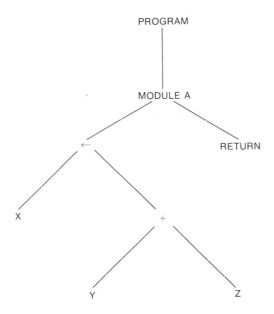

With this picture in mind, let us look at exceptions. We have already said that, for built-in operators, we have predefined the possible
exceptions and the circumstances that cause each of them to be raised.
We must also have the ability for modules to raise any of a set of exceptions. For this purpose, we define the statement

RAISEEXCEPTION(name);

Execution of this statement causes the containing module to raise the
exception that is named. The name is arbitrary; one may name an invented
exception as he chooses (or he may artificially raise a built-in exception
in this same manner).

The effect of RAISEEXCEPTION in a module execution should be
analogous to that of occurrence of an exception in a built-in operator.
What should that effect be?

We suggest that the individual to be notified if an exception arises
is the operator of which the operator raising the exception is an operand.
If, in our simple program above, the execution of + causes an overflow, the ← operator should be notified of the problem. If, on the other
hand, ← causes some exception (e.g., mismatched data types for source
and target), the operator A should be notified. If A raises some exception
(via RAISEEXCEPTION), its caller (the operator of which it is an operand)
should be notified.

We suggest further that if no action specification is encountered for the exception in the caller, no further search should be made (in the caller's caller, and so forth, out the tree). This rule stems from the philosophy that if the individual closest to a problem cannot do anything about it, no one else can either. Each exception should be local to the invoking operator activation.

We have said that an exception is fielded by the operator of which the operator causing that exception is an operand. This we provide for by allowing, in a module, a specification linking a given exception name to some attendant action. Whether such specification is with an executable statement, or has the static nature of an ALGOL declaration, depends upon the nature of the particular embedding language. In either event, we define a fielding statement of the form

EXCEPTION(name,action);

If the module containing this statement is notified of the occurrence of the named exception, the indicated action is taken.

Now we look more at that action, which we suppose to be itself a module. We suggest that the purpose of the action be, in every respect, to replace the operation that raised the exception. That operation failed in its execution for some reason, so it is reasonable to replace the operation in whatever context the exception occurred. But this replacement can work effectively only if our action has information about the failure, so that it can replace the operation intelligently. In particular, it should be able to use three special operators to obtain the following pieces of information:

- the exception name (EXCEPTIONNAME)
- the operator raising the exception (OPERATOR)
- the total set of operands of that operator (OPERAND(i))

With this information, the exception action can execute as any other module. When it completes, return is (as it would be for the failing operator) to the module specifying the exception fielding. A result may be returned if the failing operator was intended to return a result.

Let us focus this set of features on a particular example. Module M wishes to field exceptions of type ZERODIVIDE (division by zero) occurring in its operands. Division is carried out by the module DIVIDE, which at some point checks its second operand, and raises the ZERODIVIDE exception if the value of that operand is zero. The replacement of the division operation is done by FIX, as specified in M.

```
MODULE M;                              MODULE FIX;
        .                                      .
        .
        .                              IF OPERATOR = DIVIDE
        EXCEPTION(ZERODIVIDE,FIX);        ∧ EXCEPTIONNAME =
        .                                ZERODIVIDE THEN
        .                                RETURN(IF OPERAND
        .                                (1) = 0 THEN 0 ELSE
        ..DIVIDE(A,B)..                  IF OPERAND(1)>0
        .                                THEN 999 ELSE
        .                            .   −999);
END M;                                 .
                                       .
MODULE DIVIDE(X,Y);                    .
        .                          END FIX;
        .
        .
IF Y = 0 THEN RAISEEXCEPTION(ZERODIVIDE);
        .
        .
        .
END DIVIDE;
```

M calls its operand DIVIDE, passing two arguments. DIVIDE checks to determine whether or not the second has the value zero. If so, DIVIDE is terminated and the ZERODIVIDE exception is raised in M. This causes FIX to be invoked. At some point, FIX interrogates the operator raising the exception and the exception itself. Finding that DIVIDE has raised ZERODIVIDE, it then checks the first operand of DIVIDE and returns a result of 0, 999, or -999 according to the value of that operand. This result returned from FIX is taken to be the result of DIVIDE(A,B) in M.

Finally let us look at a set of default actions to be performed in the absence of any exception specification. For the exceptions built in to a language, we leave reasonable decisions to the designer of that language. But for exceptions not implicitly recognized, some general action must be taken. For this purpose we define a general exception called FAILURE. If an exception arises for which no action specification is given (either built-in or user-defined), the default action is to raise the FAILURE exception in the module of which the failing operator is an operand. The caller of that module may contain an action specification for the FAILURE exception. If not, the FAILURE default is carried out (program termination). This is a general and useful technique for handling operator failures. Sufficient information is available to the exception specification actions to permit them to simulate the operators that they are replacing.

Exercises

1. How should an exception or interrupt module fit into the execution environment when it is invoked; that is, how should its global symbols be resolved?

14.2 SUPERVISION

So far we have discussed only conditions intuitively characterizable as involving errors, failures of operators to do their jobs. We classify these as *local exceptions*, local in the sense that notification of the raising of one of them is made only to the invoking operator activation; activations further out the call chain are not involved.

Now we look at a more general variety of monitoring that we shall call *supervision*. Two important differences separate supervision from local exception handling:

1. Interruption of an operator's execution need not imply error failure. Later, the operator may continue its work.

2. A hierarchy of exception handling is possible. That is, an execution may be monitored by other than the invoking operator activation. In fact, the more remote the monitoring activation, the more power it can exert. This bureaucratic kind of picture, which we are calling supervision, is also called *hypervision*, to emphasize the many levels of supervisory hierarchy involved.

The general capability that we are defining is for an activation to initiate another activation, but to retain power to suspend that latter activation and regain control upon occurrence of certain specified events. In particular, the activation can interrupt a called activation upon its execution of any operator designated in a statement of the form

       INTERRUPT(operator,action);

This statement enables the executing activation for interruption of called activations whenever they execute the indicated operator. We can later override this specification by a statement of the form

       DISREGARD(operator);

For simplicity, we assume that such specifications apply only to activations tied directly by call to the current activation. Later we shall extend this domain.

Now, as with exceptions, we examine the actions that may be performed when an activation is interrupted. Again we assume that the action specification is itself given as a module to be activated. We identify three possible types of action by the interruptor:

1. He may terminate the operator, replacing its result with his own computation.

2. He may take note of the occurrence, and then let the interrupted activation proceed normally, as though never interrupted.

3. He may decide to terminate the activation.

To support these features, we need several operators. As with exceptions, we need to be able to discover what operator caused the interruption, and we must have access to its operands. To support action 1, we must also have the statement,

RESUME(result);

which causes the interrupted activation to resume execution, with the interrupted operator canceled and its result replaced as indicated.
For action 2, we need another type of termination statement,

CONTINUE;

which causes the interrupted activation to continue execution normally.
For action 3, we have a third termination statement,

ABORT(result);

which kills the interrupted activation, and returns control to the point following the call in the current activation. The specified result is taken to be the result of the aborted activation.

A particularly useful feature available as a type of interruptor action is the specification, within the interruptor, of an action to be taken in the environment of the interrupted operator rather than in the environment of the interruptor. Such a specification is denoted syntactically to be for this use; the undeclared symbols within it are resolved as though they appeared within the interrupted operator. This gives the interruptor a stylized way of accessing data of the interrupted operator—data that normally might not be available to him.

These are the basic features required for simple single-level supervision. But how do we support the multiple-level picture we spoke of?
Two significant generalizations are needed:

1. Enabling for an operator extends not only to immediately called activations, but also to all activations further down the call chain.

2. If several activations are enabled for an operator, then its execution is interrupted by that activation furthest up the call chain from the current operator activation.

To support the first generalization above, we simply generalize ABORT, which we now define to abort all activations below the current one, rather than just the activation interrupted.

For the second generalization, we complicate our model slightly in the interest of a more workable bureaucracy. We would like to be able to have a situation in which all interruptors are notified of an event, and all may take some action. Nevertheless we want to retain the supervisory principle that the highest ranking of contending interruptors (the one remotest from the current activation in the call chain) is given control.

To this end, we extend the definitions of two of our interrupt-terminating operators, RESUME and CONTINUE. When a RESUME or CONTINUE is executed, the next activation down the chain from the current interruptor is inspected and, if it is enabled for the interrupted operator, its indicated action is taken. The search continues on down toward the interrupted activation. Thus a succession of interruptions may be honored, from top to bottom in the chain.

Of course we must have some tight protocol to govern this freedom. No enabled activation can be allowed to undo the action of a prior one (and, in the case of ABORT, a later activation cannot get interrupt control at all). So we establish the following conventions:

■ An interruptor can determine whether there has been a prior higher-level interruption, and, if so, what type of termination was indicated for it.

■ If a prior interruptor terminated with RESUME(result), the current interruptor must terminate with RESUME with no result value. The value is taken from above.

■ If a prior interruptor terminated with CONTINUE, the current interruptor may terminate in any way he desires.

These conventions establish our hierarchical control picture, giving greatest power to the highest-level interruptor, but with potential for action by all interruptors.

The features that we have described so far involve no intelligence or cooperation on the part of the interrupted activation. Modules can be written without knowledge of any interrupt enabling that will have ensued prior to their activation. We would like to add one feature that does involve cooperation, the statement operator

PAUSE(integer);

This operator can be enabled for interruption just as any other. The interrupt occurs when the PAUSE is executed. The interruptor has access to the qualifying integer for use in analyzing the interruption. The purpose of PAUSE is to cause an interruption and thus inform the interruptor of the executing activation's progress. If there is no enabled interruptor, the PAUSE has no effect.

Let us conclude this discussion of supervision with an example illustrating some of the features described. Suppose we have a call chain in which activation A_1 has called B_1 which has called C_1. Both A_1 and B_1 are enabled for interruption of the operator $+$. A_1 wishes to replace sums by differences, while B_1 wishes only to count occurrences of $+$.

```
MODULE A;                    MODULE X;

    .                            .
    .                            .
    INTERRUPT( + , X);           IF OPRTR = + THEN
    .                            RESUME(OPND(1)-OPND(2));
    .                            .
END A;                           .
                             END X;
MODULE B;
    .                        MODULE Y;
    .                            .
    INTERRUPT( + ,Y);            .
    .                            IF OPRTR = + THEN DO;
    '                               COUNT←COUNT + 1;
END B;                              IF TERMTYPE = RESUME THEN RESUME;
                                    CONTINUE;
MODULE C;                        END;
    .
    .                            .
    ... + ...                END Y;
    .
    .
END C;
```

When $+$ is executed in C_1, the enabling in A_1 causes an activation for x. x interrogates the operator and defines its result as the difference of the operands. This result is used in the RESUME command.

Now the call chain is searched; it is determined that B_1 is also enabled for $+$ by module Y. So Y is invoked, and it updates a counter. It checks to see whether a previous RESUME has been given. If so, it terminates by RESUME, otherwise by CONTINUE; in the latter case, the $+$ is done normally where it appears.

Exercises

2. It might be useful to tie together the concepts of exception handling and supervision by allowing the interruptions not only of certain operators, but also of specified exception occurrences.

(a) Define an extension providing this extended supervision.

(b) In what ways does this supervision differ from normal operator interruption?

14.3 COROUTINES

In this chapter we have seen that control within an activation need not always consist of entering at the start, proceeding to the end, and then returning to the point of call. Exceptions and interruptions may cause different kinds of control flow. Now we shall discuss a similar concept, differing by the fact that activations proceed in complete cooperation with each other, with control switching periodically between them. Usually called the *coroutine concept*, this approach is related to supervision and used commonly as a programming technique. Since it is not generally available directly in high-level languages, it is often simulated.

We envision two activations A and B, interacting as shown below:

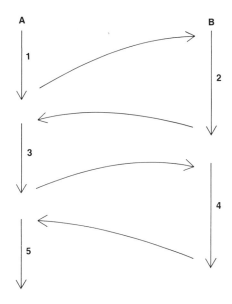

A is executing first (1) and eventually calls B. B executes until it reaches some agreed upon point (2), at which time, control is returned to A, following the point of call. A executes until a subsequent agreed upon point is reached (3). Then control returns to B, and execution of B resumes at the point where it had halted (4). This control exchange process continues until both A and B have completed—in our example, first B, and then A (5).

The interesting aspect of this execution mode is the symmetry of the cooperating activations. Aside from the fact that control must enter and leave through the same activation (a formality that is easily obtainable), each activation has the same degree of autonomy, the same ability to monitor the other's progress. And surely this is a natural mode of communication, simulating such real-life processes as telephone conversations or two-party discussions in which only one person speaks at a time.

What language operators do we need to support the coroutine concept? To answer this question, we again assume a simple case of two participating activations. The initial calls and final returns need no new definitions, except for a flag appended to the initial call of the second routine (B above) to say that the called and calling routines are to act as coroutines. Establishing this information here obviates the need for passing it at each switch of control.

Only one new statement operator is needed:

REVERSE(result);

This operator suspends the currently executing member of the coroutine pair, and returns control to the other, possibly passing a result value for this portion of the execution. REVERSE can be used identically in either member, there is no supervisory concept here of one activation interrupting execution of another.

A and B above might be coded as follows, presuming A to be entered first:

```
MODULE A;                        MODULE B;
       .                                .
       1                                2
       .                                .
   CALL B, COROUTINE;              REVERSE;
       .                                .
       3                                4
       .                                .
   REVERSE;                        RETURN;
       .                                .
       5                           END B;
       .
END A;
```

This modest-sized language extension is adequate to carry our program bureaucracy picture from one of error recovery and supervision to one also involving cooperation. All of these features, together, facilitate programmed modeling of systems involving supervision and cooperation among various processes. Further treatment of execution monitoring, supervision, and coroutines can be found in [Fis70].

Exercises

3. How might PL/I label variables be used to simulate the effect of co-routines?

4. Generalize the coroutine picture to allow any number of intercommunicating coroutines.

CHAPTER 15

Multiprocessing

We have progressed in our development of control structures from the simple sequential ones of chapter 10 through the features for exception handling and supervision in chapter 14. But in all of our discussions, we have recognized only the possibility of a single executing stream of instructions. Whenever one activation (say, of an operator) begins to execute, another stops at least temporarily to allow that execution. There may be, at some time in execution, many activations, but only one is executing.

Now we go a step further, and investigate the language impact of considering different program execution streams proceeding at the same time, that is, in parallel. Of course, such simultaneity requires multiple logical processors, each capable of executing instruction streams. The term *multiprocessor* is used to denote a computer with this capability.

Ideally, when parallel execution is involved, exactly one processor can be used for each of the parallel processes. But this is not possible when the number of processes exceeds the available number of processors. In this case, pure multiprocessing is simulated by sharing processors across processes according to some algorithm. This sharing technique is called *time-sharing*, and, in general, the simulation of multiprocessing (especially when only one processor is available) is called *multiprogramming*.

We investigate three language aspects of multiprocessing: (1) the logical language structures supporting it, (2) the features available for communication between processes executing in parallel, and (3) the protocols regulating such processes' access to common, shared data.

Finally, we look briefly at multiprogramming. Let us emphasize now that the language relevance of multiprogramming is indistinguishable from that of true multiprocessing. The simulation results only in increased execution times and some decrease in problems normally associated with multiprocessing. But, multiprogramming and multiprocessing are to the user, logically, the same.

Before proceeding to look at multiprocessing as a language feature, we should observe that it can be examined from other points of view. If two processes are executing concurrently only because the processors for executing them are available, and if those processes are totally independent of, and unrelated to, one another (they neither communicate nor have access to common data), then there need be no language significance to the multiprocessing involved. Viewed in this way, multiprocessing is a computer system capability, governed by rules for allocating processors to programs in some optimal manner.

At an intermediate stage of interaction is the environment in which two processes are unaware of each other's existence, yet they happen to be executing concurrently and accessing a common library of data, perhaps for reading that data, perhaps for updating it. It would be ideal if we could divorce this situation from language consideration. Unfortunately, this is usually impossible. The system must worry about cases in which one process may be updating or writing data that another is trying either to use or to update. Safeguards must be provided to ensure validity of all references in this potentially chaotic environment. Usually, a system trying to provide this safety requires that users of such data provide "helpful hints" as language addenda to their programs (e.g., a certain datum will be read and used but never updated by a certain program).

Of importance to us is the situation in which a single application is using multiprocessing. Various processes within the application communicate with one another and have access to common data. Here, multiprocessing serves as a set of features for use by multiple concurrent processes who desire to work together effectively. This situation is quite different from the previous case in which the system tries to provide safety for independent users who neither know nor care about one another.

15.1 LANGUAGE STRUCTURES FOR MULTIPROCESSING

Let us look first at the basic language requirements for multiprocessing. These are basic in that we do not initially consider problems either of common data access or of process synchronization. We need first a way for an executing process to request the execution, in parallel with his own, of some other process. We consider this feature within the confines of a single program, since that is the largest execution unit defined.

Our multiprocessing structure can be conveniently defined in terms of the execution model of chapter 11. Suppose that some activation A_3 of the call chain is in execution, and a command is encountered for creating a new activation A_4 (e.g., a CALL statement). Further suppose that the command has appended to it the designation NEWPROCESS (name). This means that a new, named process (call it P_2) is to be created, headed by the named invocation; that new process is to execute in parallel with the current one, P_1. We diagram this as follows:

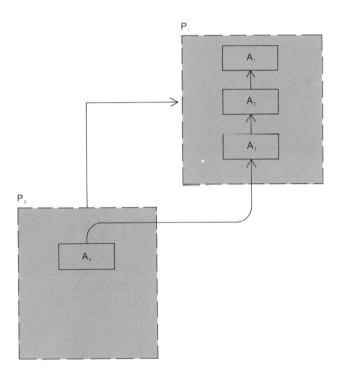

Activation A_3 within process P_1 used CALL NEWPROCESS to initiate process P_2, whose head activation is A_4. Since P_2 will execute concurrently with P_1, there is no concept of A_4 returning to A_3, and thus no link between the two activations. We do, however, link P_2 to its initiating process P_1, and we say that P_2 is a subprocess of P_1.

Notice our superimposing of a process structure on our activation model. Any executing process has an activation chain as in our simple model. And no activation can be split across processes; CALL NEWPROCESS always initiates a new process and a new activation.

Now we extend our picture, omitting the individual activations that may occur by normal calls within a process. P_1 and P_2 continue to execute.

At some point, P_1 issues another CALL NEWPROCESS; P_2 does likewise. Then our picture expands into the following:

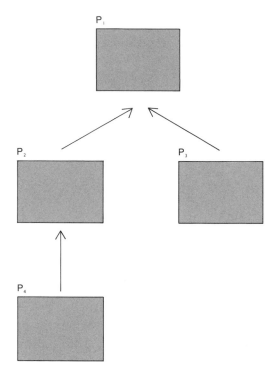

P_1 has initiated another subprocess, P_3; P_2 has initiated P_4.

Our ultimate generalization is a process tree, with each process (except the root process P_1) being a subprocess of exactly one other process. And note that all of the processes of such a tree may be executing simultaneously.

Why have we linked the processes into a tree structure? What use do we make of these links? Surely, since they are proceeding simultaneously, they must have a relatively high degree of execution independence from one another. The answer is that we want to introduce two simple kinds of supervisory features directly related to the process structure. First, we propose that a process have the ability to terminate execution of any of its immediate subprocesses. For this purpose, we define the command

    KILL(processname);

which is honored so long as the named process is an immediate subprocess of the process issuing the KILL.

This feature has the potential of creating orphan processes. If, for example, the processes in our last picture are named P1, P2, P3, and P4, and P1 issues the command KILL (P2); what happens to P4? There are two reasonable possibilities:

> 1. P2 and the entire process tree below it (in this case only P4) is terminated.
>
> 2. P2 is terminated, and its immediate subprocesses (here only P4) are made subprocesses of the killer (P1).

Notice that this situation arises not only when a process is killed, but also when it completes prior to completion of certain of its subprocesses. We offer our two possibilities as reasonable in either case of termination.

A second feature required for multiprocessing is the ability of a process to stop and restart its subprocesses as they proceed. A STOP command stops the execution of a subprocess. A START command can be given later to continue the execution of that subprocess from the point at which it was stopped.

So we are providing only a minimal capability for a process to supervise a subprocess. Next we look at techniques for communication between processes; these involve cooperation rather than just a one-way capability.

15.2 PROCESS COMMUNICATION

Now we look at communication between two processes, both presumably desiring such communication. We must make a strong premise about the parallel nature of two process executions, assuming that they are not communicating using the special techniques that we describe in a moment:

> Suppose we have a process tree with executing processes P1 and P2. Given a point in the execution of P1, there is no way to determine, at the time P1 reaches that point, where in execution P2 may be. Furthermore, unless one is a descendant (subprocess, subprocess of a subprocess, or more distant offspring) of the other, there is no way to state any limit on where P2 may be.
>
> If P1 initiates P2, we can make the following limits:
>
> > 1. At any point in P2, it is certain that P1 is not at any point prior to its initiating of P2.

2. At any point in P1 prior to initiating P2, it is certain that P2 does not exist.

This premise is not overstated; it cannot be viably replaced in a multi-processing system by any weaker statement, such as "if P1 has executed only one statement, then P2 has executed no more than three statements." No programming system and no language can embody any such promises relating to time-dependencies.

We look in section 15.3 at the obvious need for processes to communicate information by use of common data. But first we must specify an even more basic communication capability, that of synchronization. Consider two cooperating processes, P1 and P2, initially proceeding independently of each other. P1 and P2 have prearranged, however, that P1 must not continue beyond a given point in its execution until P2 has performed some critical function required for P1 to proceed. We speak of this function of P2's as an *event*, and we use an EVENT datum to communicate the event. An EVENT datum has one of two values: It is either *pending* or *transpired*.

We define three statement operators for use with event variables:

POST(event) sets the event to transpired.

CANCEL(event) sets the event to pending.

WAIT(event) prevents the executing process from proceeding until the event is transpired.

Suppose that an event datum EV is known to both P1 and P2 and initialized to pending before activation of either P1 or P2. Our above case can be programmed as follows:

```
P1    .              P2   .
      .                   .
      WAIT(EV);           critical function
      .                   POST(EV);
      .                   .
      .                   .
                          .
```

P1 and P2 proceed independently until P1 issues the WAIT. If, at that time, P2 has not completed the critical function, EV will have a value of pending, and P1 will not proceed. When the critical function is completed, the POST sets EV to transpired; the WAIT is satisfied and P1 continues.

We have stressed the importance of cooperation between P1 and P2. If confusion arises, many synchronization problems can develop, the worst of which is the deadlock problem. Suppose that P1 and P2 are cooperating processes and that E1 and E2 are event data, both initially pending. Consider the following:

```
P1    .                 P2    .
      .                       .
   WAIT(E1);             WAIT(E2);
      .                       .
      .                       .
   POST(E2);             POST(E1);
      .                       .
      .                       .
```

Both P1 and P2 proceed until they reach their respective WAIT's. At those times, neither can proceed until one has posted the event on which the other is waiting. A deadlock results.

This example shows the simplest case of deadlock. With many processes involved, the situation can be much more complex. System diagnosis and resolution of such a situation can be a major design problem in a multiprocessing system.

15.3 SHARED DATA

We proceed now to the general case of data communication between processes. To begin, we must define an *atomic operation sequence*. We say that a sequence of one or more operations within a process is atomic if other processes may access data known to that sequence perhaps before, perhaps after, but never during, execution of the sequence. The sequence thus appears to others to be indivisible, a single atomic operation.

Unfortunately the gap between physically atomic operations and logically atomic ones is as great as the programmer makes it. The interrelationships among elements of a huge array or string may be such that interrogation of it during an operation sequence that updates it may give nonsensical and inconsistent values. The updating process is far from atomic, physically, yet it may be desirable to consider it logically atomic. This desire expresses the essence of the problem of data sharing among processes. For such sharing, involving both interrogation and updating, we must provide for certain critical sections of code to appear atomic, so that other processes cannot view that section's data while the code is executing.

Of course, an ideal solution to the problem would be a linguistic ability to use syntactic bracketing to indicate that a section of code is to be considered atomic. Unfortunately, this solution is far too difficult to support with current computer hardware and operating systems. A compromise solution, one that involves cooperation, can be arrived at:

> A code sequence is effectively atomic only if both
> the coder of that sequence and the coders of all

other processes accessing its data treat it as atomic.

We define two operators, OBTAIN and RELEASE, which must be atomic. Each works with a datum of type RESOURCE (really just an integer), initialized to the value 1. Intuitively, we associate a RESOURCE with the data of a code sequence that is to be atomic. **OBTAIN(resource)** requests exclusive rights to that data until a subsequent **RELEASE(resource)** is issued to relinquish those rights. OBTAIN is successful for the executing process unless the resource has already been obtained, in which case the process attempting to obtain it must wait until the resource is released. OBTAIN and RELEASE are used both by a process executing an atomic operation sequence, and by a process accessing its data (the access, as well as the updating, is critical and should appear atomic).

More formal definitions of OBTAIN and RELEASE are given by the expansions below. The module ENQUEUE causes an obtainer to be placed in a queue (in this case, always a simple queue of length 1) until a RELEASE is issued for the resource to be obtained. At that time, the obtainer obtains the resource (via DEQUEUE) and proceeds.

```
MODULE OBTAIN(RES);            MODULE RELEASE(RES);
   DECLARE RES RESOURCE;          DECLARE RES RESOURCE;
   RES←RES-1;                     RES←RES + 1;
   IF RES≥0 THEN RETURN;          IF RES>0 THEN RETURN;
   CALL ENQUEUE(RES);             CALL DEQUEUE(RES);
   RETURN;                        RETURN;
END OBTAIN;                    END RELEASE;
```

Let us trace a simple example involving processes P1 and P2. P1 has an atomic section of code to protect, and P2 makes references to data of that section. We assume P1 and P2 to know a common RESOURCE named R.

```
P1   .                P2   .

     .                     .

     OBTAIN(R);            OBTAIN(R);
     critical code         references to
     RELEASE(R);             critical-code data
     .                     RELEASE(R);

     .                     .

                           .
```

There are, of course, many possible orderings of execution between P1 and P2. Let us assume that R has been initialized to 1, and that P2 is first to try to obtain R. OBTAIN decrements R to 0 and, since R is nonnegative, returns; P2 proceeds. Before P2 has released R, P1 tries to obtain R. OBTAIN decrements R to -1 and, therefore, calls ENQUEUE, passing R.

ENQUEUE causes P1 to be stopped and enqueued. Now P2 finishes his references to critical-code data and releases R. RELEASE increments R to 0 and calls DEQUEUE, passing R. DEQUEUE allows P1 to obtain R and proceed.

It is easy to see that when P1 obtains R, P2 is blocked similarly from access until P1 releases R. The control enforced via the resource datum ensures sequential, rather than parallel, accesses to the critical code by cooperating processes. Thus we speak of OBTAIN and RELEASE as sequencing operators.

The reader has probably noticed a strong similarity between sequencing and synchronizing, a close analogy between OBTAIN and WAIT, and between RELEASE and POST. In fact, they are nearly identical. If we initialize our resource to 0 instead of 1, and consider pending to be 0 and transpired to be 1, then it is easy to verify that OBTAIN(resource) is exactly the definition of WAIT(event), and RELEASE(resource) is exactly POST(event). Synchronization and sequencing are logically the same phenomenon, though intuitively they may seem quite distinct. Further discussions of synchronization and sequencing can be found in [Fis70], [And65], [Dij65], [Knu66], [Dij68(May)], and [Hab67].

Exercises

1. Generalize the definitions of OBTAIN and RELEASE to an environment of N processes sharing accessibility to a resource, and in which not more than K<N of these processes are allowed simultaneous access.

2. Define the functions ENQUEUE and DEQUEUE for the generalized case above.

3. Why must the functions OBTAIN and RELEASE be atomic operations?

15.4 MULTIPROGRAMMING

Strictly speaking, multiprogramming, or time-sharing, is not a language issue. It is a system technique for supporting multiprocessing in the absence of enough processing units to go around. We look at the subject because of the common use of its terminology and techniques in discussions related to programming languages.

Let us take a simple case of two processes supposedly executing together, but in a system having only one processor. What requirements must this processor meet to simulate the multiprocessing environment?

If the processes are totally independent, having no communication, the processor may execute all of one, then all of the other, or alternate between them in any fashion. There are no constraints in this case (recall the total indeterminacy of relative execution points of independent processes).

The only situations in which we must be careful are those that involve WAIT or OBTAIN. Our processor interprets a WAIT or OBTAIN by executing our expansion for OBTAIN. If an ENQUEUE is necessary, the processor must switch to the other process and execute it until it issues a POST or RELEASE on the event or resource datum named in the WAIT or OBTAIN. At that time, the selection of which process to continue is again theoretically arbitrary.

The discussion above is a gross oversimplification of multiprogramming. We have oversimplified in three major areas:

1. Decisions of when to execute which process are often important in practice.

2. There may be any number of extant processes, not just two.

3. There may be any number of processors available.

These considerations are part of the general problem of allocating processors to processes optimally. Two goals affect this optimization, with varying weights dependent on the entire computer installation environment:

■ high total throughput (total amount of code executed per unit of real time)

■ fast apparent response time for all system users

If execution is proceeding in an interactive environment with a single processor and a number of users typing in requests and expecting answers at terminals then obviously that processor should switch frequently among the users (processes). They cannot distinguish between computer response times of microseconds or milliseconds, or even of a second or two. And they certainly cannot enter their requests with computer speed. There is no reason to dedicate a processor to one user throughout his terminal session or even through processing of a single request. It is better to allot time more evenly by giving brief time-slices to all the users. Obviously the desirability of servicing multiple users affects the processor allocation algorithm.

In the general case of n processes and a pool of $m < n$ processors, the allocation algorithm becomes even more complicated, to satisfy varying response requirements. To help the system allocate processors intelligently, it is common for processes to specify priorities for their executions. Assume, for example, that one process has a lower priority than another, and both wish to proceed (no WAIT's or OBTAIN's are pending). If only a single processor is available, it will be dedicated to the second process, until it completes or must wait, or until another process having an even higher priority is ready for execution.

We repeat that multiprogramming is not a language issue; it is a problem of optimization in matching processors to processes. Such problems need not concern us directly in our study of languages. We remain not only independent of physical machines and processors, but also independent of the number of them available for our use. Language development can be totally sheltered from the many problems associated with system support for multiprogramming.

CHAPTER 16

List Processing in LISP

The programming languages we have examined thus far, and most of the language concepts we have developed, have been, as we have labeled them, "general-purpose"; they have been developed for use in a wide variety of interdisciplinary programming applications. While such study is an effective approach to the vast area of programming languages, the general-purpose language is not the optimal answer to all problems of the future. While general concepts may be used to build physical or conceptual machines for language interpretation (as we indicated in the introduction), the emphasis in the future must be on the development of highly specialized languages with which users who are not necessarily programmers can communicate problems effectively. In the next two chapters, we look at two such specialized languages, and in chapter 18, we investigate techniques for building such languages out of more general concepts.

The first specialized language that we look at is LISP, a language intended specifically for, and named for, list processing. LISP was first developed in 1960. We discuss only those aspects of the basic language providing directly for list processing. If the reader desires to know more of its conventional features such as variables and arithmetic, he can investigate the references given at the end of this chapter.

It is perhaps unfortunate for teaching, though certainly complimentary to the LISP language, that we must immediately emphasize three important concepts native to LISP, concepts that we have not encountered previously:

1. the specialized list-processing capabilities of LISP

2. the radically different type of control flow within LISP programs

3. the critical ability to represent LISP programs as LISP data structures

While these ideas are related, and embedded within a very small language, they are distinct concepts to which we might devote separate chapters. Instead, we ask that the reader bear in mind the distinctions among these concepts as we present them; LISP combines them so elegantly that one tends to lump all together and call the resultant language concept LISP.

If LISP were a large and cumbersome language, we would now return to the three concepts above, and dwell further on them in abstract before undertaking a language description. But since LISP is small, we prefer to give a short description of the important aspects of the language, and then to discuss the concepts, illustrated with LISP itself.

16.1 THE LISP LANGUAGE

We now examine the basic features of the LISP language.

16.1.1 SYMBOLIC EXPRESSIONS

All LISP data are represented syntactically by *symbolic expressions (S-expressions)*. An S-expression consists of either an *atomic symbol* or a pair of S-expressions. (Note that this definition is recursive.)

An atomic symbol is just a string of characters, arbitrary in information content, and scalar in having no internal structure. Examples of LISP atomic symbols are:

```
A
2.3
XYZ
B2
```

The second kind of expression (a nonatomic S-expression) is written as a pair of S-expressions separated by a period, and surrounded by parentheses. The following list shows increasingly complex S-expressions, the simplest of which is the atomic symbol A.

```
A
(A.B)
(A.(B.C))
```

((A.B).(C.D))
(((A.B).C).D)

Structurally, S-expressions can be characterized as binary trees, with atomic symbols as leaves and nonatomic S-expressions as intermediate nodes. Our above examples can be represented in tree form as follows:

A

A

(A.B)

(A.B)

(A.(B.C))

(A.(B.C))

((A.B).(C.D))

((A.B).(C.D))

(((A.B).C).D)

(((A.B).C).D)

16.1.2 OPERATORS ON SYMBOLIC EXPRESSIONS

Two operators are available in LISP for dissecting S-expressions. If we let the variable name e denote an S-expression of the form (e1.e2) then

$$CAR[e] = e1$$
$$CDR[e] = e2$$

CAR returns the left half of a binary tree, CDR the right half. These operators can be applied to our above examples as follows:

CAR[A] is undefined	CDR[A] is undefined
CAR[(A.B)] = A	CDR[(A.B)] = B
CAR[(A.(B.C))] = A	CDR[(A.(B.C))] = (B.C)
CAR[((A.B).(C.D))] = (A.B)	CDR[((A.B).(C.D))] = (C.D)
CAR[(((A.B).C).D)] = ((A.B).C)	CDR[(((A.B).C).D)] = D

The mnemonic value of the terms CAR and CDR is questionable; words like HEAD and TAIL would be more suggestive of their functions. Actually, the terms CAR and CDR were derived from the original LISP machine implementation as abbreviations for "contents of address in register" and "contents of decrement in register," respectively. They are by now well-established in the world of computer science.

A single operator is avilable for building new S-expressions from old ones. If e1 and e2 are S-expressions, then

$$CONS[e1;e2] = (e1.e2)$$

Again we look at our previous examples, noting that CONS can never yield an atomic symbol:

$$CONS[A;B] = (A.B)$$
$$CONS[A;(B.C)] = (A.(B.C))$$
$$CONS[(A.B);(C.D)] = ((A.B).(C.D))$$
$$CONS[((A.B).C);D] = (((A.B).C).D)$$

If e1 and e2 are S-expressions and e is a nonatomic S-expression, it is easy to verify the following identities:

$$CAR[CONS[e1;e2]] = e1$$
$$CDR[CONS[e1;e2]] = e2$$
$$CONS[CAR[e];CDR[e]] = e$$

CONS, incidentally, stands for "construct" and thus appears to be a more appropriate acronym than CAR or CDR.

The operator EQ checks two atomic symbols to see whether or not they are identical, and returns the atomic symbol T (true) or F (false) accordingly. EQ is not defined for nonatomic S-expressions.

$$EQ[A;B] = F$$
$$EQ[AB;AB] = T$$
$$EQ[A;(A.B)] \text{ is undefined}$$
$$EQ[(A.B);(A.B)] \text{ is undefined}$$

CAR, CDR, and EQ are defined only for atomic symbols. So LISP includes another operator that can be used to determine whether or not an S-expression is atomic.

$$ATOM[(A.B)] = F$$
$$ATOM[A] = T$$

Another operation, which for readability we show as a type of notation, is the conditional expression:

$$[p_1 \rightarrow e_1; p_2 \rightarrow e_2; ..., p_n \rightarrow e_n]$$

Here $p_1, p_2, ..., p_n$ are S-expressions, or operations yielding values of T or F (thus we speak of them as *predicates*), and $e_1, e_2, ..., e_n$ are arbitrary S-expressions, or operations. The value of the entire conditional expression is the value of the e_i corresponding to the leftmost p_i whose value is T. In ALGOL notation, this would be expressed by

IF p_1 THEN e_1 ELSE IF p_2 THEN e_2 ELSE...ELSE IF p_n THEN e_n

The value of a conditional expression is undefined if all p_i's evaluate to F.

16.1.3 NOTATIONAL SHORTHANDS

Before proceeding to a few examples, we introduce several notational conveniences. These are in no way basic to the language itself—just shorthand notations recognized by the LISP interpreter and translated into language equivalents.

One often finds it necessary to nest groups of CAR's and CDR's, as in

CAR[CDR[CAR[CAR[X]]]]

This cumbersome notation can be avoided by stringing together A's (for CAR) and D's (for CDR) between a C and an R indicating a single apparent operator. Thus the notation above can be abbreviated to

CADAAR[X]

The other notation we wish to use is called list notation. The reader may wonder why we have spoken of LISP as a list-processing language—binary trees are the only kind of data structure that we have described. But such trees are a medium for representing lists. Suppose we have a list of symbols A, B, C, D, and E. We can represent the list in tree form as

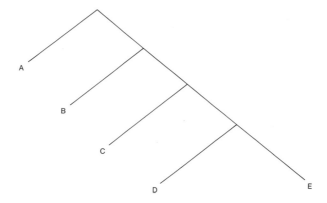

or in S-expression form as

(A.(B.(C.(D.E))))

This way of representing lists is awkward. Consider the means of obtaining each element. Let x represent (A.(B.(C.(D.E)))). Then

CAR[X] = A
CADR[X] = B
CADDR[X] = C
CADDDR[X] = D
CDDDDR[X] = E

We almost have a pattern above, in which the nth element of the list is given by CAD...DR[X], where n-1 D's are present. This pattern holds except for the last element. One cannot use the pattern to obtain an arbitrary element of an arbitrary list. If the element to be obtained is the last one, the retrieval scheme does not work. This deficiency is not overcome easily, because there is no convenient way of determining beforehand which is the last list element.

An alternative approach that solves these problems is represented in tree form as

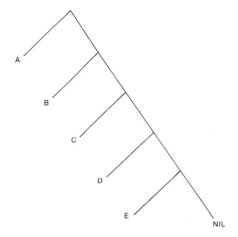

NIL Is a special symbol known as a *list terminator.* It signals the end of a list, and its presence ensures that our above pattern works for retrieving all elements of the list, including the last, which immediately precedes NIL.

LISP provides a shorthand list notation according to this representation. One can write the *list expression*

(A B C D E)

as shorthand for the equivalent S-expression

(A.(B.(C.(D.(E.NIL)))))

Exercises

1. Express the following lists as S-expressions:

(a) ()
(b) (A)
(c) ((A))

16.1.4 EXAMPLES

Now we look at some examples of function definitions in LISP, all of which are built from the operators (primitive functions) that we have described.

Example 1.

We define a function FA, which returns the leftmost atomic symbol (atom, for short) of its S-expression operand x.

$$FA[x] = [ATOM[x] \rightarrow x;$$
$$T \rightarrow FA[CAR[x]]]$$

Suppose that FA receives as operand the S-expression ((A.B).C). Then we evaluate FA[((A.B).C)] as follows:

FA is defined as a conditional expression. ATOM[((A.B).C)] = F so we pass on to the next case, T, which is, of course, T (true). So FA[((A.B).C)] = FA[CAR[((A.B).C)]] = FA[(A.B)] (note the recursive call of FA). ATOM[(A.B)] = F so FA[(A.B)] = FA[CAR[(A.B)]] = FA[A]. ATOM[A] = T so FA[A] = A so FA[CAR[(A.B)]] = A, so FA[(A.B)] = A, so FA[CAR[((A.B).C)]] = A, so FA[((A.B).C)] = A.

Example 2.

Recall that the EQ operator is defined only for atomic symbols. We find it useful to define a function EQUAL that takes arbitrary S-expression arguments and indicates whether they are identical.

$$EQUAL[x;y] = [ATOM[x] \rightarrow [ATOM[y] \rightarrow EQ[x;y];$$
$$T \rightarrow F];$$
$$EQUAL[CAR[x];CAR[y]] \rightarrow EQUAL[CDR[x];CDR[y]];$$
$$ATOM[y] \rightarrow F;$$
$$T \rightarrow F]$$

EQUAL is defined as a four-way conditional expression: (1) If x is atomic and y is atomic, then EQUAL[x;y] = EQ[x;y]. But if x is atomic and y is not, then the value returned by the function is F. (2) If y is atomic, then the value is F (since x is at this point known to be nonatomic). (3) The third possibility in the conditional is recursive on both the "if" and "then" sides: If the CAR's are EQUAL, then EQUAL[x;y] is T if and only if the CDR's are EQUAL. (4) Finally, if x and y are not atomic, and if their CAR's are not EQUAL, then x and y are not EQUAL.

The reader should endure the tedium of tracing a moderately complex example to ensure himself that this definition works, that the recursions do, in fact, eventually unwind satisfactorily. This function definition is typical of the recursive complexity of many LISP functions, and it is necessary before continuing to feel comfortable with this recursive style of definition.

Example 3.

We define a third function, MEMBER[x;y], which determines whether x is a member of the list identified by y.

MEMBER[x;y] = [NULL[y]→F;
EQUAL[x;CAR[y]]→T;
T→MEMBER[x;CDR[y]]]

NULL is an auxiliary function that indicates whether or not its argument is the null list. If y is null, obviously, x is not a member. Otherwise we test whether x is EQUAL (as defined above) to CAR[y] (the first member of y). If not, we test whether x is a MEMBER of CDR[y] (the remainder of y, omitting that first member).

Again the reader is encouraged to trace several examples to become familiar with the definition technique.

16.2 LISP PROGRAM STRUCTURE

We have defined the primitive operators of the LISP language, and a few other functions using them, but we have said nothing about a LISP program. The loose answer is that a LISP program consists of a function definition followed by the list of arguments to that function. We formalize this notion somewhat in the paragraphs below.

The syntax of a LISP program is more strict than we have indicated with our variety of notation for showing arguments, definitions, and so forth. We have described LISP using a metasyntax rather than the actual LISP syntax. Within a LISP program, every operation to be performed is represented as a LISP list, of which the first element is the operator, and the remainder of the elements are its operands. For our simple operators, this translation is fairly obvious. CAR[x], for example, is written in a program as (CAR X); CONS[x;y] is written as (CONS X Y). A conditional expression [P1→E1;P2→E2;P3→E3] becomes (COND (P1 E1) (P2 E2) (P3 E3)).

We have also defined functions in an informal manner, giving names, argument lists, and then definitions. We must find a consistent way to treat these features.

We observe first that often there is no reason to name a function (i.e., program) to be executed. It must be named only if called by itself during execution (a recursive call), or if we want to introduce it to the computing system and later call it by name. Our problem is simplified, but we must have a way of indicating how operands of the function are to be matched against parameter names used to define the function. It is ambiguous to define a function as x-y and apply it to the list (2 3). We do not know (1) whether x and y are intended to represent the operands, or (2) if they are, which name corresponds to which operand. This is taken care of in our informal terminology, in which we define FUNC[x;y] = x-y. We could write (FUNC 2 3) and be assured of the correspondence of 2 to x and 3 to y.

The LISP solution to this problem is adapted from the lambda-calculus ([Chu41]), which uses the operator λ. With this operator,

$$\lambda[[x;y];x-y][2;3]$$

indicates application of the function defined by x-y to the indicated operands. The λ indicates that x and y are names of the two operands of the function. The x and y are *bound variables* of the function. If the function were instead defined by x-y + n, with n unmentioned in the λ operand, the n would be a *free variable* of the function. Its definition would have to come from outside the function definition.

Similarly, in our formal syntax, we write a function definition followed by its operands as

$$(\text{LAMBDA}(name_1...name_n) \text{ function definition}) (opnd_1...opnd_n)$$

But now take our simple example, the function FA, which finds the first atom of an S-expression. Since FA calls itself recursively, we must have some way to give it a name for reference. We use the LABEL operator. It takes two operands, a name (the name of the function) and its definition. A complete formal definition of FA, which is named and has a bound variable x, follows.

$$(\text{LABEL FA}(\text{LAMBDA}(X)(\text{COND}((\text{ATOM X})X)((\text{QUOTE T})(\text{FA}(\text{CAR X}))))))$$

One point in the above needs explaining, the substitution of QUOTE T for T. The QUOTE is needed to indicate that T represents the literal value true, rather than a variable named T.

Now we have defined our function. We wish the LISP interpreter to execute our function by applying it to the operand (A B C). To this end, we invoke the interpreter, EVALQUOTE. We now have a complete LISP program:

$$(\text{EVALQUOTE}(\text{LABEL}...) ((\text{A B C}))$$

We have indicated the great pains taken in LISP to arrive at its program syntax, which clearly was not designed for readability. A program is just a list, with deeply nested sublists. These lists are S-expressions, which in turn are, structurally, binary trees. There are two important aspects to this language structure.

We notice first that a LISP program consists totally of functional notation. A program is a complete nest of functions, or operators, and their operands, which in general may themselves be functions. LISP has no concept of a statement as we have seen it in other languages and no kind of explicit branching capability. The flow of control can be described in a straightforward manner, as a succession of evaluations of operators and their operands.

The second, more significant aspect of the language structure is that a LISP program is neither more nor less than a LISP data structure that we may choose to execute. Programs are structurally and syntactically indistinguishable from data. The importance of this identity cannot be overemphasized; its implications are staggering.

What, after all, are the differences between programs and data? The job of each is to produce information on request; it just happens that this job is more straightforward in the case of data. Or is it? Consider the access to an element of a complicated PL/I array of structures. Certainly, some intelligence is required to select the appropriate element, given the source reference. Yet that reference is considered to be a data reference rather than a function call.

Consider, on the other hand, a program to be entered into a computing-system program library. The mechanism taking care of this job views the program as just a piece of data; it is not to be executed, but only to be stored somewhere and cataloged.

The situation is analogous to that of constants and variables as discussed in chapter 5. One man's program is another man's data. Distinction comes only from points of view, not from the data or program.

Having isomorphic data and programs in a language eases the problems of treating one entity, at one time, as data and, at another time, as program material. It also eases system transitions. For example, system data available to a user may be supported initially as a program generating the data; later, the system design may be modified so that the data is actually stored and available in its stored form.

In no other languages that we have looked at does this program/ data identity exist, except trivially in languages allowing character strings as data structures. Such representation of a program is rather useless, since it fails to indicate the structure of the program, and its operator-operand associations.

Now we observe an interesting outgrowth of program/data identity, as evidenced in LISP. Suppose we plan to write an interpreter to execute LISP programs. What language might we use to write our code?

We approach this design decision by looking at the LISP language that we are to interpret. We would like to write our interpreter in a language that facilitates work with the LISP program structure. But that structure is, as we have seen, just a LISP data structure. And what language could be more convenient for working with LISP data structures than LISP itself?

The LISP interpreter (EVALQUOTE) is, in fact, defined as a LISP program. It takes two arguments: (1) a LISP program to be executed, and (2) the argument list for that program. EVALQUOTE executes the program, which operates on the list of arguments. We speak of EVALQUOTE as a universal function, in that it can perform any function defined as a LISP program, by interpreting that program.

The reader may wish to look at EVALQUOTE, described and specified in appendix 4. We applaud its elegant brevity, which we attribute both to the elegance of the LISP language, and to the natural benefits of its being a LISP program.

The definition of a LISP interpreter, or compiler, as itself a LISP program does not, of course, suddenly give us a usable LISP language on a machine. For what intelligence understands our interpreter, which is still a LISP program? What we have described so far is perhaps interesting, but it is not a magical way of introducing LISP on a machine without knowing the language of that machine. To actually acquire our LISP support, we must take our interpreter, as defined by LISP, and do a manual translation of that program into machine language. The resultant machine-language program serves as our LISP processor. The hand translation should not be difficult—if we have described a LISP processor in LISP, we must understand LISP processing well enough to process a particular LISP program, namely, our LISP processor.

The technique of describing a language processor as a program in that language, and then manually translating the processor into machine language to obtain an executable processor, is called *boot-strapping*. This technique has many advantages in compiler writing, a particularly important one of which is exemplified by the following:

> Suppose that we are to write a FORTRAN compiler that produces, from a FORTRAN source program, extremely efficient target machine code—an optimizing FORTRAN compiler. Suppose further that we are able to write this compiler entirely, or at least chiefly, in FORTRAN. After doing so, we hand translate our compiler into machine code to get an executable compiler. Remember that this optimizing compiler produces very efficient machine-code translations of FORTRAN source programs. Now comes our coup de grace: We compile the FORTRAN version of our compiler, using our hand-translation version as our compiler. This yields a very efficient machine-code translation of that FORTRAN program (the compiler). Thus we have obtained a very efficient FORTRAN compiler.

This is one of many fallout advantages of being able to use a given language to process programs of that language. LISP is an excellent example of a language in which that approach is eminently practicable, because of its ability to handle the data structures that represent LISP programs.

16.3 LISP APPLICATION AREAS

LISP's list-processing capabilities cover a wide range of application areas: symbolic data processing, theorem proving, differential and integral calculus, formula manipulation, circuit logic, game playing, and other areas in which the application data structures are readily representable as S-expressions, particularly lists. To acquire a flavor for its features, we look at a simple example of logical expression processing. For convenience, the program is described in our loose metasyntax rather than in the strict functional notation.

Assume that we wish to describe a collection of LISP functions that evaluate certain expressions to the result T or F, depending on their truth or falseness. Any of the following kinds of expressions may be evaluated:

1. the atom TRUE or FALSE
2. a two-element list, the first element being the atom NOT, and the second an expression
3. a three-element list, the first element being the atom OR or AND, and the second and third elements being expressions

We use the normal rules for logical expression evaluation. If the expression in a NOT list evaluates to T, the NOT list evaluates to F; otherwise it evaluates to T. If both expressions in an OR list evaluate to F, the OR list evaluates to F; otherwise it evaluates to T. If both expressions in an AND list evaluate to T, the AND list evaluates to T; otherwise it evaluates to F. Examples of expressions and their values follow:

Expression	Value
TRUE	T
(AND TRUE FALSE)	F
(OR FALSE(AND TRUE TRUE))	T
(NOT(OR(AND TRUE FALSE)(NOT FALSE)))	F

We define our program as LOGIC. It uses the functions EITHER, BOTH, and OPPOSITE, which evaluate OR, AND, and NOT lists respectively.

$$LOGIC[x] = [ATOM[x] \rightarrow [EQ[x;TRUE] \rightarrow T;$$
$$T \rightarrow F];$$
$$EQ[CAR[x];OR] \rightarrow EITHER[CDR[x]];$$
$$EQ[CAR[x];AND] \rightarrow BOTH[CDR[x]];$$
$$EQ[CAR[x];NOT] \rightarrow OPPOSITE[CDR[x]];$$
$$T \rightarrow F]$$

$$EITHER[x] = [LOGIC[CAR[x]] \rightarrow T;$$
$$T \rightarrow LOGIC[CADR[x]]]$$

$$BOTH[x] = [LOGIC[CAR[x]] \rightarrow LOGIC[CADR[x]];$$
$$T \rightarrow F]$$

$$OPPOSITE[x] = [LOGIC[CAR[x]] \rightarrow F;$$
$$T \rightarrow T]$$

LOGIC is the driver of the mechanism. He checks the list argument; if it is an atom, he evaluates it himself. If TRUE, the result is T; otherwise the result is F. Thus, F is returned if a list error has yielded some strange illegal entry. If the list argument is not an atom, LOGIC uses CAR[x] to see which type of list is present and calls the appropriate function, passing the remainder of the list. Again, if a strange entry is found (other than AND, OR, or NOT), LOGIC returns F.

EITHER checks CAR of his argument list (the first expression) by invoking LOGIC to evaluate that expression; if the evaluation yields T, EITHER returns T, without looking at the second argument. Otherwise EITHER returns the value of the second expression. (Why is the second expression of the list given by CADR rather than CDR?)

BOTH is functionally similar to EITHER. If the value of the first expression is T, the value of BOTH is that of the second expression; otherwise it is F.

OPPOSITE evaluates his only expression. (Why is it given by CAR?) If it yields T, OPPOSITE returns F; otherwise OPPOSITE returns T.

This example is typical of processing applications well-suited to LISP processing. For further history and detail of the LISP language, see [McC60], [Ber64], and [McC65]. For a general discussion of list processing, see [Fos67].

Exercises

2. Consider a LISP representation of arithmetic sums and products in which the first of three members of a list is the operator, and the other members are its operands. Let the atomic data for these LISP representations be limited to the variable x, and the constants 0 and 1. Thus, for example, $(x + (1*x))*(0*x)$ would be represented by the expression:

    (MULTIPLY(ADD X (MULTIPLY 1 X))(MULTIPLY 0 X))

    Write a LISP routine SIMPLIFY(expression) to do algebraic simplifications on such expressions. In particular, the following identities should be realized:

    (ADD expression 0)   = (ADD 0 expression)   = expression
    (MULTIPLY expression 0) = (MULTIPLY 0 expression) = 0
    (MULTIPLY expression 1) = (MULTIPLY 1 expression) = expression

    Thus our above example would be simplified by the routine to the expression:

    (ADD X X)

3. Considering expressions as represented in exercise 2, write a LISP function DERIV(expression) to take the symbolic derivative of such an expression with respect to x, then simplify the result. The result of DERIV should be an expression represented in the way that we have described. Assume the following rules:

$$
\begin{aligned}
\text{DERIV}(0) \ &= \ \text{DERIV}(1) \ = \ 0 \\
\text{DERIV}(x) \ &= \ 1 \\
\text{DERIV}(e1 + e2) \ &= \ \text{DERIV}(e1) \ + \ \text{DERIV}(e2) \\
\text{DERIV}(e1 * e2) \ &= \ e1 * \text{DERIV}(e2) \ + \ e2 * \text{DERIV}(e1)
\end{aligned}
$$

4. Use FORTRAN, rather than LISP, to formulate and solve the problem of exercise 3. Define any mapping desired, to represent an expression in terms of FORTRAN arrays.

CHAPTER 17

String Processing in SNOBOL

In chapter 7 we looked at strings as a data type, and at a set of common operations natural to their manipulation. We emphasized that the features were adequate for using strings within general-purpose programming tasks involving some string handling; they were not intended to streamline solutions to problems highly specific to string manipulation.

In this chapter we discuss a language with highly extended string-handling features, a language designed specifically for string handling. The language is SNOBOL, developed in 1962. We look in particular at SNOBOL 4, the fourth evolutionary step in the language's development. We need not cover some aspects of the SNOBOL language, features such as arithmetic which are common elsewhere. But we emphasize features specific to string processing, along with some attendant concepts of control flow that we have not seen before.

For those who might consider strings a rather uninteresting data organization, we hope that this chapter liberalizes such views somewhat. While strings are admittedly rather uninteresting in form, the meanings associated with them can be of unlimited complexity—strings are, after all, the basis for written communication of information. One can do more with them than just define them, concatenate them, dissect them, and search within them. Those operations are the primitive ones in terms of which all else can be defined, but they are in no practical sense adequate for applications involving heavy use of strings. SNOBOL is designed expressly for allowing the superimposing of sophisticated semantics on simple strings; such semantics are specified as SNOBOL programs.

17.1 STATEMENT TYPES

We start by grossly characterizing SNOBOL by two types of statement: (1) the assignment statement, and (2) the pattern-matching replacement statement. The assignment statement simply assigns some expression value (string, integer, real, or pattern) to a specified variable:

> A = expression

The expression is evaluated, and the result is assigned to A.

A statement of the second type specifies a subject string, a pattern to be searched for within that string, and a string to replace the pattern if found:

> subject pattern = replacement

We might, for example, execute the following sequence:

> SUB = 'RAISE'
> SUB 'IS' = 'Z'
> OUTPUT = SUB

The variable SUB is assigned a string value. SUB is then searched for the pattern string 'IS', which in this case is found; that pattern is replaced by the string 'Z'. Thus SUB is given the new string value 'RAZE'. Assignment to the specialized variable OUTPUT indicates that the newly assigned value of SUB is to be printed out. Thus the string 'RAZE' is printed out on a standard output medium.

> Z = 'TSTS'
> P = 'TS'
> Z P = 'AR'

This sequence updates Z to 'ARTS', not to 'TSAR' or 'ARAR'. The leftmost occurrence of the pattern string is matched and acted upon.

17.2 PATTERN STRUCTURES

A string expression to be used as a pattern need not be a single string. The operations of *alternation* and *concatenation* are available to construct more complex patterns.

> PAT1 = 'OV'
> SUB = 'POVERTY'
> SUB PAT1 'E' = 'A'

SUB is searched for the pattern string consisting of the concatenation of the pattern value of PAT1 ('OV') and the pattern string 'E'. This composite pattern 'OVE' is changed to 'A', so the new value of SUB is 'PARTY'. Concatenation is indicated by adjoining patterns; no explicit operator is required.

```
PAT  =  'EA' | 'AI'
SUB  =  'TREAT'
SUB PAT  =  'OU'
```

The variable PAT is given the alternation (indicated by |, the alternation operator) of the strings 'EA' and 'AI' as a pattern value. This means that when PAT is used subsequently as a pattern, a match will be made if either string is found in the subject. In this case 'EA' is found in SUB, and changed to 'OU'. Thus SUB is given the new value 'TROUT'.

More complex patterns can be built with combinations of alternations and concatenations. The pattern

'A' 'B' | 'C' 'D'

matches either of the strings 'AB' or 'CD', while

'A' ('B' | 'C') 'D'

matches 'ABD' or 'ACD'. In the absence of parentheses, concatenation precedes alternation in pattern interpretation.

17.3 CONDITIONAL AND IMMEDIATE VALUE ASSIGNMENT

Conditional value assignment involves the association of a variable name with a pattern. If a match is found during subsequent scanning for that pattern, the string containing the matching pattern is assigned to the variable.

```
X  =  ('E' | 'I' | 'O').VAR
BASE  =  'FO'
BASE X  =  'UM'
```

The variable VAR is associated (via the period) with the pattern 'E' | 'I' | 'O'. When BASE is searched for the pattern X, a match is made with the 'O'. Thus VAR is given the value 'O' and BASE the value 'FUM'.

```
X  =  'E' | 'I'.VAR | 'O'
BASE  =  'FO'
BASE X  =  'UM'
```

Here VAR has been associated with the single-string pattern 'I'. The subsequent search matches pattern X, but it does not match the pattern 'I', so VAR remains unchanged, though BASE is updated as before.

The replacement could have been omitted from our last statement in the above example. That is, we could write

        BASE X

This is a pattern-matching statement, with no replacement. In simple cases, it has no effect, but if variables have been associated with pattern segments, assignments may be made to them, even though the subject string is not modified. Other cases in which the simple pattern-matching statement can be of use are described later in the chapter.

Suppose that we are searching for the pattern string 'ANDY'. We can use conditional value assignment to let us know if the string is found. But if the string is not found, we would still like to know how close we came ('A', 'AN', or 'AND'). This we cannot readily determine with conditional value assignment, since assignment is made only if the entire pattern is matched. But we can use *immediate value assignment*, which is similar to conditional assignment, but takes place if a subpattern associated with the variable is found; however, the entire pattern need not match.

        P = (('A' $ OUTPUT) ('N' $ OUTPUT) ('D' $ OUTPUT)'Y').OUTPUT

We denote our pattern 'ANDY' by a concatenation of patterns 'A', 'N', 'D', and 'Y'. And with each subpattern we specify the immediate-value-assignment operator $, requesting immediate value assignment to the variable OUTPUT if the subpattern is found. OUTPUT is also conditionally associated with the entire pattern. We assign a value to the variable S and match our pattern against that value as follows:

        S = 'NADANDNAY'
        S P

The result is the set of outputs:

        A
        A
        N
        D
        A

The pattern 'ANDY' was not matched, but we see that three 'A's, one 'AN', and one 'AND' were found. Immediate value assignment is generally useful for monitoring matching progress through a pattern.

17.4 SUCCESS AND FAILURE OF STATEMENTS

Thus far we have said nothing directly about flow of control through a
SNOBOL program; we have assumed that statements are executed sequentially in order of occurrence. And this is true if nothing further is
specified. It is possible, however, to attach labels to statements and
specify control transfer via those labels.

```
        LAB    statement1
               .
               .
               .
        statement2    :(LAB)
```

After statement2 is executed, control is transferred to the statement
labeled LAB. Control transfer is thus achieved by a statement appendix
indicating the target statement for the transfer.

A more interesting conditional transfer feature is based upon the
outcome of the statement being executed. We speak of each execution
of a statement in a SNOBOL program as either *succeeding* or *failing*.
While there are a number of minor conditions determining success or
failure, the primary one is the successful or unsuccessful matching of the
pattern in a pattern-matching or replacement statement. If a match is
made, the statement is said to have succeeded; if not, it has failed. SNO-
BOL exploits this characterization of statements by allowing control transfer to be conditional upon success (S) or failure (F) of a statement.

```
        statement    :S(LAB1)F(LAB2)
```

If the above statement succeeds in execution, transfer is made to the
statement labeled LAB1; if the statement fails, transfer is made to LAB2.

```
        statement    :F(LAB)
```

If this statement succeeds, execution continues with the next statement;
otherwise transfer is to LAB. Similarly one can specify only a success
transfer, in which case failure results in normal sequential processing.

The concept of success and failure of statements is applicable to
all SNOBOL statements. Even those not involved with pattern matching
may have execution contexts in which they are considered to have failed.
Our emphasis, however, is on the success or failure of pattern matches.

17.5 INDIRECT REFERENCING

SNOBOL has a completely dynamic feature for naming objects. The
transition of a string from value to name is executable with the unary

indirect-addressing operator $ (not to be confused with the binary immediate-value-assignment operator $ of section 17.3).

$$\text{LANGUAGE} = \text{'SNOBOL'}$$
$$\text{\$LANGUAGE} = \text{'STRINGY'}$$

This sequence assigns the string 'SNOBOL' to the name LANGUAGE. It then assigns the string 'STRINGY' to the name given as the string value of LANGUAGE, that is, to SNOBOL. Thus the second statement is equivalent to

$$\text{SNOBOL} = \text{'STRINGY'}$$

The indirect-addressing operator $ provides a dynamic indirect-addressing capability allowing total string flexibility in use between values and names.

17.6 SOME PRIMITIVE FUNCTIONS

SNOBOL has a large number of useful built-in functions. We shall mention several of the more common ones.

SIZE(string) returns the length of its string argument.

$$\text{SIZE('FIVE')} = 4$$

DUPL(string,integer) returns a string of duplications of its argument string.

$$\text{DUPL('TSE',2)} = \text{'TSETSE'}$$

REPLACE(string1,string2,string3) replaces within string1 each character of string2 with the corresponding (in order) character of string3.

$$\text{REPLACE('TSETSE','EST','UAM')} = \text{'MAUMAU'}$$

A *predicate function* returns a null string if a tested condition is true; otherwise the statement containing the function is considered to have failed. We can use these functions to direct control flow by also specifying success and failure labels in containing statements. They include DIFFER, IDENT, and LGT, as explained below.

DIFFER(string1,string2) is true if its argument strings are different.

$$\text{DIFFER('DING','DONG')} = \text{''} \quad \text{(the null string)}$$

IDENT(string1,string2) is the converse of DIFFER.

    IDENT('DING','DONG') fails.

LGT(string1,string2) is true if string1 lexically follows string2.

    LGT('DING','DONG') fails.

Another class of built-in functions return commonly useful patterns for subsequent matching use. But before we discuss these, we must introduce the notion of the SNOBOL cursor and scanning positions.

    We have thus far indicated that a pattern being searched for may be found anywhere within the subject string. If there are several occurrences of the pattern, the leftmost is recognized. This scanning mode is known as *unanchored mode*.

    It may often be useful to search for a pattern only at the start of the subject string (many languages indicate comments, labels, and the like, by indications in column 1 of an input line). When this requirement arises, one must enter *anchored mode*, in which all pattern searches are limited to the start of strings. Anchored mode is efficient for execution because there is no need to search through an entire string.

    Either of these two modes can be selected by assignment to the system variable &ANCHOR. If &ANCHOR has a value of 0, execution is in unanchored mode; otherwise execution is in anchored mode.

    So the choice between anchored and unanchored mode allows the programmer to limit the domain of scan for patterns. The *cursor*, in a complementary role, allows the programmer to monitor, during scanning, the subject-string position currently under scan. This is done by way of the operator @. Thus @x, where x is a variable, returns a pattern matching the null string (a match that always succeeds) and assigns to x the current cursor position within the scan of the subject string.

    Suppose that we want to search the string 'ABRACADABRA' for the substring pattern 'ADA' and obtain the position within the subject string of the match. We must first ensure that we are in unanchored mode (in future examples we shall assume this unless stated otherwise), and then we execute the pattern-matching statement.

        &ANCHOR = 0
        'ABRACADABRA' @WHERE 'ADA'

The search for 'ADA' is made left to right. The first attempt is with the cursor at position 0: the position just prior to the first character 'A'. The attempt to match 'ADA' (preceded by a null string) fails at that point, but WHERE is assigned the value 0. The match is again attempted with the cursor at position 1; it fails, but WHERE is updated to 1. Finally the match succeeds when the cursor has the value 5. Exit is made from the statement at that point, with WHERE equal to 5.

With this background, we return to our discussion of functions that return patterns.

LEN(integer) returns a pattern structure defined to match any string of characters of the indicated length. Suppose STR is a string consisting of a sequence of words separated by commas. Then the statement

LAB   STR ',' LEN(4) ',' = :S(LAB)

removes all four-letter words from the sequence (excluding the first and last words of the sequence, since they are not flanked by commas). Note that the null replacement string can be indicated by not specifying any string to be assigned as a replacement for matched strings of characters.

SPAN(string) returns a pattern defined to match the longest substring of the subject string, starting from the current cursor position and containing only characters of the argument string. Suppose STR has the value '$ 00345'. Then the statement

STR '$' SPAN('0 ') = '$'

strips off the leading blank and 0s, replacing '$' and them by '$', thus leaving STR equal to '$345'. Note that the order of characters in the argument string is not significant.

BREAK(string) provides the converse function of SPAN. Its pattern is defined to match the longest substring containing only characters not in the argument string. If STR has the value '123,456' then

STR BREAK(',') = '0'

translates STR into '0,456'.

ANY(string) is defined to match any single character that is contained in its argument, while **NOTANY(string)** matches any character not in its argument. If STR is equal to 'c12HA3R456s' then

LAB   STR ANY('0123456789') =   :S(LAB)

strips out the digits, leaving STR equal to 'CHARS'. In contrast, given the same initial string value,

LAB   STR NOTANY('0123456789') =   :S(LAB)

strips out all characters other than digits, leaving STR equal to '123456'.

TAB(integer) matches all characters from the current cursor position up to the indicated position. TAB is useful during a pattern match for positioning the cursor to a certain position in matching against column-sensitive data formats.

        LINE TAB(17) 'MALE'

yields a successful match if the substring 'MALE' immediately follows the seventeenth character of LINE.

RTAB(integer) matches all characters from the current cursor position up to the indicated number of positions prior to the end of the string. Thus RTAB(0) matches everything to the end of the subject string. Using TAB and RTAB in combination,

        LINE TAB(17) RTAB(0).LAST

assigns to LAST the substring of LINE beginning with the character immediately following the seventeenth character to the end of LINE.

POS(integer) matches the null string if the cursor is located at the point of the subject string indicated by the argument. Whereas TAB is used to move the cursor, POS is used to test its current position.

        &ANCHOR = 1
        LINE SPAN('X') POS(3)

succeeds only if LINE begins with exactly three 'X' characters.

FAIL yields a pattern guaranteed not to match any characters of the string being searched. This is useful in a search for a set of alternative patterns when one wishes to know all of the alternatives that are present. Appending FAIL to the total pattern causes each alternative to fail so all alternatives are searched for in the subject string.

        'SYZYGY' ('SY' | 'ZY' | 'GY') $ OUTPUT FAIL

'SY', 'ZY', and 'GY' are printed out enroute to the pattern's failure.

ABORT yields a pattern defined to cause immediate failure of the entire pattern match. This differs from FAIL, which causes failure of only the current alternative. ABORT is useful in defining patterns of which some subcases are not intended to match. Suppose that we have a pattern P, but we want to attempt matches with P only if the subject string is less than seven characters long. Then we define and use a new pattern P1:

        P1 = LEN(7) ABORT | P

If a match of P1 is attempted against a subject string of length at least seven, the first alternative causes the entire pattern to fail. Otherwise a match with P is attempted.

17.7 DATA AGGREGATES

SNOBOL has explicit operators for dynamically creating arrays or tables of data. The statement

$$MAT = ARRAY('2,3')$$

creates a 2 × 3 array and assigns it to the variable MAT. Elements are subsequently referred to by indices within the dimensions, for example, MAT<2,1>. (The symbols < and > enclose indices in SNOBOL.) The string indicating the array shape may itself be variable, so not only the individual bounds, but also the dimensionality of a created array may be determined during execution. Another degree of flexibility allows array elements to be heterogeneous with respect to data type.

A table is a collection of data elements referred to by a string key, rather than by indices within an ordering. Thus tables are analogous to PL/I structures in that references are made by names rather than by positions.

Again we see in tables the dynamic naming capability of SNOBOL. We can create an empty table by executing

$$T = TABLE()$$

We can subsequently add or delete elements at will, naming them at time of assignment:

$$WHEN = 'DAY'$$
$$T<WHEN> = 'MONDAY'$$

An element of the table T, namely, T<DAY>, is set equal to 'MONDAY'.

17.8 FUNCTION DEFINITION

A SNOBOL programmer can define new functions for use in his programs.

$$DEFINE('FUNC(X,Y)A,B','FSTART')$$

Here a function identified as FUNC is being defined, with arguments X and Y and local variables A and B. FSTART is a label designating the entry point to FUNC.

The termination of FUNC can be designated by a transfer label of either RETURN or FRETURN. RETURN is used to indicate a successful completion, in which case the returned value is that currently stored in the name FUNC. FRETURN indicates a failure of FUNC. There is no returned value.

As an example, we define and call a function REV, which reverses the characters of any string other than a null string, or returns with failure if its argument is a null string.

```
        DEFINE('REV(STR)C1,S1')
        .
        .
        .
        S  =  INPUT
        OUTPUT  =  REV(S)          :S(OK)F(BAD)
REV     STR LEN(1)                 :F(FRETURN)
        S1  =  STR
L1      S1 LEN(1).C1  =            :F(RETURN)
        REV  =  C1 REV             :(L1)
        .
        .
        .
OK      . . . . .
        .
        .
BAD     . . . . .
        .
        .
        END
```

We define REV to take one argument and to have local variables S1 and C1; these, along with REV itself, are initialized to contain null strings. No entry point is specified so REV is taken to be the entry point.

Our calling routine, after defining REV, reads a string into S, and requests output of REV(S), then a transfer to OK if REV succeeds, or to BAD if REV fails.

REV begins by checking to see whether its argument string is null. This is done with the simple pattern-matching statement, which specifies a failure return if LEN(1) is not satisfied, that is, if there are no characters in the argument string. Otherwise the local variable S1 is assigned the argument string. Now a two-statement loop is executed to delete characters from the argument, one at a time, storing each into C1, which is then prefixed to the string REV. When no characters are left, a successful return is made with the reversed string in REV.

17.9 DATA DEFINITION

In addition to defining new functions, a SNOBOL programmer can define new data types.

```
DATA('COMPLEX(REAL,IMAG)')
```

Here we are defining a new data type, COMPLEX. A complex datum contains two fields, referenced by REAL and IMAG, respectively.

```
C1  =  COMPLEX(7,9)
```

The operator COMPLEX creates a COMPLEX datum C1 with subfield values 7 and 9, respectively. These subfields are subsequently retrievable as

```
REAL(C1)
IMAG(C1)
```

If we define complex data in a SNOBOL program, we, of course, have to define as functions the various operators to manipulate it.

17.10 UNEVALUATED EXPRESSIONS

The operator ∗, when encountered, postpones the evaluation of its argument expression. That argument is carried along in unevaluated form, and is finally evaluated only when encountered during scanning through a pattern.

```
C  =  '#'
P  =  ∗C
```

These statements assign '#' to the variable C and the pattern given by the variable C to P. But P is not given the simple character pattern '#'. If P is used later, in a pattern match, then C is evaluated at that time.

```
S '5' P ' '
```

Thus, if C is updated to contain '%' subsequent to the assignment to P but prior to the pattern match above, the pattern being searched for in S is '5% ', not '5# '.

So, with ∗, a pattern variable can represent a number of different patterns, as determined by matching-time evaluations of unevaluated expressions it contains.

A particularly useful application of unevaluated expressions is in the recursive definition of patterns.

```
PAT  =  'X' | ∗PAT 'X'
```

A pattern PAT has been defined to involve the unevaluated pattern expression ∗PAT. This recursive definition becomes resolved at pattern-matching time, when PAT is evaluated. PAT matches either 'x' or anything matched by PAT followed by 'x'. Since PAT matches 'x', our second possibility means that PAT matches 'xx'; this similarly implies that PAT matches 'xxx'. This recursive definition defines PAT as matching any string of 'x's.

Let us look at a more interesting example.

$$ P \;=\; \text{ANY('ABC')} \;|\; \text{'('} \;\ast\text{P} \;\text{'+'} \;\ast\text{P} \;\text{')'} $$

Here we are recursively defining a pattern P that matches either one of the characters 'A', 'B', or 'C', or a pair of patterns matched by P, separated by ' + ', and enclosed in parentheses. When evaluated in a subsequent pattern match, P matches any of a large class of strings such as the following:

```
A
(B + C)
(B + (A + C))
((A + C) + (B + C))
 .
 .
 .
```

This example illustrates the use of recursive pattern definition in recognizing various expression syntaxes.

17.11 CONCLUSIONS

It is a misleading oversimplification to classify SNOBOL as a string-manipulation language. We could just about as well classify in this fashion all languages that operate on one-dimensional data. SNOBOL's importance lies in its elegant features, which permit the overlaying of complex structures on simple forms. The language is also noteworthy for its totally dynamic approach to naming of data and for its control features: Every statement may succeed or fail, in either case with a well-defined successor statement. Control transfer is an inherent part of the semantics of all statements, rather than relegated to specialized statements such as the usual GO TO. A final feature of significance is the unevaluated expression, which represents a late-binding analog to ALGOL's call-by-name feature.

For a full description of the SNOBOL language, see [Gri68].

Exercises

1. Write a SNOBOL program to return a pattern that matches any permutation of the characters of its string operand.

2. Describe SNOBOL functions for performing the substring replacement, insertion, and deletion operations of chapter 7.

3. Write a SNOBOL program to evaluate Boolean expressions similar to those that can be evaluated by the LISP routine LOGIC of section 16.3.

For simplicity, we modify the syntax of the expression to the following, using the symbols T, F, ~, &, and | for TRUE, FALSE, NOT, AND, and OR, respectively, and omitting the parentheses:

       1.   T or F
       2.   ~ expression
       3.   & expression
       4. | expression

Thus an expression to be evaluated might be

       & T ~ | F T

CHAPTER 18

Language Extensibility

We have now looked at six programming languages, which we consider to be representative in both style and features of a very large class of languages. We have tried to develop, in general terms, a set of features rather comprehensive in their application to algorithmic problem solution. We have stopped short of actually defining a "total" language, ideal for all problem solution. The style that a language should best assume is far too dependent on the human and machine environment in which it is used. And that environment must also affect the level of sophistication of the features of a language. To say that a language has a generally acceptable set of arithmetic features is not to say that it is ideal for use in work totally oriented to numerical analysis. The less general the applications of a language, the less adequate a general-purpose language for those applications.

So we have been driven to a fairly primitive level in our development of a set of features. We have provided building blocks, rather than all the imaginable application superstructures definable from those building blocks. The number of blocks may be finite, but the number of conceivable buildings certainly is not.

Every machine language serves as a set of building blocks, with compilers serving as builders. But most machine languages are oriented, not toward problem expression and solution, but toward hardware considerations. We have tried to indicate features of a machine language directed toward the former rather than the latter.

It is critical that a language designed to provide building blocks provide a comprehensive set of them, a set from which all envisioned superstructures within some application discipline can be built. To claim that most machine languages do this is often true in a theoretical sense but a leap of faith in any more practical sense; we have already mentioned the extreme mismatch between machine-language features and problem expression. We intentionally neglect the amusing exception to this: the machine-language programmer who characterizes problems in terms of their machine-language descriptions. While language may direct our thoughts, we should at least be able to evolve cyclically to languages that reflect our thoughts better than those with which we started—better tools of the intellect, languages easier and more natural to think in.

So we have emphasized building blocks for problem solution, but we have stressed their inadequacy for direct use in particular application areas. The usual bridge between blocks and applications is a compiler that translates specialized application-language programs into building blocks of the underlying machine language.

At the risk of slight exaggeration, we must chastize, in today's programming environment, the process of compilation and the very word itself, which is the grand euphemism of computer science. Compilation is like an alchemistic art of transforming gold into lead, to obtain pencils and hence to communicate information. The task of a compiler is to take programs of a high-level, relatively problem-oriented language, and mutilate them beyond recognition, distorting them finally into sequences of unrecognizable codes comprehensible only to elements of electronic circuitry capable of actual execution. Incredibly, the high-level intent is simulated in this world of wires, and the program is executed as desired. The compilation process is magic. A translation has been made between two representations with no apparent similarity of form or of content, yet those representations are in a global sense equivalent in their executions.

Of course, this process is a bleak necessity in a world of problem-oriented thought and machine-oriented execution. It is bleak both to the compiler designer, who must go to amazing contortions to guarantee the simulation with such foreign constructs; and to the user who, faced with the seemingly unavoidable requirements of relating obscure execution-time messages to his program, must come to understand the machine translations of his programs.

This technique of compilation, of translation from one language to a dissimilar one, is what we wish to discount in this discussion of language extensibility. Compilers will always have an important role in the language picture, and we discuss that role later. But here we wish to talk about language extensibility as a process of graceful enhancement of some base language, not a process of turning it into a completely different language to be compiled back down. We view extensibility as an inherent part of a language, whereby the programmer can define language extensions in terms of his base language. To the extent to which a language possesses features of this kind, it may be called a *self-extending language*.

18.1 COMMON TYPES OF CURRENT LANGUAGE EXTENSIBILITY

We now look at three areas of extensibility in language: (1) definition of new operators, (2) definition of new data types, and (3) definition of new notational forms. The first two of these are the critical semantic areas for extension of language, which we have characterized simply as collections of operators and data. The third area permits the user to define notational conveniences: abbreviations, terminology changes, statements with unusual formats, and the like.

Before we investigate these areas, it is useful to look at the features commonly available for extension of today's languages. In a simple sense, the very act of programming is a language extension, an empowering of a language with problem-solving features not before realized. To write a program in some language, and then to name that program and thus allow its invocation from elsewhere, is a language extension involving creation of a new operator; that operator is realized algorithmically by the program defining it. So all languages in which one can write and invoke programs possess a simple kind of semantic operator extensibility. In some languages (e.g., APL), the new operator is indistinguishable syntactically from a base operator, while in others (e.g., ALGOL or FORTRAN), it is distinguished syntactically, with the operator first, followed by a parenthesized set of operands.

Whether a new operator is indistinguishable semantically from base operators of a language is an issue critical to language development. It is desirable for a language to lend itself to growth from a small initial nucleus. Extensions first realized only through programming may later be built in to the language if their use warrants. But for such inclusions to be made without impact to users of extensions, transparency between extensions and built-in features must be inherent to the language design.

We note at this point a distinction between two types of operator extensions, a distinction we emphasize repeatedly. The programming community speaks of two types of programmed routines, characterizing them as *in-line* and *out-of-line*. The distinction lies in the time at which the defined operator is expanded into its defining program. If an operator is referenced in-line within another program, it means that prior to execution of the referencing program, the operator reference is replaced with its definition. Thus, in the executable expansion of the referencing program, there is no evidence of the newly defined operator, per se. This type of extension may be considered syntactic only; the executing machine has no provision for handling the new operator.

If an operator is referenced out-of-line, the referencing program contains, even in its executable form, a reference to that operator. The executing machine employs various communication conventions for linking to that operator, and for returning from it when it has completed. This variety of operator extension is truly semantic in that the extensibility is reflected in the definition of the executing machine.

Data extensibility is provided in a similar way in most languages. The base language typically provides a nonextensible set of primitive scalar data types (e.g., numbers and strings), and schemata for building a variety of data aggregates from these. The schemata are typically rigid (multidimensional arrays or structures, referenced in a stylized way by index or name), but the particular shapes describable as dimension bounds are unlimited. Thus extensibility is provided in the ability of the programmer to specify, within the aggregate schemata provided, particular shapes for his data aggregates.

As was true for operator extensions, the user of a defined data aggregate may view that aggregate as an inherent part of the system, for which he has been provided referencing capabilities (subscripts, qualified names, cross-section references, and the like).

Again we note a difference—this time, between syntactic and semantic data extensions. A primitive executing machine may recognize no concept of aggregation more sophisticated than that of ordering; a compiler may be required to translate all aggregate references into appropriate indexes into vectors that it has created to simulate the aggregates. In this case, the data extensions are syntactic, not processed by the executing machine. If, however, that machine is more intelligent, it may have aggregate-oriented features that allow leaving the aggregate processing to the machine. In this case, the extensions are truly semantic.

Features such as PL/I pointer data, used to define and manipulate other kinds of aggregates, do not provide data extensibility as we are describing it. They are coding tools only, used to simulate complicated structures through programming. They in no sense allow the definition of such structures within any data structure schema provided by the language.

One additional comment about data extensibility is in order. We noted for primitive scalar data types only that the types available here are usually not extensible, though aggregates are. We hope to build a more general picture in which the set of scalar data types is also extensible.

In only a very trivial way do most languages allow definition of new notational forms. A programmer usually has the ability to define any of a virtually unlimited set of names for his use, within a restrictive format requiring first an alphabetic character, followed by a number of characters from some character set. Thus naming is an extensibility feature, but more interesting extensions of notation are not provided. New statement definitions in particular are not ordinarily allowed as syntactic extensions. We return to this subject later in development of our model for extensibility.

18.2 A CLASSIFICATION OF EXTENSIBILITY

We now begin to look at a general picture of language extensibility, characterizing extensions in two ways:

1. What is the nature of the extension?
    a. operator
    b. data primitive
    c. data aggregate
    d. notational

2. Where is the extension realized?
    a. syntax only
    b. execution only
    c. both syntax and execution

The combinations that we shall examine are indicated in the following table. Notational extensions are by definition not noticeable at execution time; data primitive extensions, for reasons we shall see later, must have execution time ramifications.

NATURE OF EXTENSION / WHERE REALIZED	Operator	Data primitive	Data aggregate	Notational
Syntax only	*		*	*
Execution only	*	*	*	
Syntax and execution	*	*	*	

18.3 AN EXTENSION EXAMPLE

As the first step in developing our extension model, we shall provide some motivation for our above classification scheme with a tangible example of an extension area and the various techniques that can be used to realize the involved extensions. We relate these techniques to our classification as described.

Suppose that we have one of the popular high-level languages, say, FORTRAN, ALGOL, or PL/I, and we wish to add to it a set of features for handling complex data (we assume that no such features are available). More precisely, we wish to add the data type **COMPLEX** and five attendant operators as listed below. (CE stands for a complex expression, CN for a complex name, and RE for a real expression.)

> **ADD(CE1,CE2)** adds two complex numbers.
> **MULTIPLY(CE1,CE2)** multiplies two complex numbers.
> **STORE(CE,CN)** stores a complex number in a complex target.
> **COMPLEX(RE)** translates a real number to complex.
> **REAL(CE)** translates a complex number to real.

We proceed informally through several approaches to our task.

Approach 1.

We define a new language with complex data, and use a compiler to translate programs of that language into programs of the base language. But this is exactly the technique that we are trying to discourage. In no sense does it provide a graceful extension of the existing language.

Approach 2.

We make a purely notational extension in which the type attribute COM-PLEX is translated into the base-language notation for a two-element vector. We use the two elements to hold the real and imaginary parts of a complex number. Next we provide operators ADD, MULTIPLY, STORE, COMPLEX, and REAL, using functional notation. Here we are likely to encounter an annoying problem: Programmer-defined operators of our language may not be able to return aggregate results. If we must live with this restriction, we make our operators like subroutines, returning no results, instead of like functions returning results. We may define (1) that we pass a target to such an operator explicitly, or (2) that each operator overwrites an operand for a target. If we do the former, our operators are invoked as follows:

```
CALL ADD(CE1,CE2,CN);
CALL CMULT(CE1,CE2,CN);
CALL STORE(CE,CN);
CALL COMPLEX(RE,CN);
CALL REAL(CE,RN);
```

A number of points are interesting in this approach:

> 1. Since STORE names a target explicitly, we do not need to add a target argument.

2. The REAL operator could have been retained with functional notation, since its result is not complex and thus not an aggregate. Thus we could define the function REAL(CE) to return a real number (presumably the real part of the result of the complex expression).

3. The annoying requirement of an explicit target field for ADD and MULT precludes complex expressions with more than one operator. To add complex numbers A, B, and C, we must write

   ADD(A, B, TEMP); ADD(TEMP, C, TEMP);

4. If our host language provides operators that accept aggregate arguments and perform the operation on an element-by-element basis, we might be able to use the built-in addition operator to provide for ADD (with an aggregate result) and the built-in assignment operator to provide for STORE. Unfortunately, the built-in multiplication operator would not suffice for MULTIPLY, since complex multiplication is not done on an element-by-element basis.

5. These extensions, using statements for the operators, might be realized either as syntactic or semantic extensions—an operator could be replaced by its expansion either in the text or only when it is called at execution time. If, however, the operators were definable, not as statements, but as functions returning results, then our host language could probably not accommodate the extensions syntactically. One cannot usually substitute a program to perform an operation for that operation within an expression. Language syntax generally precludes this at present.

6. This approach assumes no sophisticated extensibility features in the host language. We are assuming only a capability for subroutine call and a simple notational convenience for specifying the type COMPLEX.

7. There can be no type-checking in this approach. Any two-element vector can pass for COMPLEX, and any COMPLEX value can be treated simply as a two-element vector, with arbitrary violation of the rules for COMPLEX arithmetic.

Approach 3.
For this approach, we assume some more novel extensibility features to be embedded within the host language. We first insist on a host language

whose operators, whether extensions or basic, may return aggregate results. We cannot tolerate an operator extension environment in which the target fields of approach 2 arise. Graceful enhancement must be provided in a natural way.

We propose to associate, with each operator of a language, an attribute describing whether that operator is a scalar or an aggregate operator; this attribute must be specified as a part of any new operator definition.

If an operator is declared to be a scalar operator, the presence of aggregate operands signals the system to perform the operation on an element-by-element basis, using distribution as discussed in chapters 7 and 8. The result is an aggregate of the common shape of the aggregate operands.

This base-language feature eases some of the burdens encountered in our last approach. We can now write multiple-operator expressions such as ADD(MULTIPLY(A,B),C). Furthermore, we can use the built-in operators for addition and assignment, rather than invent new ones (assuming those operators in the base language are defined to be scalar operators). Thus, instead of the above, we can write MULTIPLY(A,B) + C.

We would also like to modify our host language so that the extension operators can be expanded in-line (syntactically) rather than only out-of-line (semantically). The choice here involves space/time trade-offs, as do all decisions on whether and when to use subroutines in programming, but at least, the choice should be available. Of course, if an extension operator is defined recursively, it cannot be expanded in-line.

We make a syntactic addition to our host language to allow us to replace an operator and its operands, at any point, with the programmed definition of that operator. The definition, of course, must indicate in some fashion the value to be taken as the result of the operator's execution. Then, instead of writing

$$A + B * F(C,D) - E$$

and elsewhere defining F by

```
MODULE F(X,Y);
   .
   .
   ...X...Y...
   .
   .
   RETURN(value);
   .
   .
END F;
```

it is possible to write

A + B ✳ [...C...D...RETURN(value)...] − E

We can now allow syntactic operator extensions.

Now let us consider the operator MULTIPLY, with which there are still problems. Recall that we cannot simply use the base-language scalar multiplication operator in its place, since that results in element-by-element multiplication, which is not appropriate. If we view complex numbers from the point of view of MULTIPLY (or of REAL), we find it awkward to describe COMPLEX as just a two-element vector. We certainly view complex multiplication as a scalar operator (it should distribute appropriately when we have an operand that is an array of complex numbers), yet we cannot define it in that way. So we must get by with defining MULTIPLY to be an aggregate (nondistributive) operator, and we must be careful in our use of arrays of complex numbers—they cannot be given as operands of MULTIPLY.

Although we haven't really solved this problem, we now try to settle two smaller inconveniences in use of MULTIPLY. One is the obvious preference for use of symbols that "look like" operators. Why should base operators be represented by useful special symbols (+ , −, /, and the like), but our defined operators be limited to names? Our host language should be liberalized so that operator definitions can be represented by special symbols if desired. Of course, we cannot use our basic operator symbol for multiplication (normally ✳ or ×). We must use something new, whether it be a special symbol or a name.

A second inconvenience lies in the syntactic requirement that MULTIPLY and its set of operands look like a conventional function reference, while the luxury of infix form is available for binary operators of the base language. One may write A + B + C, but we cannot write A MULTIPLY B MULTIPLY C. Instead we must resort to cumbersome functional notation:

MULTIPLY(MULTIPLY(A, B),C)

Here we suggest augmentation of our host language in either of two ways:

1. Allow any operator occurrence to be written either in functional notation or in infix (if binary) or prefix (if unary) notation.

2. Require a declared attribute for each defined operator, indicating in which form it is to be specified.

If an operator is specified to be infix, we may have to provide more information (recall our discussions of operator priority and associativity in chapter 6). If our language is APL-like in its uniform right-to-left association, then nothing is required. But otherwise we must define with our operator its precedence relative to other operators of the language. We declare it to be in precedence equal to, next higher than, or next lower than, some other specified operator. We also indicate whether its association is to be left-to-right or right-to-left.

This third approach solves several important problems of the previous extension approaches, but leaves others still unsettled. We have augmented the base-language extensibility features, but more is needed.

Approach 4.

All of our approaches to introducing complex data have involved extending our language operator set in significant ways. We have not, however, tried to exploit any capabilities for extending the set of data types available. The convenience of being able to write COMPLEX rather than ARRAY(2) was only a bit of notational trivia, devoid of semantics. Our executing machine saw no type COMPLEX, and had no features for handling such a data type. Now we look at a more sophisticated approach to our problem, using features for new data definition.

Recall our unsettled problems with MULTIPLY in our last approach:

■ MULTIPLY could not be defined to be a distributive operator, since COMPLEX was defined to be an aggregate. Thus we could not handle multiplication of aggregates of complex numbers.

■ We could not use the normal multiplication symbol for complex multiplication.

Our introduction of a new data type for COMPLEX enables us to resolve both of these difficulties.

We chose in chapter 8 to characterize data aggregates by the distributive effect of their presence as operands of scalar operators. This leaves us with our old problems if we describe COMPLEX as any type of aggregate; later in this chapter we discuss new data aggregate definitions, but they are not the answer here. What we need now is the ability to describe COMPLEX, not as an aggregate of any kind, but as a scalar. Then we can define our complex operators to be distributive and use aggregates of complex numbers with them. Since the operators will not naturally distribute over the components of a complex number, MULTIPLY will work as desired.

We now endow our base language with a feature allowing definition of new scalar data types to be recognized by the executing machine.

```
DECLARE COMPLEX DATATYPE;
DECLARE X COMPLEX;
```

COMPLEX is defined to be a new scalar data type, and x is defined to be of this new type. More information must be given to tell our executing machine what to do when it encounters COMPLEX operands during execution. Hence the definition of this new data type must include specification of the action to be taken when an object of this type is encountered during execution. This specification is in the form of a reference to an operator, presumably defined elsewhere to support operators with COMPLEX operands.

The action of the system when an operator with COMPLEX operands is encountered during execution is to invoke the operator accompanying the COMPLEX type declaration. That operator simulates the application of the encountered operator to its operands.

In order to execute the expression containing COMPLEX operands, the COMPLEX operator must have two pieces of information: (1) the operator of which the COMPLEX objects are operands, and (2) the operands themselves. This information is passed to the COMPLEX operator via parameters when it is invoked. It executes the expression and returns a result taken to be the result of applying the encountered operator to its operands.

Note that we have associated the intelligence required to execute expressions involving COMPLEX operands, with definition of the COMPLEX type, rather than with individual operators. Thus we speak of this extension technique as being data-driven, rather than operator-driven.

An implementation issue involves the desirability of specification of the storage-allocation requirements for data of a newly defined type. If the type is one whose allocation requirements may vary during execution (e.g., a variable-length string or list), then allocation considerations must be handled by the type operator at execution time in response to operators that may require changing the allocation (e.g., INSERT). In these cases an arbitrary initial allocation, providing only a basic resolution, may be the only reasonable recourse. In less dynamic cases, however, it may be desirable to indicate the allocation requirements by declaration of some data structure known to the language. Then, for our COMPLEX case, in which allocation requirements do not vary, one might write

DECLARE COMPLEX DATATYPE (type operator, (2) INTEGER);

This declaration indicates that allocation requirements are as for a two-element integer vector. Less rigidly, one might instead give this specification individually with each declaration of a datum of this type. Then different data of the same type might have different allocation requirements; a possible example is an extension analogous to fixed-length strings. We emphasize that this specification in no way gives logical structure to the data. They are scalar and hence cannot be dissected by any general indexing mechanism.

Another option arises in this picture regarding a potential ambiguity. What if an operator encounters a mixture of operand types, for example, a triadic operator with one operand of a built-in type and two of different extended types? We suggest either of two approaches to this issue:

1. Require all operands to be of the same type.
2. Use the type operator of the first operand to perform the operation.

With this model of data definition, let us now take a new approach to introducing COMPLEX into our base language.

We have to take one step backward from our previous approach. Since we are defining COMPLEX semantically rather than just notationally, we are denied the luxury of using directly the built-in operator for addition. For assignment a question arises. It might seem reasonable to consider that assignment works in a manner independent of the semantics of its operands. It simply moves the data identified by its source operand to the location reserved for its target operand. We might, more generally, define for each operator of a language whether or not it is sensitive to data types of its operands.

We choose, however, a more open position. We have not required that the storage component of a newly defined name indicate all of the data physically comprising the object. That component may itself identify other data of arbitrarily complex structure. Only the operator component of a new data type knows how to use the storage component of a name declared to be of that type. Thus even operators such as assignment must use that operator, in order to ensure that the correct data are moved.

We start by defining our new data type COMPLEX as we indicated, identifying with this type the two-element vector providing for storage allocation. Our action component is the interesting part of our definition. We have identified five operators for use with COMPLEX operands, and our action component must be able to handle each of them. For addition and assignment, it can indirectly use the distributive built-in operators, providing, as operands, descriptions of the COMPLEX data as two-element vectors.

We must write a new operator to perform the MULTIPLY function, but we are free to use the built-in multiplication operator symbol, which remains distributive. Consider the sequence of actions prescribed by the following code:

```
DECLARE COMPLEX DATATYPE (type operator, (2) INTEGER);
DECLARE A(10) COMPLEX, B(10) COMPLEX;
    .
    .
    .
.....A ∗ B.....
    .
    .
    .
.....REAL(A).....
```

Upon encountering A ∗ B, the system notes that ∗ is distributive, and that A and B are aggregates. It thus performs the operation element-by-element over the aggregates A and B. But when performing A(i) $*$ B(i), the system notes that each operand is, not an aggregate, but a new scalar data type. Thus the action component indicated for A(i) is invoked to perform the operation. It is passed the information that $*$ is the operator, and that A(i) and B(i) are the operands. That action specification we have defined in this case to call an operator MULTIPLY to perform the operation.

The REAL operator works analogously. It is defined to be distributive, so the operation is performed element-by-element over A. REAL(A(i)) involves a new scalar data type; the action component is invoked to perform the operation.

The COMPLEX operator takes a REAL operand, so the above mechanisms are not involved. The operator definition creates a COMPLEX datum from the REAL operand, and returns this datum as its result.

18.4 DEFINITION OF NEW DATA AGGREGATES

In addition to defining new scalar data types not subject to distribution by scalar operators, we would like to be able to define new types of data aggregates. For nondistributive operators, these new aggregate types will be treated exactly as new scalar types (we re-emphasize that we have defined aggregates in terms of distribution), but for distributive operators, we wish still to be able to exploit the distribution mechanism as it applies to built-in aggregates.

Suppose that we are involved in an application discipline making heavy use of symmetric matrices (two-dimensional square arrays for which, at all times for an array A, A(i,j) = A(j,i)). We wish to refer to elements of such an array in the usual manner, yet we wish not to be so wasteful as to carry in storage the entire array. We solve this problem by defining a new aggregate data type **SYMMAT(shape)**, where shape indicates the common number of rows and columns of the aggregate.

Our desire is to carry physically only the components of a SYMMAT object for which i≥j in a reference A(i,j). If then, in such a reference, i<j, we will transpose the indices to retrieve the appropriate element. Obviously, this requirement implies that a prime characteristic of our defined aggregate is the interception of the built-in indexing operation, when its operand is a newly defined aggregate.

Defining our new aggregate data type involves two specifications:

1. specification of the action to be taken when the aggregate appears as an operand of a nondistributive operator (in particular, the indexing operator, whose operands may be unlimited in number and format)
2. information for the distributor to use when this aggregate appears as an operand of a distributive operator

As for scalar types, we might also include a declaration indicating the storage-allocation requirements for our aggregate.

Suppose that we wish to define a symmetric matrix of shape 3. Then our storage allocation specification might name a vector v of six elements used in order for A(1,1), A(2,1), A(2,2), A(3,1), A(3,2), and A(3,3). These comprise the bottom triangle of our matrix:

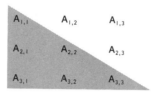

$$A_{1,1} \quad A_{1,2} \quad A_{1,3}$$
$$A_{2,1} \quad A_{2,2} \quad A_{2,3}$$
$$A_{3,1} \quad A_{3,2} \quad A_{3,3}$$

Recall that $A_{1,2} = A_{2,1}$, $A_{1,3} = A_{3,1}$, and $A_{2,3} = A_{3,2}$.

Our action specification (again a reference to an operator) indicates the action to be taken upon reference to A(i,j). (If $i < j$, then the reference is taken to be A(j,i).) It is easy to verify that, in terms of our vector representation, we wish to interpret A(i,j) as $v(i + j - 1 + (i-1) * (i-2)/2)$. Our newly defined operator for indexing need only evaluate the indexed reference according to this formula, returning the appropriate element.

Finally, we must give some information to the distributor. Suppose the system encounters the expression x + A where x is a 3 × 3 matrix and A is as defined above. The distributor is invoked to perform the operation on an element-by-element basis, but it must know how to pair up elements of x with elements of A. We take care of this by specifying, in the definition of A, an operator which, when invoked repeatedly by the distributor, in each case returns identification of the "next" element of A in accordance with a desired canonical linearization of A.

If we assume that our language naturally orders built-in aggregates in row-major order ($x_{1,1}$, $x_{1,2}$, $x_{1,3}$, $x_{2,1}$, $x_{2,2}$, $x_{2,3}$, $x_{3,1}$, $x_{3,2}$, $x_{3,3}$ in this case), then we naturally define our ordering operator in such a way that successive calls on it produce, in order, returned identifications of v_1, v_2, v_4, v_2, v_3, v_5, v_4, v_5, and v_6. We get this ordering by associating v_1 with $A_{1,1}$, v_2 with $A_{2,1}$ (and $A_{1,2}$), v_3 with $A_{2,2}$, v_4 with $A_{3,1}$ (and $A_{1,3}$), v_5 with $A_{3,2}$ (and $A_{2,3}$), and v_6 with $A_{3,3}$.

$$A_{1,1} = v_1 \quad A_{1,2} = v_2 \quad A_{1,3} = v_4$$
$$A_{2,1} = v_2 \quad A_{2,2} = v_3 \quad A_{2,3} = v_5$$
$$A_{3,1} = v_4 \quad A_{3,2} = v_5 \quad A_{3,3} = v_6$$

We have now given all information needed by the system to handle our new aggregate satisfactorily. In particular, we can still take advantage of the distributor, and we can handle indexing in any fashion we desire. Our declarations might look as follows:

```
DECLARE SYMMAT AGGREGATETYPE (type operator, ordering
      operator);
DECLARE A SYMMAT;
```

But note that there is no indication in the declaration of A that it has the logical shape of a 3 × 3 matrix. Therefore the type SYMMAT cannot describe symmetric matrices in general, but only 3 × 3 ones. Both the type operator and the distribution operator must be sensitive to the shape of the aggregate type.

If we wish to generalize our picture to allow these operators to work with a symmetric matrix of any size, we must provide a shape specification with the declaration of each datum of type SYMMAT. That specification can be passed to each operator, which can therefore treat the shape parametrically in carrying out distribution, subscript range checking, and so on. Note in this particular case that shape is not needed to do indexing.

In general, we suggest that a shape specification be given as a vector in which each element contains one shape parameter. This vector is used only by the type operator and the distribution operator associated with a particular aggregate type.

Our above declaration for A is modified accordingly to

```
DECLARE A SYMMAT(3);
```

where the qualifier represents a single-element vector with the element value 3.

18.5 A GENERALIZED EXTENSION MODEL

We now summarize the points of our example to provide a general model for language extension. We cover extensions of operators and data and then look at notational extensions. We assume in our model the previously mentioned language additions allowing return of aggregates and in-line expansion of operators.

An operator definition involves the following specifications:

1. the algorithm used for defining the operator semantics
2. whether the operator definition is to be expanded in-line or out-of-line
3. whether the operator is distributive
4. the number of operands of the operator and, if binary, whether it is to be in infix form; if unary, whether it is to be in prefix form
5. if the operator is to be in infix form, its precedence and associativity

A new scalar data-type definition includes the following items:

1. an action specification used to execute all operators of which a datum of this type occurs as an operand
2. an optional declaration indicating storage allocation requirements for data of this type

A new aggregate data-type definition is comprised as follows:

1. an action specification used to execute all nondistributive operators of which the aggregate occurs as an operand
2. an ordering operator to be used by the distributor
3. an optional declaration indicating storage-allocation requirements for data of this type

Exercises

1. Use the extension features described in this chapter to define the extensions required to introduce the forward-linked lists of chapter 8 into a language. Any extant language may be used to define the extension semantics.

2. Define extensions adequate to introduce ordered sets of integers into a language as a new type of aggregate. Operators provided should include union, intersection, and indexing, a query function to obtain the number of elements of a set, functions EQUAL and SUBSET for comparing two sets, and some way to speak of the null set.

18.6 NOTATIONAL EXTENSIONS

It is quite straightforward to introduce, as PL/I has done, features allowing replacement of a symbol in text by the result of executing some operation whenever that symbol is encountered. This type of feature we call *text-editing*. It can be very useful and almost totally independent of the language over which it is defined. It has no effect on the executing machine for that language, or even on the language processor that puts a legible program in that language into machine-language form.

A more sophisticated type of notational extensibility involves actual additions to the collection of syntactic forms available in the language. Ideally one might define a new syntactic form, however complex, and then give its expanded definition in terms of syntactic forms already understood as part of the language. Thus it might, for example, be possible to define a PL/I DO loop (if not already present in the language) in some fashion and then express that definition in terms of existing PL/I syntactic forms. As a first step, let us define a syntactic form for the DO as follows:

    DO V = e1 TO e2; S...END

Now we expand our definition in terms of existing syntactic forms:

    V = e1; L:S...V = V+1; IF V< = e2 THEN GO TO L;

where v is a variable
        e1 is an expression
        e2 is an expression
        s is a statement

Here we are using a loose hypothetical format for describing a syntactic form representing a DO loop and its expansion. The names v, e1, e2, and s represent various syntactic forms already understood within PL/I.

We would be most fortunate if extension definitions of this type could be incorporated easily into languages. A language processor understanding a language with some basic set of syntax rules might suddenly understand a language with that set of rules and a few more. But this general capability is not realizable for a large number of reasons. The basic problem is that definition of a new syntactic form generally results in havoc with regard to old defining forms of the language. A Pandora's box of syntactic ambiguities arises, for which no general resolution techniques work satisfactorily. Hence we must discourage the notion that syntactic extensions to a language are straightforward; they are not, except in highly stylized contexts that we have seen (replacement of symbols, definition of new symbols, admission of infix operators, and the like). The techniques available for language syntax description are themselves extremely primitive and inflexible. Techniques for modifying language descriptions of those kinds are almost nonexistent.

18.7 A VIEW OF COMPILERS

We began this chapter with an assault on compilers as they are usually understood. We conclude this discussion with a more constructive view of the role that compilers should play in language support of the future.

We feel strongly that operator-extension and data-extension mechanisms as we have described them provide the road to graceful enhancement of languages. The user of a language cannot tell whether an operator or datum that he uses is built-in or an extension, whether it is realized algorithmically or by physical hardware. Thus a language can be augmented periodically in a fashion transparent to its previous, current, and future users. A language far-extended in this fashion still will bear a close resemblance to the base language. The executing machine still will be well-equipped to handle it, through the mechanisms inherent in that machine.

But in the area of notational extensions, we see a different picture. General techniques for such extensions are not available. Furthermore, extant techniques for describing syntax are insufficient for many desirable types of language notation. Yet the variety of notational forms continues to grow, particularly as computer use expands to other than programmers. More and more specialized languages arise, with syntactic nuances covering a broader and broader spectrum that we simply cannot handle with current techniques for syntax description.

We suggest that the role of compilers in the future should evolve more and more into a role dealing only in syntax translation, but not dealing in the decisions of how to represent the semantic features of user languages as remote sequences of seemingly unrelated machine code. Compilers should deal, not with translation of meanings of constructs, but only with translation of their syntactic representations.

As techniques for describing and modifying syntax become more sophisticated and are incorporated into compilers, compilers will become more general in use. A single compiler will be able to handle a number of different user languages (this is already the case for some very limited languages). But the day when a single compiler will be adequate for all language translation is far distant. On that day, we will be able to formally incorporate the all-sufficient compiler into our basic executing machine. Until then, we must continue to separate compiler discussions from those of executing machines. We must continue to view a compiler as a black box that performs, in whatever manner, either private or shared with other compilers, the service of translating programs of its designated source language into programs of a machine language. We ask now only that that compiler find it easy to model the semantics of the various constructs of the source language.

18.8 SOME TERMINOLOGY

A multitude of terms are in vogue, all relating to features that we have been describing. To help the reader avoid frustrating points of confusion arising in discussions of extensibility, we identify and differentiate the following:

language extensibility	function
macro capabilities	subroutine
definitional facilities	operator
self-extending language	built-in function
self-defining language	operator definition
syntax-directed compiler	data definition
table-driven compiler	
compiler-compiler	

The terms in the left-hand column are used to designate general properties of a language or compiler; those in the right-hand column refer to particular types of extension.

Oddly enough, in computing literature, the general subject of extensibility is usually assumed to deal only with syntactic extensions as we have described them: in-line operator definitions and notational data definitions. There seems to be a widespread reluctance to investigate extensibility realized through the executing machine for a language. As we have emphasized repeatedly, we regard the rationale of "machine-independence" to be pure nonsense. In any event, the term *language extensibility* usually connotes the ability to make syntactic extensions to the operator and data-type domains of a language.

The term *macro capability* is even more tied in connotation to syntactic extensions. It also often relates to notational extensions of the sort available in PL/I.

Definitional facilities is a more general term than either of the above. It is used to refer collectively to the spectrum from text-editing notational extensions to syntactic extensions of data or operators. Semantic extensions are still, however, generally excluded.

A *self-extending language* is one that includes, as part of its base definition, features for language extensibility as defined above.

A *self-defining language* is one whose syntactic description can be given in terms of data structures of the language, and whose executing machine can be defined by a program in the language. An example is LISP.

A *syntax-directed compiler* is one that uses directly a syntactic description of a source language to effect its translation. It does not inherently know of the various syntactic forms of a particular language; it knows only of a standard way of describing those forms, which, for a particular source language, are provided as input to the compiler. Thus a syntax-directed compiler can be used to compile programs for any set of languages whose syntactic forms are describable in its standard way.

A *table-driven compiler* is one that executes largely as a function of data given it, rather than according to a predetermined sequence of actions. A syntax-directed compiler is table-driven with respect to its reliance upon a particular syntax description for its execution. In general, use of the term *table-driven* for a program connotes a high flexibility in that program's ability to respond in widely differing ways to different data.

A *compiler-compiler* is a program that takes as input a syntactic and semantic description of some language, and produces as output a compiler for that described language.

Turning now to extension specifics, we recognize *function* and *subroutine* as almost universal operator-extension features, differing in whether they return a result. In keeping with the avoidance of semantic extensions, these are usually not thought of as features providing language extensibility.

The usual distinction between *operators* and *built-in functions* of a language is purely a notational one. A built-in function is represented by a name followed in parentheses by its set of operands. An operator is represented by a name or special symbol, in prefix, infix, or suffix form with regard to its operands, and with no parentheses involved. Thus one tends to think of FACTORIAL(A) as a reference to a built-in function, but of A! as a reference to the ! operator. Both operators and built-in functions are assumed to be built-in to a base language, and are usually differentiated from functions and subroutines on this basis.

The terms *operator definition* and *data definition* are used in language-extensibility discussions to describe syntactic operator-extensions and notational data-extensions, respectively. A function or subroutine, being semantic, is not usually thought of as being a type of operator definition.

We have not presented these terms to impress the reader with any absolute distinctions involved; we feel the distinctions are in many cases artificial. But we have presented them to prepare the reader, educated by the approach that we have used in this chapter, to communicate with those educated in environments emphasizing different terminology to describe features otherwise similar to what we have discussed here. Language extensibility is the bright hope for the future of programming languages. The area presents enough intellectual challenges without the common misunderstandings arising from differences in terminology.

Language extensibility is a very popular subject in computer science today, and much has been written about it, both in general terms and by specific features for a number of languages. The following set of references provides a good background into what has been done and proposed in the field: [Gal70], [Gar68], [Gal67], [Che66], [Ard69], [Str65], [Lea66], [Sta67], [Bro67], [Hal68], [Mcl60], [Rey70], [Bra71], [Wul71], [Wij69], [Wir66], and [Chr69].

APPENDIX 1

Programming Language Syntax

A1.1 SYNTAX VERSUS SEMANTICS

Throughout our language study we have used the words *syntax* and *semantics* with no attempt to make a formal distinction between the terms. We indicated in chapter 18 that syntax relates to aspects of a language not seen by its executing machine, to notation which is translated away before execution; semantics, on the other hand, relates to language aspects reflected at execution time; semantics deals with how things work, rather than how they look.

We have hesitated to be more explicit in our differentiation because the issue is not the black/white one that so many people often see. For a programming language, the usual simple-minded rule intended to separate its syntax from its semantics is given roughly as follows:

> The syntax of a language determines the well-formed (grammatically correct) programs of that language; its semantics describe how such programs will execute.

As a general observation on syntax, this rule is not too bad, but we must not read into it any definitive precision that is not there. For what, after all, is a grammatically correct program of some language? A look at several examples should dispel any intuitive notions of grammar as an absolute concept. We consider some cases of erroneous FORTRAN statements, trying to decide whether the errors are violations of the language's syntax (grammar) or of its semantics.

Example 1: A←2B + C;

Here we see three errors that are obviously syntactic: use of ← for assignment; the illegal name 2B; and a semicolon to terminate the statement. FORTRAN allows none of these.

Example 2: I = J + 2.1

Here I and J are integers, while 2.1 is a floating-point number. It is illegal to add integers to floating-point numbers. Is the error syntactic or semantic? The statement looks more reasonable than that in the last example, but we contend that the syntax of FORTRAN precludes this statement.

Note, however, that the intelligence required to diagnose this syntactic error is somewhat greater than that required in the previous example, where illegal symbols were used. Here, all symbols are legal; we note the error only by examining the context of the symbols, and thus finding J + 2.1.

Example 3: INTEGER I

.

.

GOTO I

In this example, I is declared to be an integer, but is used in a position where a label is required. One cannot transfer to an integer. Our determination of error type begins to get difficult. All symbols are legal, and all statements are legal, viewed in isolation. To discover the error, we must investigate the GOTO statement in the context of a declaration appearing at the beginning of the program. Can we speak of the error as syntactic? Is the program ungrammatical?

Example 4: DIMENSION A(10)

.

.

I = 11
...A(I)...

Here not only a broad context is required to recognize the error in the reference to A(I), but also some knowledge of how the execution must proceed. Careful scrutiny may reveal that since the reference to A(I) is in the statement following the assignment, and since that statement cannot be reached from elsewhere, the reference must be to A(11), which is illegal.

But now we are really stretching our notion of syntax. If the statement referring to A(I) had been labeled, so that transfer could have been made to it from elsewhere, then we might have tried to trace all possible paths of flow to determine whether the variable I would always have the value 11 at this point. But such searches eventually are foiled. Generally, it is not possible to trace all flow of control through a program without actually executing it; its execution may, for example, depend on values read in at execution time. Our rule is:

> When we cannot determine that some construct
> is erroneous without executing the program, we
> must call the error, if it then does occur, a semantic
> error.

So we see a spectrum of error types, ranging from the obviously syntactic to the necessarily semantic. Intermediate types may intuitively fit into either category, depending on the beholder.

A pragmatic distinction between syntax and semantics can be made as a function of a language and a compiler for that language:

> Errors detected by the compiler are syntactic,
> while those that escape the compiler but are de-
> tected during execution are semantic.

This distinction is absolute, but only as a function of the intelligence embedded within a particular compiler for a particular language. Rather than use this route to an absolute distinction, we prefer to live with certain language characteristics definitely semantic, others definitely syntactic, and others in between. We can already classify as definitely semantic, portions of a language definition dependent upon values of data acquired during execution. We will classify as definitely syntactic, portions specified by a simple kind of language syntax description that we examine below.

A1.2 CONTEXT-FREE GRAMMARS

We now discuss a simple type of grammar for defining the syntax of a programming language. Anyone who has diagrammed sentences has made use indirectly of *Backus-Naur Form* (BNF) as a tool for defining and structuring languages. BNF is the primary tool in current use for formally describing programming-language syntax. Let us first look at BNF in a simple context of English grammar. Later we formalize it and apply it to some programming-language definitions.

Our English grammar, given in BNF, defines a collection of what we call sentences. We first define a sentence to be a subject followed by a predicate followed by a period:

SENTENCE: : = SUBJECT PREDICATE.

The terms SENTENCE, SUBJECT, and PREDICATE are called *nonterminals* of our grammar. Each is a construct to be defined. The term SENTENCE is, in addition, distinguished by the fact that it is not used to define any other nonterminals. It is the *root* of our grammar.

The period is a *terminal* of our grammar. It is a symbol actually appearing in sentences of the language being defined; it is therefore not defined elsewhere.

Our next step in building our grammar is to define the nonterminals SUBJECT and PREDICATE.

SUBJECT: : = SIMPSUB|SIMPSUB *and* SUBJECT

The vertical bar above indicates that a SUBJECT may be either the construct to the left of the bar (SIMPSUB) or the construct to its right. Thus we are defining a SUBJECT to be either a SIMPSUB, or a SIMPSUB followed by the terminal *and* followed by a SUBJECT. Note the recursive aspect of this definition, in which SUBJECT is partially defined in terms of the same construct, SUBJECT. We examine this in detail in a moment.

So that our definition of SUBJECT is meaningful, we continue by defining SIMPSUB:

SIMPSUB: : = QUALIFIERS NOUN|NOUN

A SIMPSUB is either a QUALIFIERS followed by a NOUN, or just a NOUN.

QUALIFIERS: : = ADJECTIVE|ADJECTIVE,QUALIFIERS

QUALIFIERS consists either of an ADJECTIVE, or of an ADJECTIVE followed by a comma (a terminal of the grammar) followed by a QUALIFIERS.

ADJECTIVE: : = *big*|*little*

NOUN: : = *dinners*|*books*|*Snoopy*|*Linus*|*Charlie*

An ADJECTIVE consists of either of two terminals, *big* and *little*. A NOUN consists of any of the five terminals indicated above.

Having examined all constructs pertinent to SUBJECT, we turn now to definition of the nonterminal PREDICATE:

PREDICATE: : = VERB|VERB DIROBJ|VERB DIROBJ ADVERB

Here there are three alternatives. A PREDICATE may be either a VERB, a VERB followed by a DIROBJ, or a VERB followed by a DIROBJ followed by an ADVERB.

DIROBJ: : = SUBJECT

A DIROBJ may be any construct that is valid as a SUBJECT.

VERB: : = *eats|reads*
ADVERB: : = *with feeling|reluctantly*

This completes our grammar. Let us consider some sentence candidates and try to determine whether, according to this grammar, certain strings are SENTENCE's of the language being defined.

Example 1: *Snoopy eats.*

We ask of our grammar whether this phrase is a SENTENCE. We know that a sentence must consist of a SUBJECT followed by a PREDICATE followed by a period, so we first check whether *Snoopy* can serve as a valid SUBJECT. A SUBJECT can be either of two constructs, but the second is obviously not satisfied, so we check to see whether *Snoopy* satisfies the first alternative, SIMPSUB. It cannot satisfy the first alternative for a SIMPSUB, but we find that it does satisfy the construct NOUN. Thus *Snoopy* is a valid SIMPSUB and therefore a valid SUBJECT.

    Similar analysis shows *eats* to be a valid PREDICATE. The period is present so we conclude that our candidate is in fact a valid SENTENCE of our grammar.

    Let us depict the structure of our SENTENCE by a tree. Nodes in the tree are terminals and nonterminals, while a connection from a nonterminal node to a collection of nodes indicates that the collection comprises the definition of the nonterminal node.

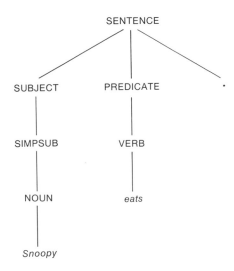

Recall that *Snoopy* is a NOUN, which is in turn a SIMPSUB, which is in turn a SUBJECT. We know that *eats* is a VERB which is in turn a PREDICATE. The collection SUBJECT PREDICATE. comprises our SENTENCE. We started with the terminal phrase *Snoopy eats.* and built it up with our grammatical definitions into a SENTENCE. The definitions of our grammar are often more procedurally called rewriting rules. We succeeded ultimately in re-writing our phrase as SENTENCE, by successively rewriting sets of con-structs as the constructs which they defined.

Our use of the grammar in this example was as a "recognizer." Our task was to take a phrase and recognize whether it was a SENTENCE. We proceeded, with the goal of SENTENCE in mind, to build up our tree from the bottom, consisting only of our phrase, to the top, which we hoped would be SENTENCE. Had this construction been impossible, we would have concluded that our phrase was not a SENTENCE. Note that we did more than just recognize whether the phrase was a SENTENCE. We created the tree representing the phrase structure of the sentence candi-date.

Grammars may be used alternatively as "generators" for construct-ing sentences of a language. In this approach, one builds a tree from top to bottom, starting with SENTENCE and progressing downward by select-ing some alternative defining each nonterminal appearing in the tree. Eventually this process results in a string of terminals which comprise a SENTENCE of the grammar.

Example 2: *Snoopy eats Linus reluctantly.*

Our first example was easy, since our phrase contained only two words. If it was a SENTENCE, then *Snoopy* had to be the SUBJECT, and *eats* had to be the PREDICATE. Thus we had no problem in making the proper choices among alternatives in our definitions. Now we look at a more complicated case, involving greater possibility of dead ends in investigation.

Again we know that we need a SUBJECT and PREDICATE, and in-tuitively we know, by examination, which parts of our phrase satisfy these requirements. But suppose that, without intuition, we were to guess, unfortunately, that *Snoopy eats* is probably the SUBJECT. Then we would start down our definitions by assuming that *Snoopy eats* is a SIMPSUB (it lacks the terminal *and*), and thus a QUALIFIERS NOUN, since two terminals are present. But we would then see that *eats* is not a NOUN (and *Snoopy* is not a QUALIFIERS). So we would have to go back and start over, discarding our choice for the SUBJECT.

From here on through our examples, we assume intelligent choices at all times, but we realize that mechanical processors performing this recognition task may not be so perceptive. Hence we look at this problem later.

If we postulate *Snoopy* as our SUBJECT, we meet with success. We are left with the task of recognizing whether the remainder of our phrase comprises a valid PREDICATE. Of our choices for a PREDICATE, we intelligently look at VERB DIROBJ ADVERB and eventually find that *Linus* is in fact a valid DIROBJ. The other terminals fit immediately as VERB and ADVERB. Our phrase structure in this case is represented as follows:

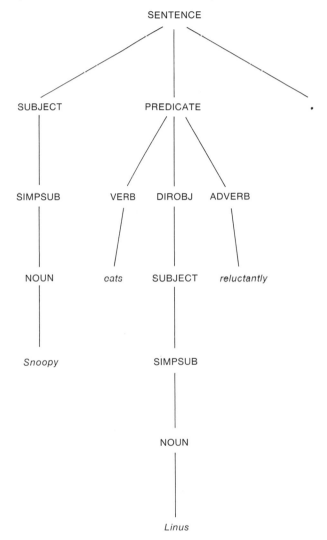

Example 3: *Linus and Snoopy and Charlie reads dinner.*

Here we have our first use of a recursive definition for our SUBJECT. With our usual clairvoyance, we choose *Linus and Snoopy and Charlie* as our candidate for SUBJECT. We then check this against the second SUBJECT alternative, SIMPSUB *and* SUBJECT.

If we propose *Linus* as our SIMPSUB, we must check *Snoopy and Charlie* as a SUBJECT. This checks satisfactorily, using *Snoopy* as a SIMPSUB and *Charlie* as a SUBJECT in the second alternative for SUBJECT.

This recursive definition of SUBJECT allows as a SUBJECT any collection of SIMPSUB's separated by *and*'s. Thus this grammar allows an infinite number of possible SUBJECT's and hence of possible SENTENCE's.

Our phrase structure in this example is shown by the tree on the following page.

We emphasize that BNF as a type of grammar is not adequate for description of natural-language syntax (according to any intuitive notion of syntax). We have used it to illustrate BNF, not English. More sophisticated types of grammars are available for describing more sophisticated languages. Our preoccupation with BNF derives from its overwhelmingly common use in definition of programming-language syntax.

Before discounting other types of grammars, however, we should explain our use of the term *context-free* in describing BNF. This refers to the requirement that the left-hand side of a BNF definition contain precisely one nonterminal. This restriction means that the nonterminal is always taken to be comprised of one of its alternative definitions, regardless of the context in which it occurs. A generalization to *context-sensitive* grammars allows the left-hand side of a definition to include the left and right context (as strings of terminals and nonterminals) of the defined symbol for which the definition is valid. Such grammars are clearly more powerful in the classes of languages that they can define, but they are also much more difficult to realize in actual programs for performing syntactic analysis.

Now we turn from our English-language example to the use of BNF for defining languages more related to programming. Let us start with a simple language consisting of expressions containing + and ∗ as operators and the names *a, b,* and *c* as operands. Examples of sentences in this language are:

$$a$$
$$a + b$$
$$b * a + c$$
$$a + b + c * b$$

We propose a simple BNF grammar for defining all such strings, using SENTENCE, as before, as our distinguished nonterminal.

```
SENTENCE: : = EXPRESSION
EXPRESSION: : = NAME|EXPRESSION OPERATOR EXPRESSION
NAME: : = a|b|c
OPERATOR: : = + | ∗
```

Note the recursive definition of EXPRESSION, which allows us to write arbitrarily long strings of names and operators.

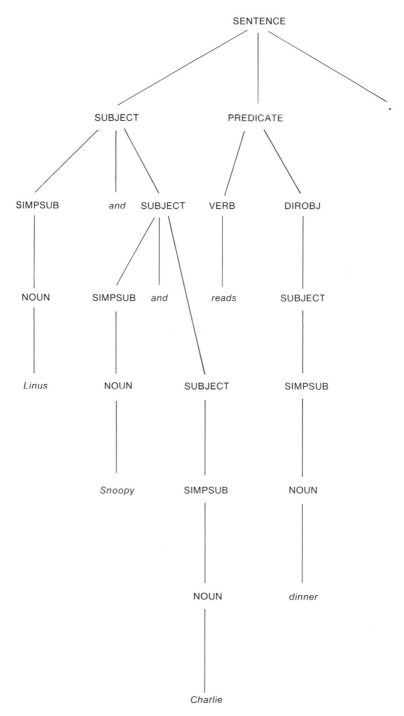

We now consider the simple string $a + b*c$, using our grammar to recognize whether it is a SENTENCE and, if so, what its phrase structure is. We check $a + b*c$ against the definition EXPRESSION OPERATOR EXPRESSION, choosing to try a as the first EXPRESSION, $+$ as the OPERATOR, and $b*c$ as the second EXPRESSION. This works well, producing the following tree:

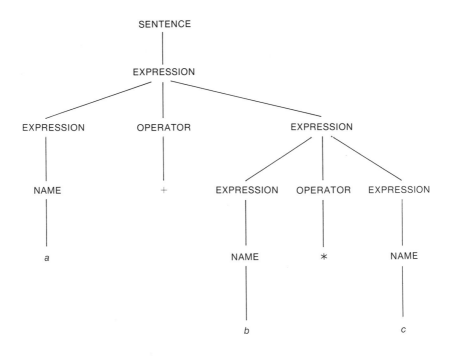

Suppose that instead of choosing a as the first EXPRESSION and $b*c$ as the second, we had tried $a + b$ as the first EXPRESSION, $*$ as the OPERATOR, and c as the second EXPRESSION. All would have worked satisfactorily, and we would have produced the following tree:

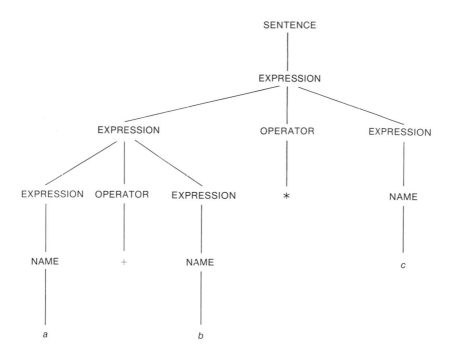

Our grammar allows the recognition of $a + b * c$ as a sentence with either of two different phrase structures. We say that the grammar is ambiguous.

The ambiguity in this example is clearly more than just a formality. The phrase structure illustrates the logical operator-operand relations within the expression. The first phrase structure represents the following expression tree:

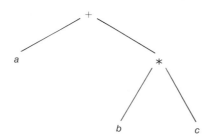

The interpretation is as though the expression had been written $a + (b * c)$. The second phrase structure represents the following tree:

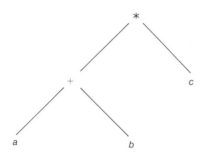

This interpretation is as though the expression had been written $(a + b) * c$. The difference between these interpretations is, of course, monumental.

Let us respecify our grammar in an attempt to eliminate the ambiguity:

SENTENCE: : = EXPRESSION
EXPRESSION: : = NAME|EXPRESSION OPERATOR NAME
NAME: : = $a|b$
OPERATOR: : = $+|*$

Only our second phrase can now be obtained, and we claim this grammar to be unambiguous. It provides a phrase structure dictating that any expression is evaluated in a left-to-right manner. The expression $a + b * c + b$, for example, is interpreted as $((a + b) * c) + b$. If we had given our definition of EXPRESSION as EXPRESSION: : = NAME|NAME OPER-ATOR EXPRESSION, we would have established a right-to-left ordering, yielding $a + (b * (c + b))$.

In chapter 6 we looked at associativity and precedence as factors involved in definition of an operator. We now see that associativity can be handled in BNF by appropriate specification of recursive definitions. Our left-to-right ordering was obtained by left-recursion of EXPRESSION. Right-to-left could be obtained by right-recursion.

Our latest grammar gives $+$ and $*$ as having equal precedence. But suppose that, as is usual, we wished $*$ to have higher precedence than $+$; suppose further that we wished $+$ to be left-to-right associative, $*$ right-to-left associative. Can we use BNF to give these characteristics to our language?

In our phrase-structure tree, we wish $+$ always to be above $*$, that is, nearer to EXPRESSION. We accomplish this by introducing $+$ as a direct constituent of EXPRESSION, and placing ✱ at a deeper level in the definitions.

SENTENCE: : = EXPRESSION
EXPRESSION: : = TERM|EXPRESSION + TERM
TERM: : = FACTOR|FACTOR ✱ TERM
FACTOR: : = a|b|c

With this new grammer, look again at our simple case of $a + b ✱ c$. If we attempt to analyze this phrase as $(a + b) ✱ c$, we immediately fail, since it is not of the form EXPRESSION + TERM, or of the form TERM ($a + b$ cannot be a FACTOR). We are forced to analyze it as $a + (b ✱ c)$, with the following phrase structure:

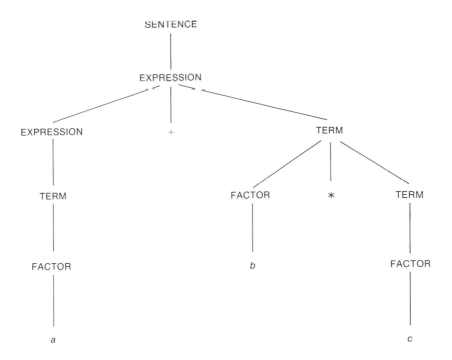

Furthermore, our left-recursive definition of EXPRESSION guarantees the left-to-right associativity of +, while our right-recursive definition of FACTOR guarantees the right-to-left associativity of ✱.

We have touched on the definitional powers of BNF for defining programming-language syntax. We have alluded to the possibility of building processors that take (as input) a BNF language description and candidate programs of that language, and produce (as output) either the phrase-structure translations of those programs or explanations of why they are grammatically erroneous. Such processors are in a sense language-independent: The processor logic is not specific to any language, only to BNF as a means of describing languages.

The problem of building processors to work efficiently from context-free language descriptions is a large area that we shall not cover here. It has led to many subcategorizations of BNF-like grammars, and subcategories are usually built around the ease with which a processor can analyze the phrase structure. The primary problem is, of course, that of making intelligent selections of definition alternatives, and of being able to back up if a poor selection is made and eventually fails. Various restrictions can be placed on grammars to ensure that only a certain number of adjacent symbols need be retained during scanning, to guarantee that the processor can have the kind of clairvoyance that we assumed in our examples.

Exercises

1. Revise our BNF grammar for expressions, in which $+$ has low priority and $*$ has high priority, so that it also allows a SENTENCE to contain parentheses, forcing certain operator-operand orderings. Construct definitions such that $a*(b+(c+b))$ is a valid SENTENCE.

2. Attempt to give unambiguous BNF grammars to define each of the following collections of SENTENCE's.

   (a) $\underbrace{a \ldots \ldots \ldots a}_{m \text{ occurrences}} \underbrace{b \ldots \ldots \ldots b}_{m \text{ occurrences}} ,m>0$

   (b) $\underbrace{a \ldots \ldots \ldots a}_{m \text{ occurrences}} \underbrace{b \ldots \ldots \ldots b}_{n \text{ occurrences}} ,m,n>0$

   (b) $\underbrace{a \ldots \ldots \ldots a}_{m \text{ occurrences}} \underbrace{b \ldots \ldots \ldots b}_{m \text{ occurrences}} \underbrace{c \ldots \ldots \ldots c}_{m \text{ occurrences}} ,m>0$

   (d) $\underbrace{a \ldots \ldots \ldots a}_{m \text{ occurrences}} \underbrace{b \ldots \ldots \ldots b}_{n \text{ occurrences}} \underbrace{a \ldots \ldots \ldots a}_{m \text{ occurrences}} ,m,n>0$

   (e) $\underbrace{a \ldots \ldots \ldots a}_{m \text{ occurrences}} \underbrace{b \ldots \ldots \ldots b}_{n \text{ occurrences}} \underbrace{a \ldots \ldots \ldots a}_{m \text{ occurrences}} \underbrace{b \ldots \ldots \ldots b}_{n \text{ occurrences}} ,m,n>0$

(Hint: Two of the above are impossible to describe with BNF.)

3. Give a BNF grammar allowing as SENTENCE's all nonnegative integers divisible by 4. In doing so, assume that the integers are represented to the base 2.

4. Repeat exercise 3, but assume that the integers are represented to the base 10.

A1.3 ALTERNATE REPRESENTATIONS OF PHRASE STRUCTURE

We have frequently used trees to denote the phrase structures for language constructs. They are a convenient way to illustrate general operator–operand relationships without use of precedence and associativity tables, parentheses, and various syntactic quirks. Trees are also used extensively for this purpose in many language processors. They are not, however, the simplest representation vehicle for structure, because they have an inherent two-dimensional trait often inefficient to realize with common data structures.

   We now discuss several varieties of a linear phrase-structure representation, looking at their derivation from external-language syntax, and the convenient ways in which they can be directly executed. These text representations show unambiguously the operator–operand structure of programs, and are equivalent in their information content. Simple techniques are available to map between pairs of these representations.

   Linearization of phrase structure is generically called *Polish form*, after its inventor, the Pole, Lukasiewicz ([Luk51] and [Bur54]). It provides a linear operator–operand format in which each operator of a language immediately precedes its ordered set of operands (prefix Polish) or succeeds them (postfix or reverse Polish). Let us look at several examples of these forms:

Source text	Prefix Polish	Postfix Polish
$a + b$	$+ab$	$ab+$
$(a + b) * c$	$* + abc$	$ab + c*$
$a + (b * c)$	$+ a * bc$	$abc * +$

The first example consists of a single operator and two names, and the two Polish forms are self-explanatory. The second example involves two operators, $+$ and $*$. The operands of $+$ are a and b, while those of $*$ are $a + b$ and c. Since $a + b$ is represented in prefix Polish as $+ab$, the entire expression consists of the $*$ followed by its operands, $+ab$ and c in that order. The Polish representations maintain operand order as well as operator–operand relations.

The third example illustrates the sensitivity of the Polish forms to parenthesization (and, as we shall see, to associativity and precedence) in the source form. Here b and c are operands of $*$, while a and $b*c$ are operands of $+$.

Consider now a language of operators and names for which the relative precedence of each operator has been given, along with the direction of each precedence level. Our task is to describe an algorithm for translating sentences of such a language into postfix Polish form (each operator immediately follows its operands). We have available an output queue in which to build our Polish string, and we use an internal stack to hold operators temporarily during our analysis. Our approach is diagrammed in the flowchart shown on the following page.

Let us work through our previous example of a language with two operators: $+$, left-to-right associative and of low priority; and $*$, right-to-left associative and of high priority. We take as source input the string $a+b*c*d+e$. For convenience of observing movements of the specific operators, we index them to separate each from other occurrences of the same operator. (Thus, with spacing for readability, our first entry in the source queue is $a +1\ b *1\ c *2\ d +2\ e$.)

We leave individual steps through the flowchart to the reader, and record only the changes to the source and output queues and the stack.

Step	Source queue	Output queue	Stack
	$a + 1b*1c*2d + 2e$	empty	empty
1	$+ 1b*1c*2d + 2e$	a	empty
2	$b*1c*2d + 2e$	a	$+ 1$
3	$*1c*2d + 2e$	ab	$+ 1$
4	$c*2d + 2e$	ab	$+ 1*1$
5	$*2d + 2e$	abc	$+ 1*1$
6	$d + 2e$	abc	$+ 1*1*2$
7	$+ 2e$	$abcd$	$+ 1*1*2$
8	e	$abcd*2$	$+ 1*1$
9	e	$abcd*2*1$	$+ 1$
10	e	$abcd*2*1 + 1$	$+ 2$
11	empty	$abcd*2*1 + 1e$	$+ 2$
12	empty	$abcd*2*1 + 1e + 2$	empty

The reader should convince himself that our result is in fact a postfix Polish representation of our input string. He should work through a number of examples in this manner to become familiar with the use of the stack and its relation to precedence and associativity.

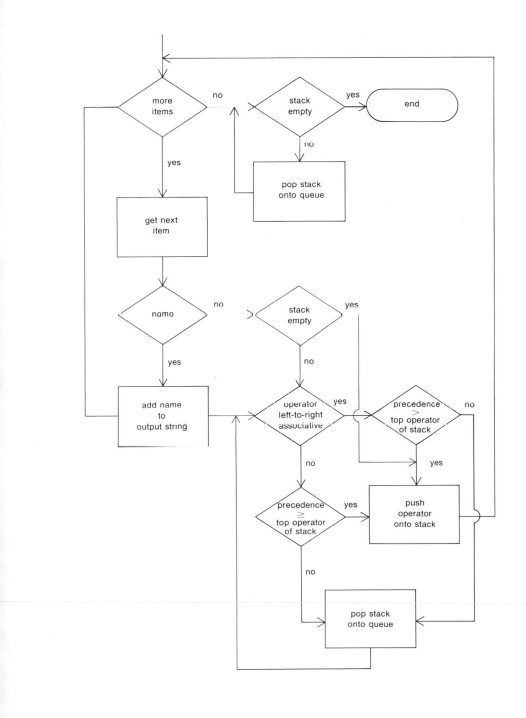

Suppose now that we have the converse situation, namely, a postfix Polish representation of some expression sentence that we are to execute. Again we use a stack, but this time to hold operands temporarily, rather than operators. Our approach can be flowcharted as follows.

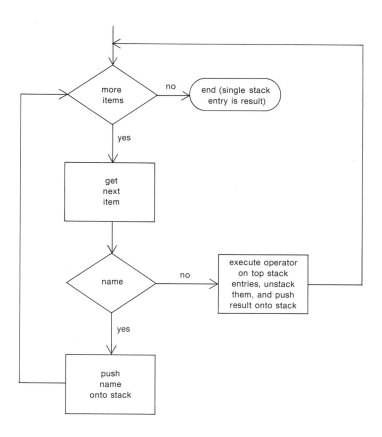

As an example, we trace the execution of the postfix Polish representation that we created above.

Step	Polish queue	Stack
	$abcd**+e+$	empty

1	$bcd**+e+$	a
2	$cd**+e+$	ab
3	$d**+e+$	abc
4	$**+e+$	$abcd$
5	$*+e+$	$ab(c*d)$
6	$+e+$	$a(b*(c*d))$
7	$e+$	$(a+(b*(c*d)))$
8	$+$	$(a+(b*(c*d)))e$
9	empty	$((a+(b*(c*d)))+e)$

Here we can see clearly the ease of execution of Polish strings, using only a stack to hold operands until time for their use with an operator.

We have now traced two processes from source to execution. We have started with a language of operators and names, complete with precedence and associativity information. That has allowed us to generate Polish representations of programs of that language, after which it is easy to execute the Polish forms. With the knowledge of how this approach works, we can now consider a more direct execution mechanism, working directly from a BNF language description.

Recall our grammar for our above language with $+$ and $*$ and their given precedences and associativities. We rewrite that grammar trivially, specifying alternatives as though they were separate definitions. We number the definitions for reference purposes. Further, we introduce an actual execution semantics specification into the grammar, by describing an action to be taken upon each use of a definition during syntactic analysis. As usual, we use a stack (s) as an aid, and we employ our stack operators from chapter 8.

	Definition	Execution semantics
1	SENTENCE: : = EXPRESSION	END (result is on stack)
2	EXPRESSION: : = TERM	no action
3	EXPRESSION: : = EXPRESSION + TERM	P2←POP(S)
		P1←POP(S)
		PUSH(S, P1 + P2)
4	TERM: : = FACTOR	no action
5	TERM: : = FACTOR * TERM	P2←POP(S)
		P1←POP(S)
		PUSH(S, P1 * P2)
6	FACTOR: : = a	PUSH(S, a)
7	FACTOR: : = b	PUSH(S, b)
8	FACTOR: : = c	PUSH(S, c)

Now let us trace the steps in building and executing the phrase-structure tree for our simple expression $a+b*c$.

	Definition	Tree	Stack

Initial

state $a + b * c$ empty

```
              FACTOR
                |
Step 1   6    a + b * c          a


              TERM
                |
              FACTOR
                |
      2   4   a + b * c          a


         EXPRESSION
              |
            TERM
              |
           FACTOR
              |
      3   2  a + b * c           a


         EXPRESSION
              |
            TERM
              |
        FACTOR    FACTOR
           |         |
      4   7  a   +   b  *  c      ab


         EXPRESSION
              |
            TERM
              |
      FACTOR  FACTOR  FACTOR
         |       |       |
      5  8  a  +  b  *  c         abc


         EXPRESSION
              |
         TERM           TERM
          |              |
      FACTOR  FACTOR  FACTOR
         |       |       |
      6  4  a  +  b  *  c         abc
```

```
        EXPRESSION              TERM
            |                  / | \
          TERM              /    |   TERM
            |             /      |     |
         FACTOR        FACTOR    |   FACTOR
            |             |      |     |
7   5       a      +      b      *     c                a(b*c)
```

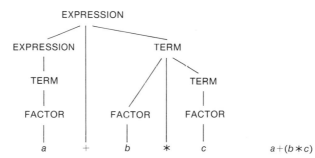

```
                    EXPRESSION
                  /     |      \
         EXPRESSION     |        TERM
             |          |      / | \
           TERM         |    /    |  TERM
             |          |  /      |    |
          FACTOR        | FACTOR  | FACTOR
             |          |   |     |   |
8   3        a      +   b   *     c              a+(b*c)
```

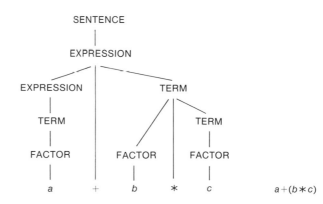

```
                     SENTENCE
                        |
                    EXPRESSION
                  /     |      \
         EXPRESSION     |        TERM
             |          |      / | \
           TERM         |    /    |  TERM
             |          |  /      |    |
          FACTOR        | FACTOR  | FACTOR
             |          |   |     |   |
9   1        a      +   b   *     c              a+(b*c)
```

At the expense of being somewhat oversimplistic, we can claim to have specified, with our set of BNF rules and the action specifications accompanying them, a complete language definition for our simple language. We can now envision writing a processor that accepts a definition such as ours as input, and uses that definition to analyze programs written in the language defined by it. This processor would then serve as an automated language-translator constructor. Given a language definition, it would produce a comprehensive translator for that language.

Our oversimplification lies both in the inadequency of BNF for describing many language phenomena, and in its overcomplexity for use by a processor such as we have described. As we indicated earlier, numerous restrictions and stylizations may be placed on BNF to make its handling easier, but these may at the same time reduce its descriptive power even further.

Nevertheless, this approach to automated language-translator production is promising, and a number of techniques have been developed for this purpose ([Iro61], [Ing66], [Fel66], [Pol72], [Coc70], and [Fos70]). There is every reason to hope that the general approach may be extended to serve as a very useful tool for automated translator-building.

For thorough treatments of grammars and language translators, see [Hop69], [Fel68], [Cho62], and [Gri72].

Exercises

5. Assume that we have a language with three infix operators of precedences and associativities as follows:

$+$	lowest	left-to-right
$*$	middle	right-to-left
$\uparrow$	highest	left-to-right

Give prefix Polish representations of the following expressions:

(a) $a + b + c$
(b) $a * b * c$
(c) $a * b + c \uparrow d$
(d) $a + b * c \uparrow d$
(e) $a \uparrow b * c + d$

6. Assuming the same language, give postfix Polish representations of the expressions above.

7. Flowcharts involving stacks and queues were presented for translating infix notation into postfix Polish, and then for executing the postfix Polish. Define analogous flowcharts, also using stacks and queues (several may be required), for translating instead to prefix Polish and then executing that.

8. Revise our flowchart for translating infix notation to postfix Polish so that the source text may include parentheses to govern the operator-operand associations.

9. Given a string of operators and names, and assuming each operator to take exactly two operands, describe an algorithm for determining whether that string is a valid postfix Polish representation of an expression. For example, $ab + cd + *$ represents $(a + b) * (c + d)$, but $ab + *c$ represents nothing.

10. Give an algorithm for translating a tree representation of an expression into its postfix Polish equivalent.

APPENDIX 2

Theories of Computation

In the 1930s there arose among mathematical logicians an interest in the theory of computability of functions. It became necessary to formalize the intuitive concept of computability to be able to determine whether certain functions were "effectively computable," that is, whether it was possible to describe a mechanical algorithm for computing values of such functions. This formalization took the form of definitions of a number of models for computability; it then became possible to speak formally of computability in terms of these models.

An encouraging aspect of much of this continuing work has been the surprising equivalence of theoretic capabilities of the models proposed. Even models differing widely in appearance, and in data and control structures, were proven to be equivalent in power. For all sets of arguments for which a certain function was defined, its computability with one of these models implied its computability with others. Such consistencies tended to bolster the credibility of the term *computability* as more than an intuitive notion.

We are not concerned in our discussion with formal equivalences. Instead, we investigate three of these models from a language point of view. We look at their control and data structures, and we use each to solve several problems. In doing so, we see ways in which they relate to programming languages we have studied. These models are functionally equivalent; each can simulate the effects of the other two. Yet in the pragmatics of their approaches to solving problems, they are totally dissimilar.

A2.1 MARKOV ALGORITHMS

The first model we look at is that of Markov algorithms. This model is particularly interesting because of its elegant rendering of a number of types of algorithms. While this model is functionally equivalent to the others, it appears less primitive and higher-level in terms of ease of programming with it. There is a striking similarity between this model and the SNOBOL language; both the data and control structures of Markov algorithms are modeled quite closely in SNOBOL.

The input to a Markov algorithm is a single string of characters, each of which is included in an alphabet designated by the machine; we denote this alphabet with uppercase letters: A, B, C, and so forth. The output of the algorithm is that string, as modified by the algorithm. The single string is the only data structure available with the model; it is, however, flexible in its capacity to stretch or shrink in length according to its contents.

A Markov algorithm consists of an ordered set of statements specifying modifications to be made to the string:

$$string1 \rightarrow string2$$

This statement specifies that within the input string, the leftmost occurrence, if any, of the substring string1 is to be replaced by the string string2. The two strings need not be of the same length. The space occupied by string1 will be expanded or contracted as required to exactly accommodate string2.

Suppose that we start with the input string DABCAB. Let us look at several replacement examples. Each (except the first) takes the result string of the preceding example as input. For each, the statement to be executed and the result string produced by its execution are indicated.

$$AB \rightarrow XYZ \qquad DXYZCAB$$

The leftmost occurrence of the substring AB is changed to XYZ. This requires expanding the input string.

$$XYZ \rightarrow AB \qquad DABCAB$$

Here the input string DXYZCAB is contracted as required.

$$AB \rightarrow \wedge \qquad DCAB$$

The special character $\wedge$ indicates the null string. The first AB is simply deleted from the input string.

$$\wedge \rightarrow XY \qquad XYDCAB$$

The character ∧ can be used either as in the previous example or alone on the left-hand side of a statement. The effect in the latter case is to introduce the indicated replacement characters at the start of the string.

AD→EFG   XYDCAB

Here there is no occurrence in the input string of the substring to be replaced. Thus the input string is not modified.

The flow of control through a Markov algorithm depends on whether or not substrings are found and replaced successfully. Execution begins with the first statement. Subsequently, if a statement succeeds, that is, if a substring to be replaced is found and replaced, execution resumes with the first statement of the algorithm. If, on the other hand, a statement fails (a substring to be replaced is not found), execution continues with the next statement.

A Markov algorithm terminates in either of two ways:

1. The last statement is executed and fails.
2. A statement terminated with a period is executed successfully.

To write string-manipulation algorithms on this machine, it is necessary to have available a set of symbols from a character set disjoint from that of the input strings. Such symbols can then be used as punctuation characters in many ways, with the certainty that they are not initially contained in any input strings. We denote such symbols with Greek letters: α, β, γ, and the like.

Finally, a third disjoint alphabet of characters must be available for representing character parameters within a statement. We denote these characters by lowercase letters: a, b, c, and so forth.

AXB→CX

This statement specifies replacement for the three-character string consisting of A, followed by any single character, followed by B; that string is to be replaced by the string consisting of C followed by the character found between A and B, whatever it was.

This completes our description of Markov algorithms. Let us look at several program examples.

Example 1.
All occurrences of the character A are to be deleted from an input string.

A→∧

This one-statement program accomplishes the task. Its first execution deletes the leftmost A (if any). This success sends control to the first (and in this case only) statement of the program. The single statement is executed repeatedly as long as A's remain. When the statement fails, the program terminates.

Example 2.
This program moves the first character of an input string to the end of the string. The numbers at the left of the program statements are included for reference purposes.

1. $\alpha xy \rightarrow y\alpha x$
2. $\alpha \rightarrow \wedge$.
3. $\wedge \rightarrow \alpha$

Suppose that we have an input string ABCD. Let us trace the execution of our program.

Statement	Success or failure	String contents
1	f	ABCD
2	f	ABCD
3	s	αABCD
1	s	BαACD
1	s	BCαAD
1	s	BCDαA
1	f	BCDαA
2	s	BCDA

Initially, statements 1 and 2 fail. Statement 3 is executed successfully, placing the punctuation symbol α at the beginning of the string and transferring control to statement 1. Now, statement 1 is executed successfully. (It replaces α followed by any two characters, by the second of these characters followed by α and the first.) This statement is executed repetitively (reversing the order of successive characters) until it fails because there are no longer two characters following α. Statement 2 is executed successfully, deleting α. By definition, successful execution of a statement followed by a period terminates the program.

Note in this example the importance of ordering statements appropriately. The rather inflexible control flow rules, not allowing labeling and transfers, make ordering difficult, particularly before one is accustomed to using the language.

Example 3.
Our task is to reverse the characters of a string. We do this by moving the first character to the end as before, then moving the next character down to the position just preceding the first character, and so on.

1. $\alpha\beta \rightarrow \wedge$.
2. $\alpha x\beta \rightarrow \beta x$
3. $\alpha xy \rightarrow y\alpha x$
4. $\alpha x \rightarrow \beta x$
5. $\wedge \rightarrow \alpha$

Again we follow the execution, for the input string ABCD, indicating (for brevity) only statement executions that succeed.

Statement	String contents
5	αABCD
3	BαACD
3	BCαAD
3	BCDαA
4	BCDβA
5	αBCDβA
3	CαBDβA
3	CDαBβA
2	CDβBA
5	αCDβBA
3	DαCβBA
2	DβCBA
5	αDβCBA
2	βDCBA
5	$\alpha\beta$DCBA
1	DCBA

As in the previous example, α is used to move each character along the string. But here we must also introduce a symbol β to mark the end of the original string. Each character is then moved down to the position just following β. Completion of the algorithm is signaled by the presence of $\alpha\beta$ with no intervening characters of the string.

Again the ordering problem is a severe one; before proceeding, we alleviate it SNOBOL-style. We propose the ability to label statements of a Markov algorithm and to append label references to our statements. If a statement succeeds, and a label is appended to it, then transfer of control is to the statement bearing that label. If the statement fails, or if no label is appended, execution continues as we described it previously. Our labeling technique is borrowed from the excellent development of Markov algorithms in [Gal70].

How can we justify this introduction of labels into our algorithms? Are we not altering the character of our machine by endowing it with an intelligence that it did not possess previously?

The authors of the above reference have shown that any labeled

Markov algorithm can be translated into an equivalent Markov algorithm without labels. More strongly, they have shown this by producing a Markov algorithm to effect the transformation. The algorithm takes as its input string a labeled Markov algorithm, and translates it into an equivalent unlabeled Markov algorithm. And incidentally, the Markov algorithm for doing the transformation is written with labels. This technique is analogous to the bootstrapping that we saw in LISP in chapter 16. A compiler has been written, as a labeled Markov algorithm, to translate labeled Markov algorithms into unlabeled Markov algorithms. The compiler itself must then be hand-translated to run as an unlabeled Markov algorithm.

So labels are really just a convenience. They do not introduce any new powers into the Markov algorithm structure. This might be expected, since we have already pointed out the adequacy of Markov algorithms for executing any intuitively computable function. Certainly, our intuitive notion of calculation includes an ability to transfer control within an algorithm.

With this new coding convenience at our disposal, we continue by noting an analogy between Markov algorithms and BNF. Each consists of a set of rules for rewriting symbol strings in some fashion. Of course BNF is more restrictive in the kinds of strings that can occur as left-hand sides of rules, and it lacks the parameter capability. But even more restrictive is BNF's formulation as a definitional, rather than algorithmic, language; it has no inherent rules for control flow through the definitions. Recall from exercise 2 of this appendix the attempt to describe strings $a^m b^m c^m$ by BNF rules. We could not do so, both because of the context-free nature of BNF, and because of the lack of control primitives. Using Markov algorithms, however, we can easily write both a generator and a recognizer for such strings.

$$
\begin{aligned}
&\text{M:} \quad \wedge \rightarrow ABC, L \\
&\text{L:} \quad BA \rightarrow AB, L \\
&\qquad CA \rightarrow AC, L \\
&\qquad CB \rightarrow BC, L \\
&\qquad \textit{‘write string’}, M
\end{aligned}
$$

This is almost a generator for strings $A^m B^m C^m$. The command *‘write string’* has been introduced to allow presentation of each string as it is generated. We could, with a little more effort, write the algorithm to create a growing string containing first ABC, then later AABBCCαABC, then later AAABBBCCCαAABBCCαABC, and so on.

$$
\begin{aligned}
&\text{K:} \quad A \rightarrow \wedge, L \\
&\qquad \wedge \rightarrow \sigma. \\
&\text{L:} \quad B \rightarrow \wedge, M \\
&\qquad \wedge \rightarrow \wedge.
\end{aligned}
$$

M: $c \rightarrow \wedge, \kappa$
$\wedge \rightarrow \wedge$.

This serves as a recognizer for such strings. Upon termination, a string value of σ indicates that the string was a sentence. Any other value indicates that it was not a sentence.

The authors of [Gal70] go further than just the introduction of labels in Markov algorithms. They build from them, via bootstrapped compilation as we have described it, an extended model with structure almost as complex as that of ALGOL: blocks, local variables, procedures, and so on. Development of this kind lends more than theoretic credence to the programming power of the model. It presents a usable, high-level algorithmic language adequate without significant extension for solving a large class of problems. The language is, as we emphasized, very similar to SNOBOL in its treatment of both data and control. And the basic data structure from which its power is derived is the character string. Again we see that string manipulation is a more generally useful language feature than might be supposed.

Exercises

1. Given the grammar:

> SENTENCE: : = EXPRESSION
> EXPRESSION: : = a|(EXPRESSION + EXPRESSION)

write a labeled (or unlabeled) Markov algorithm to convert any sentence of this grammar into postfix Polish (+ is to be taken as an operator, with the EXPRESSION's on either side as its two operands).

2. Given the grammar:

> SENTENCE: : = EXPRESSION
> EXPRESSION: : = TERM|EXPRESSION−TERM
> TERM: : = x|x/TERM

write a labeled Markov algorithm to convert any sentence of this grammar to postfix Polish.

A2.2 TURING MACHINES

Whereas Markov algorithms bear little resemblance to any real machines in several of their characteristics (particularly the data string), Turing machines are intuitively a bit less abstract, with properties resembling those of real computing machines. In one sense, Turing machines are harder to program than Markov algorithms because of more primitive, nonelastic storage (see below). But in another sense they are easier to program because of less awkward features for regulating flow of control through an algorithm.

The storage for a Turing machine consists of a tape divided into squares, each of which contains one symbol:

. . .	S_1	S_2	S_4		S_3	S_2		. . .

The tape is unbounded on both ends. While at any time a Turing tape contains only a finite number of symbol squares, squares may be added at either end. Any square into which a symbol has not been placed explicitly is considered to contain a blank (b).

A Turing machine has a finite set of symbols, including b, which we designate as the alphabet of the machine. The machine also has a finite set of internal states $q_0, q_1, ..., q_n$; it is always in precisely one of these states.

The machine examines and modifies squares of the tape with a read/write head under which the tape may pass in either direction. The action taken by the machine at any point during execution is totally determined by its current internal state and the symbol under the head. This action may be any one of the following:

■ Erase the symbol being scanned, write a new symbol in its place, and pass into some internal state.

■ Move left one square and pass into some internal state.

■ Move right one square and pass into some internal state.

■ Terminate execution.

At the beginning of execution, the machine is in initial state (q_0), and the head is positioned over the leftmost square of the input tape. Execution terminates if the machine passes to an internal state for which, in conjunction with the current symbol being scanned, no action has been specified in the machine algorithm. The result of the execution is the final contents of the tape.

A Turing algorithm consists of a finite set of quadruples of any of three forms:

1. q_i s_j s_k q_l

    2. q_i s_j L q_l
    3. q_i s_j R q_l

The first of these specifies that if the machine is in internal state q_i and is scanning symbol s_j, then s_j is to be erased, s_k is to be written in that square, and the machine is to pass into state q_l. The second and third quadruples are similar, but instead of modifying the scanned square, these quadruples cause the read/write head to be positioned one square to the left (L) or right (R) from the current position on the tape. (Do not associate L and R with the direction of tape movement. Moving the tape to the left would position the head to the right.)

An algorithm cannot contain two quadruples having identical pairs of first components since, as we indicated, this pair completely determines the action of the machine. Note also, in terms of our quadruples, execution ceases when an initial component pair that is not part of any quadruple arises.

It is important to observe that an initial quadruple pair q_i s_j does not completely determine the state of an execution, though it does completely determine the action to be taken. There may be multiple occurrences of the symbol s_j on the tape, so that to record completely the machine state, it is necessary to indicate both the internal state and the tape square under scan.

Let us define some simple Turing machines and algorithms to be executed.

Example 1.
A tape consists of a sequence of contiguous squares containing 1s. We are to erase the tape by changing the 1s to ƀs. We use a machine with states $\{q_0, q_1, q_2\}$ and with alphabet $\{ƀ, 1\}$. We number the quadruples for later reference.

    1. q_0 1 ƀ q_1
    2. q_0 ƀ ƀ q_2
    3. q_1 ƀ R q_0

Let us trace the sequence of state changes to see how this algorithm works on an input string. We indicate a state by showing the string, the current internal state of the machine, and the character under scan. Thus, the input tape contains the string 111, the initial internal state of the machine is q_0, and the first character to be scanned is the leftmost 1 of 111. Each state passes into the next by application of the indicated quadruple.

Note that in the next-to-last step, the head is moved to a new square that has been generated and appended to the right end of the tape. That square is considered to have been given an initial symbol ƀ.

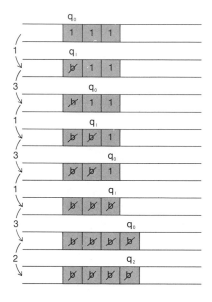

Example 2.

A tape contains a collection of 1s as before. We are to create another copy of this collection to the right of the original, with the two copies separated by $*$. We define a machine with alphabet $\{\emptyset, 1, *\}$ and states $\{q_0, q_1, q_2, q_3, q_4, q_5\}$.

1.	q_0	1	$*$	q_0
2.	q_0	$*$	R	q_0
3.	q_0	$\emptyset$	$*$	q_1
4.	q_1	1	R	q_1
5.	q_1	$*$	R	q_1
6.	q_1	$\emptyset$	1	q_2
7.	q_2	1	L	q_2
8.	q_2	$*$	L	q_3
9.	q_3	1	L	q_3
10.	q_3	$*$	1	q_4
11.	q_4	1	L	q_4
12.	q_4	$*$	R	q_1
13.	q_4	$\emptyset$	R	q_5

We trace the sequence of state changes as before, assuming an input tape containing the string 11.

A useful convention that we have followed here is to terminate an algorithm with the head stationed, as at the start, over the leftmost character of the tape. This allows successive algorithms to be merged easily.

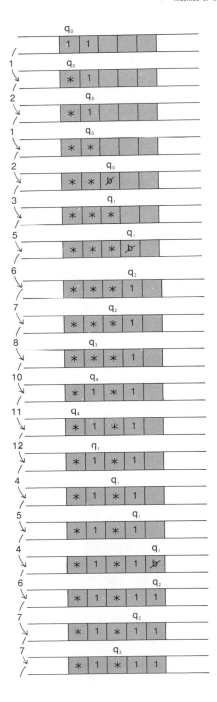

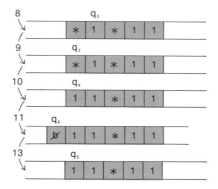

Example 3.

It is often convenient to express a nonnegative integer on a Turing tape as a sequence of 1s. So that zero is expressible, we use a sequence of n 1s to represent the integer n-1. Now we would like a Turing algorithm to add two such integers, initially separated by +. Our machine contains the alphabet $\{b,1,+\}$ and the internal states $\{q_0,q_1,q_2\}$.

1.	q_0	1	b	q_0
2.	q_0	b	R	q_1
3.	q_1	1	R	q_1
4.	q_1	+	1	q_1
5.	q_1	b	L	q_2
6.	q_2	1	b	q_2

Suppose that our tape initially contains a representation of 2 + 3: 111 + 1111. We trace the execution of our algorithm as before.

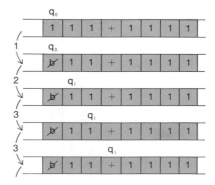

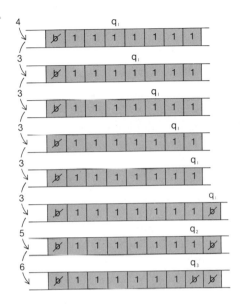

We have in the above sequence erased two 1s and added one 1 (by changing the + to 1). We started with two more 1s than the value of our sum, and arrived at the representation of that sum as one more 1 than its value.

Again we might have chosen at the end of our algorithm to move the head back to the left end of the result. We could have done so by replacing the last quadruple, q_2 1 ƀ q_2, by the sequence

$$
\begin{array}{cccc}
q_2 & 1 & ƀ & q_2 \\
q_2 & ƀ & L & q_3 \\
q_3 & 1 & L & q_3 \\
q_3 & ƀ & R & q_4 \\
\end{array}
$$

A more challenging example, but one that we shall not examine, is the definition of what is termed a universal Turing machine. This machine is an abstract analogy of the LISP interpreter discussed in chapter 17. Input to the universal Turing machine algorithm is a tape consisting of two segments: (1) a representation of some Turing algorithm and (2) an input tape for that algorithm. The task of the universal Turing algorithm is to simulate the execution of the Turing algorithm on the tape, acting on its input tape. The output of the universal Turing algorithm is the unchanged representation of the simulated algorithm, followed by the modification of its input tape as defined by that simulated algorithm.

The universal Turing algorithm is, then, truly universal in that it can simulate the execution of any other Turing algorithm.

Exercises

3. Write a Markov algorithm to perform the copying function defined by the Turing machine (example 2 in this section).

4. Write a Turing algorithm to perform binary additions on a pair of binary numbers. Thus, for example, an input string of 101 + 100 should be transformed into an output string of 1001.

A2.3 RECURSIVE FUNCTIONS

The theoretic studies of effectively computable functions originated with Church's Thesis (in [Kle52]) that every effectively computable function can be expressed as a general recursive function. This thesis is not provable because of the imprecision of the term *effectively computable*. Yet as we have emphasized, independent attempts to define abstract machines to carry out computation have resulted in identical computing capacity. Now we look at the first of those models, the one that prompted Church's Thesis and the subsequent development of the models.

Both Markov algorithms and, to a much greater extent, Turing algorithms bear some resemblance to actual machine algorithms. Each has a single unbounded data structure on which algorithms operate; and each involves certain basic control features dictating the order of execution of algorithm statements. These separate statements are the building blocks of the algorithms.

Recursive functions provide a very different approach to computation, resembling that of LISP. The notation is that of nested functions, with control a totally opaque part of the machine not available explicitly to the user. Nonnegative integers provide the infinite alphabet of the machine, with data structures occurring as ordered n-tuples of integers or of functions of integers. The nonnegative integers provide a structured alphabet, in that they are understood by the machine as an infinite ordered set. All machine features that we look at below are predicated upon this understanding.

We start with the initial functions of a machine:

1. Zero function:
   $z(x) = 0$ for all x.
2. Successor function:
   $s(x) = x + 1$ for all x.
3. Projection functions:
   $U_i^n(x_1,...,x_n) = x_i$ for all $x_1...x_n$.

Three construction rules allow definition of new recursive functions from previously defined ones:

4. Substitution functions:
   $$f(x_1...x_n) = g(h_1(x_1...x_n),...,h_m(x_1...x_n))$$
   If the functions g and $h_1,...,h_m$ are recursive, then f is recursive.

5. Recursion functions:
   $$f(x_1...x_n,0) = g(x_1...x_n)$$
   $$f(x_1...x_n,y+1) = h(x_1...x_n,y,f(x_1...x_n,y)) \text{ for } y \geq 0.$$
   If g and h are recursive, then f is recursive.
   Also allowed here is the special case of n = 0, which leaves
   us with the system
   $$f(0) = c \text{ (an integer)}$$
   $$f(y+1) = h(y,f(y))$$

6. μ-functions:
   $$f(x_1...x_n) = \mu y(g(x_1...x_n,y) = 0)$$
   Here the definition of f denotes the least y for which
   $g(x_1...x_n,y) = 0$. f is defined only if there is at least one y
   for which $g(x_1...x_n,y) = 0$, and f is then recursive if g is
   recursive.

A function f is said to be *primitive recursive* if it follows from the initial
functions by a finite sequence of substitutions and recursions as in definitions 4 and 5 above. A function f is said to be *recursive*, or *general recursive*, if it follows from the initial functions by a finite sequence of substitutions, recursions, and invocations of the μ operator as in definition 6.

Evidently any primitive recursive function is general recursive; the
converse does not hold. It can be shown that there are functions definable with use of the μ operator but otherwise undefinable by any of the
definitions 1 through 5. Thus definition 6 is not derivable from the other
definitions. An example of a general recursive function that is not primitive
recursive is Ackermann's Function, which can be shown to grow faster
with increase in its argument than any primitive recursive function of that
argument. Ackermann's Function (actually a variant of the original) is
given by the following:

$$f(0,y) = y+1$$
$$f(x+1,0) = f(x,1)$$
$$f(x+1,y+1) = f(x,f(x+1,y))$$

See [Her 65] for a proof that this recursive function is not primitive recursive.

Let us now define some simple recursive functions. Since all of
them are primitive recursive functions, the μ operator is not required.

1. **m + n**
   We note that m + 0 = m, and that m + (n + 1) =
   (m + n) + 1.

Thus we define ADD(m,n) by
$$ADD(m,0) = U_1^1(m) = m$$
$$ADD(m,s(n)) = F(m,n,ADD(m,n))$$
where F is defined by
$$F(x,y,z) = s(U_3^3(x,y,z)).$$
Thus ADD(m,s(n)) = s(ADD(m,n)).
Note that this definition uses definitions 2 through 5.

2. **m × n**

We note that $m \times 0 = 0$, and that $m \times (n+1) = (m \times n) + m$.

We define MULT(m,n) by
$$MULT(m,0) = z(m) = 0$$
$$MULT(m,s(n)) = F(m,n,MULT(m,n))$$
where F is defined by
$$F(x,y,z) = ADD(U_3^3(x,y,z),U_1^3(x,y,z)).$$
Thus MULT(m,s(n)) = ADD(MULT(m,n),m).

3. **m!**

Note that $0! = 1$, while $(m+1)! = m! \times (m+1)$.
We define FACT(m) by
$$FACT(0) = s(0) = 1$$
$$FACT(s(m)) = F(m,FACT(m))$$
where F is defined by
$$F(x,y) = MULT(s(x),U_2^2(x,y)).$$
Thus FACT(s(m)) = MULT(s(m),FACT(m)).

In these examples we can see that the problem-solving orientation of recursive functions is totally different from the orientation of Turing machines or Markov algorithms. Execution control is hidden from the user, and typical, straightforward applications revolve around integer arithmetic rather than around strings. With either Markov algorithms or Turing machines, the simulation of numerical algorithms is difficult because of their general emphasis on character manipulation. With recursive functions, we have the opposite problem: Numbers are easy to handle, but difficult simulations may be required to solve problems of a nonnumeric nature. Complicated numbering schemes must be used to map arbitrary strings unambiguously into integers, and equally complicated functions must be defined to carry out character-manipulation of these representations.

But despite these awkward tradeoffs, we must again emphasize the importance of even the purely theoretic equivalence of these models. All were intended as concrete realizations for the intuitive notion of "effective computability," and the similarity of the results is remarkable. It leaves us able to speak of computability as an intuitive notion, but one for which our individual intuitions are not likely to conflict.

Detailed formal treatment of these and other formal models of computation can be found in [Hop69], [Kle52], [Yas71], [Gal70], and [Her65].

Exercises

5. Define a recursive function to perform exponentiation EXP(m,n) defined to be m^n for integers $m,n \geq 0$. The function may use in its definition any of the functions defined in this text.

6. If we wished to use recursive functions to simulate the effect of Markov algorithms, the first problem would be finding a way to represent a given string from an alphabet unambiguously by a nonnegative integer. The correspondence must be one-to-one between strings and integers. Define such a mapping and the integer equivalent of the substitution of one substring within a given string for another.

APPENDIX 3

ALGOL 60 Syntax

ALGOL is, by today's standards, not particularly sophisticated in terms of features offered. But the language retains at least historical interest, because of the important structural concepts that it introduced into the computing world, and because of the elegance of the language definition. We reproduce in this appendix the complete BNF syntax as it appeared in the revised ALGOL 60 Report included in [Bau64]. The reader is urged to scan through it, to understand the degree of formality used in definition of the language syntax and to become familiar with its formal terminology. This description may also be used as a reference for checking syntactic correctness of programs.

In the notation, the symbols $<$ $>$ delimit nonterminals; uppercase letters represent terminals that involve alphabetic symbols. Our presentation closely parallels that of the ALGOL 60 Report. For convenience of reference, we number the language definitions.

A3.1 BASIC SYMBOLS, IDENTIFIERS, NUMBERS, AND STRINGS

1.   <empty>: : = (the null string of symbols)
2.   <basic symbol>: : = <letter>|<digit>|<logical value>|
       <delimiter>

A3.1.1 LETTERS

3.   <letter>: : = a|b|c|d|e|f|g|h|i|j|k|l|m|n|o|p|q|r|s|t|u|v|w|x|y|z|A|B|C
       |D|E|F|G|H|I|J|K|L|M|N|O|P|Q|R|S|T|U|V|W|X|Y|Z

A3.1.2 DIGITS AND LOGICAL VALUES

4. <digit>: : = 0|1|2|3|4|5|6|7|8|9
5. <logical value>: : = TRUE|FALSE

A3.1.3 DELIMITERS

6. <delimiter>: : = <operator>|<separator>|<bracket>
    |<declarator>|<specificator>
7. <operator>: : = <arithmetic operator>|<relational operator>
    |<logical operator>|<sequential operator>
8. <arithmetic operator>: : = + | − | ∗ | / | ÷ | ↑
9. <relational operator>: : = < | ≦ | = | ≧ | > | ≠
10. <logical operator>: : = | ≡ | ⊃ | ∨ | ∧ | ¬
11. <sequential operator>: : = GO TO|IF|THEN|ELSE|FOR|DO
12. <separator>: : = ,|.|₁₀ |:|;|: = |⊔|STEP|UNTIL|WHILE|COMMENT
13. <bracket>: : = (|)[|]|'|'|BEGIN|END
14. <declarator>: : = OWN|BOOLEAN|INTEGER|REAL|ARRAY|SWITCH
    |PROCEDURE
15. <specificator>: : = STRING|LABEL|VALUE

A3.1.4 IDENTIFIERS

16. <identifier>: : = <letter>|<identifier><letter>
    |<identifier><digit>

A3.1.5 NUMBERS

17. <unsigned integer>: : = <digit>|<unsigned integer><digit>
18. <integer>: : = <unsigned integer>| + <unsigned integer>
    |−<unsigned integer>
19. <decimal fraction>: : = .<unsigned integer>
20. <exponent part>: : = <integer>
21. <decimal number>: : = <unsigned integer>|<decimal fraction>
    |<unsigned integer><decimal fraction>
22. <unsigned number>: : = <decimal number>|<exponent part>
    |<decimal number><exponent part>
23. <number>: : = <unsigned number>| + <unsigned number>
    |−<unsigned number>

A3.1.6 STRINGS

24. <proper string>: : = <any sequence of basic symbols not con-

taining ' or ' >|<empty>
25. <open string>: : = <proper string>|'<open string>'
       |<open string><open string>
26. <string>: : = '<open string>'

A3.2 EXPRESSIONS

27. <expression>: : = <arithmetic expression>
          |<Boolean expression>|<designational expression>

A3.2.1 VARIABLES

28. <variable identifier>: : = <identifier>
29. <simple variable>: : = <variable identifier>
30. <subscript expression>: : = <arithmetic expression>
31. <subscript list>: : = <subscript expression>|<subscript list> ,
       <subscript expression>
32. <array identifier>: : = <identifier>
33. <subscripted variable>: : = <array identifier>[<subscript list>]
34. <variable>: : = <simple variable>|<subscripted variable>

A3.2.2 FUNCTION DESIGNATORS

35. <procedure identifier>: : = <identifier>
36. <actual parameter>: : = <string>|<expression>
          |<array identifier>|<switch identifier>
          |<procedure identifier>
37. <letter string>: : = <letter>|<letter string><letter>
38. <parameter delimiter>: : = ,|)<letter string>:(
39. <actual parameter list>: : = <actual parameter>
          |<actual parameter list>
          <actual parameter>
40. <actual parameter part>: : = <empty>|(<actual parameter list>)
41. <function designator>: : = <procedure identifier>
          <actual parameter part>

A3.2.3 ARITHMETIC EXPRESSIONS

42. <adding operator>: : = +|−
43. <multiplying operator>: : = ×|/|÷
44. <primary>: : = <unsigned number>|<variable>
          |<function designator>|(<arithmetic expression>)
45. <factor>: : = <primary>|<factor>↑<primary>

46. <term>: : = <factor>|<term><multiplying operator>
<factor>
47. <simple arithmetic expression>: : = <term>|<adding operator>
<term>| <simple arithmetic expression>
<adding operator><term>
48. <if clause>: : = IF<Boolean expression>THEN
49. <arithmetic expression>: : = <simple arithmetic expression>
|<if clause><simple arithmetic expression>ELSE
<arithmetic expression>

A3.2.4 BOOLEAN EXPRESSIONS

50. <relational operator>: : = < | ≦ | = | ≧ | > | ≠
51. <relation>: : = <simple arithmetic expression>
<relational operator><simple arithmetic expression>
52. <Boolean primary>: : = <logical value >|<variable>
|<function designator>|<relation>
|(<Boolean expression>)
53. <Boolean secondary>: : = <Boolean primary>
|¬<Boolean primary>
54. <Boolean factor>: : = <Boolean secondary>
|<Boolean factor>∧<Boolean secondary>
55. <Boolean term>: : = <Boolean factor>
|<Boolean term>∨<Boolean factor>
56. <implication>: : = <Boolean term>
|<implication>⊃<Boolean term>
57. <simple Boolean>: : = <implication>
|<simple Boolean>≡<implication>
58. <Boolean expression>: : = <simple Boolean>|<if clause>
<simple Boolean>ELSE<Boolean expression>

A3.2.5 DESIGNATIONAL EXPRESSIONS

59. <label>: : = <identifier>|<unsigned integer>
60. <switch identifier>: : = <identifier>
61. <switch designator>: : = <switch identifier>
[<subscript expression>]
62. <simple designational expression>: : = <label>
|<switch designator>|(<designational expression>)
63. <designational expression>: : =
<simple designational expression>|<if clause>
<simple designational expression>ELSE
<designational expression>

A3.3 STATEMENTS

A3.3.1 COMPOUND STATEMENTS AND BLOCKS

64. \<unlabelled basic statement>: : = \<assignment statement>
   |\<go to statement>|\<dummy statement>
   |\<procedure statement>

65. \<basic statement>: : = \<unlabelled basic statement>
   |\<label>:\<basic statement>

66. \<unconditional statement>: : = \<basic statement>
   |\<compound statement>|\<block>

67. \<statement>: : = \<unconditional statement>
   |\<conditional statement>|\<for statement>

68. \<compound tail>: : = \<statement>END|\<statement>;
   \<compound tail>

69. \<block head>: : = BEGIN\<declaration>|\<block head>;
   \<declaration>

70. \<unlabelled compound>: : = BEGIN\<compound tail>

71. \<unlabelled block>: : = \<block head>;\<compound tail>

72. \<compound statement>: : = \<unlabelled compound>|\<label>:
   \<compound statement>

73. \<block>: : = \<unlabelled block>|\<label>:\<block>

74. \<program>: : = \<block>|\<compound statement>

A3.3.2 ASSIGNMENT STATEMENTS

75. \<left part>: : − \<variable>: − |\<procedure identifier>: −

76. \<left part list >: : = \<left part>|\<left part list>\<left part>

77. \<assignment statement>: : = \<left part list>
  \<arithmetic expression>|\<left part list>
   \<Boolean expression>

A3.3.3 GO TO STATEMENTS

78. \<go to statement>: : = GO TO\<designational expression>

A3.3.4 DUMMY STATEMENTS

79. \<dummy statement>: : = \<empty>

A3.3.5 CONDITIONAL STATEMENTS

80. <if clause>: : = IF<Boolean expression>THEN
81. <unconditional statement>: : = <basic statement>
    |<compound statement>|<block>
82. <if statement>: : = <if clause><unconditional statement>
83. <conditional statement>: : = <if statement>|<if statement>
    ELSE<statement>|<if clause><for statement>|<label>:
    <conditional statement>

A3.3.6 FOR STATEMENTS

84. <for list element>: : = <arithmetic expression>
    |<arithmetic expression>STEP<arithmetic expression>
    UNTIL<arithmetic expression>
    |<arithmetic expression>WHILE<Boolean expression>
85. <for list>: : = <for list element>|<for list>,<for list element>
86. <for clause>: : = FOR<variable>: = <for list>DO
87. <for statement>: : = <for clause><statement>|<label>:
    <for statement>

A3.3.7 PROCEDURE STATEMENTS

88. <actual parameter>: : = <string>|<expression>
    |<array identifier>|<switch identifier>
    |<procedure identifier>
89. <letter string>: : = <letter>|<letter string><letter>
90. <parameter delimiter>: : = ,|)<letter string>:(
91. <actual parameter list>: : = <actual parameter>
    |<actual parameter list>
    <actual parameter>
92. <actual parameter part>: : = <empty>|(<actual parameter list>)
93. <procedure statement>: : = <procedure identifier>
    <actual parameter part>

A3.4 DECLARATIONS

94. <declaration>: : = <type declaration>|<array declaration>
    |<switch declaration>|<procedure declaration>

A3.4.1 TYPE DECLARATIONS

95. <type list>: : = <simple variable>|<simple variable>,
<type list>
96. <type>: : = REAL|INTEGER|BOOLEAN
97. <local or own type>: : = <type>|OWN<type>
98. <type declaration>: : = <local or own type><type list>

A3.4.2 ARRAY DECLARATIONS

99. <lower bound>: : = <arithmetic expression>
100. <upper bound>: : = <arithmetic expression>
101. <bound pair>: : = <lower bound>:<upper bound>
102. <bound pair list>: : = <bound pair>|<bound pair list>,
<bound pair>
103. <array segment>: : = <array identifier>[<bound pair list>]
|<array identifier>,<array segment>
104. <array list>: : = <array segment>|<array list>,
<array segment>
105. <array declaration>: : = ARRAY<array list>
|<local or own type>ARRAY<array list>

A3.4.3 SWITCH DECLARATIONS

106. <switch list>: : = <designational expression>
|<switch list>,<designational expression>
107. <switch declaration>: : = SWITCH<switch identifier>
: = <switch list>

A3.4.4 PROCEDURE DECLARATIONS

108. <formal parameter>: : = <identifier>
109. <formal parameter list>: : = <formal parameter>
| <formal parameter list><parameter delimiter>
<formal parameter>
110. <formal parameter part >: : = <empty>
|(<formal parameter list>)
111. <identifier list>: : = <identifier>|<identifier list>,<identifier>
112. <value part>: : = VALUE<identifier list>;|<empty>
113. <specifier>: : = STRING|<type>|ARRAY|<type>ARRAY|LABEL
|SWITCH|PROCEDURE|<type>PROCEDURE
114. <specification part>: : = <empty>|<specifier><identifier list>;
|<specification part><specifier><identifier list>;

115.   <procedure heading>: : = <procedure identifier>
<formal parameter part>;<value part>
<specification part>
116.   <procedure body>: : = <statement>
117.   <procedure declaration>: : = PROCEDURE<procedure heading>
<procedure body>|<type>PROCEDURE
<procedure heading><procedure body>

APPENDIX 4

The LISP Interpreter

Just as the ALGOL 60 syntactic description will live in importance long after the demise of ALGOL, so the LISP interpreter ([McC60] and [McC65]), which represents the first formal attempt to describe the semantics of a language by an actual interpreter. We have already discussed the many elegant aspects of LISP which make the interpreter feasible, and here we would like to re-emphasize that elegance by presenting the entire interpreter. Its brevity should stand as a monument to the value of good language design, in particular to the consequence of structuring a language according to the data structures available within that language.

The LISP interpreter is EVALQUOTE(fn;args). When it is given a LISP function and a list of arguments for that function, it computes the value of the function applied to those arguments.

We first introduce a pair of functions used by the interpreter:

$$\text{PAIRLIS}[x;y;a] = [\text{NULL}[x] \rightarrow a;$$
$$T \rightarrow \text{CONS}[\text{CONS}[\text{CAR}[x];\text{CAR}[y]];\text{PAIRLIS}[\text{CDR}[x];$$
$$\text{CDR}[y];a]]]$$

The argument is a list of pairs of elements. x and y are lists, and their pairs of corresponding elements are appended to the pair list a. A list of this kind is called an association list.

$$\text{ASSOC}[x;a] = [\text{EQUAL}[\text{CAAR}[a];x] \rightarrow \text{CAR}[a];$$
$$T \rightarrow \text{ASSOC}[x;\text{CDR}[a]]]$$

This function searches the association list a for the first pair whose first member is x, and it returns this pair.

An association list is used by the functions constituting EVALQUOTE to hold the associations between bound variables of a function and the arguments to be associated with those bound variables, and between function names and their definitions.

EVALQUOTE is defined by two principal functions, APPLY and EVAL. Given one of the five basic functions, APPLY applies that function to its arguments. Given any other atomic function, APPLY requests that EVAL find its definition in the association list.

If APPLY is given a LAMBDA function, it enters the bound variable/argument pairs in the association list, and then requests EVAL to handle the form. If APPLY is given a LABEL, it enters the function-name/definition pair in the association list and then proceeds normally.

EVAL handles forms, as requested by APPLY. If the form is atomic, it represents a labeled function whose definition is returned to APPLY. If the form begins with QUOTE, the "quoted" value itself is returned. Conditionals are handled by EVCON, which returns the EVAL of the form following the first true predicate of the list.

In all other cases, EVAL requests of EVLIS the evaluation of the arguments of its argument list, and then requests that APPLY apply the function to those evaluated arguments.

Following is the total formal description of EVALQUOTE, with the routines APPLY, EVAL, EVCON, and EVLIS. We use our informal syntax, and we indicate notation of the LISP program being interpreted by underscores, to avoid confusion with functions of the interpreter itself.

EVALQUOTE[fn;x] = APPLY[fn;x;NIL]

APPLY[fn;x;a] =
    [ATOM[fn]→[EQ[fn;CAR]→CAAR[x];
               EQ[fn;CDR]→CDAR[x];
               EQ[fn;CONS]→CONS[CAR[x];CADR[x]];
               EQ[fn;ATOM]→ATOM[CAR[x]];
               EQ[fn;EQ]→EQ[CAR[x];CADR[x]];
               T→APPLY[EVAL[fn;a];x;a]];
      EQ[CAR[fn];LAMBDA]→EVAL[CADDR[fn];PAIRLIS[CADR[fn];x;a]];
      EQ[CAR[fn];LABEL]→APPLY[CADDR[fn];x;CONS[CONS[CADR[fn];
                               CADDR[fn]];a]]]

EVAL[e;a] = [ATOM[e]→CDR[ASSOC[e;a]];
         ATOM[CAR[e]]→[EQ[CAR[e];QUOTE]→CADR[e];
                 EQ[CAR[e];COND]→EVCON[CDR[e];a];
                 T→APPLY[CAR[e];EVLIS[CDR[e];a];a]];
         T→APPLY[CAR[e];EVLIS[CDR[e];a];a]]

$$\text{EVCON}[c;a] = [\text{EVAL}[\text{CAAR}[c];a] \rightarrow \text{EVAL}[\text{CADAR}[c];a];$$
$$\text{T} \rightarrow \text{EVCON}[\text{CDR}[c];a]]$$

$$\text{EVLIS}[m;a] = [\text{NULL}[m] \rightarrow \text{NIL};$$
$$\text{T} \rightarrow \text{CONS}[\text{EVAL}[\text{CAR}[m];a];\text{EVLIS}[\text{CDR}[m];a]]]$$

APPENDIX 5

References

[And65]
   Anderson, J. P. "Program Structures for Parallel Processing." *Communications* of the *ACM* (hereafter cited as *CACM*) 8 (December 1965): 786–788.

[Ard69]
   Arden, B. W.; Galler, B. A.; and Graham, R. M. "The MAD Definition Facility." *CACM* 12 (August 1969): 432–439.

[Bar68]
   Barron, D. W. *Recursive Techniques in Programming.* New York: American Elsevier, 1968.

[Bat70]
   Bates, F., and Douglas, M. L. *Programming Language/One.* 2d ed. Englewood Cliffs, N.J.: Prentice-Hall, 1970.

[Bau64]
   Baumann, R.; Feliciano, M.; Samuelson, K.; and Bauer, F. L. *Introduction to ALGOL.* Englewood Cliffs, N.J.: Prentice-Hall, 1964.

[Ber64]
   Berkeley, E. C., and Bobrow, D. G. *The Programming Language LISP.* Cambridge, Mass.: The M.I.T. Press, 1964.

[Ber69]

Berns, G. M. "Description of FORMAT, a Text-Processing Program." *CACM* 12 (March 1969): 141–146.

[Bon64]

Bond, E. R. "FORMAC-An Experimental Formula Manipulation Compiler." In *Proceedings of the ACM 19th National Conference.* pp. K2.1–1 - K2.1–11. New York: ACM, 1964.

[Bra71]

Branquart, P.; Lewi, J.; Sintzoff, M.; and Wodon, P. L. "The Composition of Semantics in ALGOL 68." *CACM* 14 (November 1971): 696–708.

[Bro67]

Brown, P. J. "The ML/I Macro Processor." *CACM* 10 (October 1967): 618–623.

[Bur54]

Burks, A. W.; Warren, D. W.; and Wright, J. B. "An Analysis of a Logical Machine Using Parenthesis-free Notation." *Mathematical Tables and Other Aids to Computation.* Vol. 8. 1954, pp. 53–57.

[Che66]

Cheatham, Jr., T. E. "The Introduction of Definitional Facilities into Higher Level Programming Languages." In *AFIPS Conference Proceedings.* Vol. 29 1966 Fall Joint Computer Conference. pp. 623–638. New York: Spartan Books, 1966.

[Cho62]

Chomsky, N. "Formal Properties of Grammars." *Handbook of Mathematical Psychology.* Volume 2. Edited by Bush, R. R.; Galanter, E. H.; and Luce, R. D. New York: John Wiley & Sons, 1962, pp. 323–418.

[Chr69]

Christensen, C., and Shaw, C. J., eds. "Proceedings of the Extensible Languages Symposium." SIGPLAN NOTICES 4. New York: ACM, August 1969.

[Chu41]

Church, A. *The Calculi of Lambda-Conversion.* Princeton, N.J.: Princeton University Press, 1941.

[Chu56]

———. *Introduction to Mathematical Logic.* Princeton, N.J.: Princeton University Press, 1956.

[Coc70]
    Cocke, J., and Schwartz, J. T. *Programming Languages and their Compilers.* New York: Courant Institute of Mathematical Studies, N.Y.U., 1970.

[Cod70]
    Codd, E. F. "A Relational Model of Data for Large Shared Data Banks." *CACM* 13 (June 1970): 377–387.

[Con58]
    Conway, M. E. "Proposal for an UNCOL." *CACM* 1 (October 1958): 5–8.

[Dij65]
    Dijkstra, E. W. "Solution of a Problem in Concurrent Programming Control." *CACM* 8 (September 1965): 569.

[Dij68(March)]
    ———. "GO TO Statement Considered Harmful." *CACM* 11 (March 1968): 147.

[Dij68(May)]
    ———. "The Structure of the 'THE'-Multiprogramming System." *CACM* 11 (May 1968): 341–346.

[Ear71]
    Earley, J. "Toward an Understanding of Data Structures." *CACM* 14 (October 1971): 617–627.

[Ekm65]
    Ekman, T., and Fröberg, C. *Introduction to ALGOL Programming.* Lund, Sweden: Studentlitteratur, 1965.

[Fal68]
    Falkoff, A. D., and Iverson, K. E. *APL\360 Users Manual.* IBM T. J. Watson Research Center, Yorktown, 1968.

[Fel66]
    Feldman, J. A. "A Formal Semantics for Computer Languages and its Application in a Compiler-Compiler." *CACM* 9 (January 1966): 3–9.

[Fel68]
    Feldman, J. A., and Gries, D. "Translator Writing Systems." *CACM* 11 (February 1968): 77–113.

[Fis70]

Fisher, D. A. "Control Structures for Programming Languages." Ph.D. dissertation, Pittsburgh: Carnegie-Mellon University, 1970.

[Flo70]

Flores, I. *Data Structure and Management*. Englewood Cliffs, N.J.: Prentice-Hall, 1970.

[Fos67]

Foster, J. M. *List Processing*. New York: American Elsevier, 1967.

[Fos70]

———. *Automatic Syntactic Analysis*. New York: American Elsevier, 1970.

[Gal67]

Galler, B. A., and Perlis, A. J. "A Proposal for Definitions in ALGOL." *CACM* 10 (April 1967): 204–219.

[Gal70]

———. *A View of Programming Languages*. Reading, Mass.: Addison-Wesley, 1970.

[Gar68]

Garwick, J. V. "GPL, a Truly General Purpose Language." *CACM* 11 (September 1968): 634–638.

[Gil70]

Gilman, L., and Rose, A. J. *APL\360 - An Interactive Approach*. New York: John Wiley & Sons, 1970.

[Gol65]

Golden, J. T. *FORTRAN IV Programming and Computing*. Englewood Cliffs, N.J.: Prentice-Hall, 1965.

[Gri68]

Griswold, R. E.; Poage, J. F.; and Polonsky, I. P. *The SNOBOL 4 Programming Language*. Englewood Cliffs, N.J.: Prentice-Hall, 1968.

[Gri72]

Gries, D. *Compiler Construction for Digital Computers*. New York: John Wiley & Sons, 1972.

[Hab67]

Habermann, A. N. "On the Harmonious Cooperation of Abstract Machines." Doctoral dissertation, Technische Hogeschool Eindhoven, October 1967.

[Hal68]

Halpern, M. I. "Toward a General Processor for Programming Languages." *CACM* 11 (January 1968): 15–25.

[Hal71]

Hall, Jr., A. D. "The Altran System for Rational Function Manipulation—A Survey." *CACM* 14 (August 1971): 517–521.

[Han69]

Hansen, W. J. "Compact List Representation: Definition, Garbage Collection and System Implementation." *CACM* 12 (September 1969): 499–507.

[Har71]

Harrison, M. C. *Data Structures and Programming.* New York: Courant Institute of Mathematical Studies, N.Y.U., 1971.

[Hea72]

Heaps, H. S. *Introduction to Computer Languages.* Englewood Cliffs, N.J.: Prentice-Hall, 1972.

[Her65]

Hermes, H. *Enumerability, Decidability, Computability.* New York: Academic Press, 1965.

[Hig67]

Higman, B. *A Comparative Study of Programming Languages.* New York: American Elsevier, 1967.

[Hir70]

Hirschsohn, I. "AMESPLOT—A Higher Level Data Plotting Software System." *CACM* 13 (March 1970): 546–555.

[Hop69]

Hopcroft, J. E., and Ullman, J. D. *Formal Languages and Their Relation to Automata.* Reading, Mass.: Addison-Wesley, 1969.

[IBM65]

IBM System/360 Operating System: PL/I Language Specifications. IBM Corporation manual (GC28-6571). Data Processing Division, White Plains, New York, 1965.

[Ili68]
   Iliffe, J. K. *Basic Machine Principles*. New York: American Elsevier, 1968.

[Ing66]
   Ingerman, P. Z. *A Syntax-Oriented Translator*. New York: Academic Press, 1966.

[Iro61]
   Irons, E. "A Syntax Directed Compiler for ALGOL 60." CACM 4 (January 1961): 51–55.

[Ive62[
   Iverson, K. E. *A Programming Language*. New York: John Wiley & Sons, 1962.

[Kle52]
   Kleene, S. C. *Introduction to Metamathematics*. Princeton, N.J.: D. Van Nostrand, 1952.

[Knu66]
   Knuth, D. E. "Additional Comments on a Problem in Concurrent Programming Control." *CACM* 9 (May 1966): 321–322.

[Knu68]
   ———. *Fundamental Algorithms, Volume 1*. Reading, Mass.: Addison-Wesley, 1968.

[Kul68]
   Kulsrud, H. E. "A General Purpose Graphic Language." *CACM* 11 (April 1968): 247–254.

[Lea66]
   Leavenworth, B. "Syntax Macros and Extended Translation." *CACM* 9 (November 1966): 790–793.

[Lec66]
   Lecht, C. P. *The Programmers' FORTRAN II and IV: A Complete Reference*. New York: McGraw-Hill, 1966.

[Lec67]
   ———. *The Programmers' ALGOL: A Complete Reference*. New York: McGraw-Hill, 1967.

[Lec68]
   ———. *The Programmers' PL/I: A Complete Reference*. New York: McGraw-Hill, 1968.

[Lef69]
> Lefkovitz, D. *File Structures for On-Line Systems*. New York: Spartan Books, 1969.

[Luk51]
> Lukasiewicz, J. *Aristotle's Syllogistic from the Standpoint of Modern Formal Logic*. Oxford: Clarendon Press, 1951, p. 78.

[Lys68]
> Lysegärd, A. *Introduction to COBOL*. Lund, Sweden: Studentlitteratur, 1968.

[Mad67]
> Madnick, S. E. "String Processing Techniques." *CACM* 10 (July 1967): 420–424.

[Mar67]
> Marks, S. L., and Armerding, G. W. "The JOSS Primer." The RAND Corporation memorandum (RM-5220-PR). Santa Monica, August 1967.

[McC60]
> McCarthy, J. "Recursive Functions of Symbolic Expressions and Their Computation by Machine." *CACM* 3 (April 1960): 184–195.

[McC65]
> McCarthy, J.; Abrahams, P. W.; Edwards, D. J.; Hart, T. P.; and Levin, J. I. *LISP 1.5 Programmer's Manual*. Cambridge, Mass.: The M.I.T. Press, 1965.

[Mcl60]
> McIlroy, M. D. "Macro Instruction Extensions of Compiler Languages." *CACM* 3 (April 1960): 214–220.

[Mur71]
> Murach, Mike. *Standard COBOL*. Palo Alto: Science Research Associates, 1971.

[Neu71]
> Neuhold, E. "Formal Description of Programming Languages." *IBM Systems Journal* 10 (1971): 86–112.

[Pak68]
> Pakin, S. *APL\360 Reference Manual*. Chicago: Science Research Associates, 1968.

[Pol69]

Pollack, S. V., and Sterling, T. D. *A Guide for PL/I*. New York: Holt, Rinehart, & Winston, 1969.

[Pol72]

Pollack, B. W., ed. *Compiler Techniques*. Philadelphia: Auerbach, 1972.

[Rey70]

Reynolds, J. C. "GEDANKEN—A Simple Typeless Language Based on the Principle of Completeness and the Reference Concept." *CACM* 13 (May 1970): 308–319.

[Ros67]

Rosen, S., ed. *Programming Systems and Languages*. New York: McGraw-Hill, 1967.

[Sam67]

Sammet, J. E. "Formula Manipulation by Computer." *Advances in Computers*. Vol. 8. New York: Academic Press, 1967, pp. 47–102.

[Sam69]

———. *Programming Languages: History and Fundamentals*. Englewood Cliffs, N.J.: Prentice-Hall, 1969.

[Sta67]

Standish, T. A. "A data definition facility for programming languages." Ph.D. dissertation, Pittsburgh: Carnegie Institute of Technology, 1967.

[Ste61]

Steel, Jr., T. B. "A First Version of UNCOL." In *Proceedings of the World Joint Computer Conference*. Volume 19. pp. 371–378. WJCC, 1961.

[Ste66]

Steel, Jr., T. B., ed. *Formal Language Description Languages for Computer Programming*. Amsterdam: North-Holland Publishing, 1966.

[Str58]

Strong, J. "The Problem of Programming Communication with Changing Machines: A Proposed Solution." *CACM* 1 (August 1958): 12–18; 1 (September 1958): 9–16.

[Str66]
Strachey, C. "Towards a Formal Semantics." In [Ste66], pp. 198–220.

[Str65]
———. "A General Purpose Macrogenerator." *Computer Journal* 8 (October 1965): 225–241.

[Stu69]
Stuart, F. *FORTRAN Programming*. New York: John Wiley & Sons, 1969.

[Weg 68]
Wegner, P. *Programming Languages, Information Structures, and Machine Organization*. New York: McGraw-Hill, 1968.

[Wei66]
Weinberg, G. M. *PL/I Programming Primer*. New York: McGraw-Hill, 1966.

[Wij69]
van Wijngaarden, A.; Mailloux, B. J.; Peck, J. F. L.; and Koster, C. H. A. *Report of the Algorithmic Language ALGOL 68*. New York: ACM, Dept. AL68–M, 1969.

[Wir66]
Wirth, N., and Weber, H. "EULER: A Generalization of ALGOL, and Its Formal Definition." *CACM* 9 (January 1966): 13–23; 9 (February 1966): 89–99.

[Wul71]
Wulf, W. A.; Russell, D. B.; and Habermann, A. N. "BLISS: A Language for Systems Programming." *CACM* 14 (December 1971): 780–790.

[Yas71]
Yasuhara, A. *Recursive Function Theory and Logic*. New York: Academic Press, 1971.

INDEX

SPONSORING EDITOR: Stephen D. Mitchell
PROJECT EDITOR: Marilyn Bohl
DESIGNER: Joan Ingoldsby Brown
ILLUSTRATOR: Graphic Associates

CONCEPTS OF PROGRAMMING LANGUAGES
is set in 9/11 Helvetica body type. The book
was set by Applied Typographic Systems,
Mountain View, California, and printed
by Kingsport Press, Kingsport, Tennessee.